598.
2971
RIS

Rising, Trudy.
   Canadian songbirds and their ways / text by Trudy
and Jim Rising ; paintings by Kathryn Devos-Miller. --
Montreal : Tundra Books, c1982.
   176 p. : col. ill., maps ; 31 cm.

   Bibliography: p. 173.
   Includes index.
   ISBN: 0887761240 : $23.95

   1. Birds - Canada.   I. Rising, Jim.   II. DeVos-Miller,
Kathryn.   III. Title.
                                              561

BUS. & SCI   4263   CPLA   0100 83FEB04 95433880
          PRODUCED IN CANADA BY UTLAS   PRODUIT AU CANADA PAR UTLAS

Canadian

Songbirds
and their ways

Text by
TRUDY and JIM RISING

Paintings by
KATHRYN DEVOS-MILLER

 TUNDRA BOOKS

TO OUR PARENTS

Published in Canada by
Tundra Books of Montreal,
Montreal, Quebec   H3G 1R4

Design by Dan O'Leary, Montreal.

Printed by Herzig Somerville, Toronto.

Tundra Books Inc. has applied funds from its Canada Council block grant for 1981 and 1982 toward the editing and production of this book.

ISBN 88776-124-0

Printed in Canada

Acknowledgments

The Red-eyed Vireo illustration is redrawn by permission of the National Research Council of Canada from the *Canadian Journal of Zoology*, vol. 55, pp. 528–542, 1977.

Mrs. Margaret H. Saunders is thanked for granting us permission to reproduce from A.A. Saunders' *A Guide to Bird Songs*, Doubleday, N.Y., 1951, the rendering of songs of the Eastern Wood Pewee, the Wood Thrush and the Black-capped Chickadee, and the chickadee's call.

We thank Mr. Lincoln Chew for permitting us to discuss here his interpretations of Savannah Sparrow dialect prior to the publication of his work.

The three illustrations of warbler displays were redrawn by permission. They are based on illustrations by Dr. Dilger in Ficken, M. S. and Ficken, R. W., 1962, The comparative ethology of the wood warblers: A review, *The Living Bird*, vol. 1, pp. 102–122.

The Bell's Vireo illustration is based on an illustration by Dr. Robert M. Mengel and was redrawn by permission from the *University of Kansas Publications of the Museum of Natural History*, vol. 12, pp. 241–296, 1962.

Maps showing the westward expansion of the starling and English Sparrow were redrawn with permission from *Auk*, vol. 60, pp. 74–87, 1943.

Dover Publications, Inc., granted permission to redraw the *Archaeopteryx* skeleton from G. Heilmann's *The Origin of Birds*, D. Appleton and Company, N.Y., 1927.

Contents

PART ONE   AN INTRODUCTION TO SONGBIRDS

Birds 9   Why birds are able to fly 9   How do songbirds differ from other birds? 11   When birds came to be 12   Were the first birds able to fly? 14   Why do birds fly? 15   Convergence 16   Feathers 17 Feet of birds 18   Beaks of songbirds 19   Why birds do what they do 20

PART TWO   ANNUAL CYCLE OF SONGBIRDS

Territory 23   Why do birds sing? 26   Why do birds have color? 27 How birds woo 28   Courtship feeding 30   Mating and copulation in songbirds 31   One mate or more? 32   Nest building 34 A variety of nests 38   Egg laying 40   Incubation 41   Hatching 42 Nest sanitation 44   Keeping the nestlings warm 45   How birds respond to intruders 46   Who does the feeding — and how? 48 How nestlings get their parents to feed them 48   Helpless or independent at hatching? 49   Feathers and molting 52   The mystery of migration 54   Orientation and navigation 58   Migration kills 62 Irruptions: The unpredictable birds 64   Birds in winter 66 Amazing survival 67

PART THREE   FAMILIES OF NORTH AMERICAN SONGBIRDS

How to identify songbirds 69   How to identify a bird by its song 70 An identification quiz 71   The tyrant flycatchers 72   The larks 74 The swallows 76   The shrikes 80   The waxwings 82   The wrens 84 The mockingbirds and thrashers 86   The thrushes 88   How do animals recognize one another? 90   Attracting bluebirds to birdhouses 93   Why are bird eggs different colors? 95   The kinglets and gnatcatchers 96   The creepers 98   The titmice and the nuthatches 100   The crows, jays and magpies 102   Anting— the mystery 105   The starlings and mynas 108   The weaver finches 110   Bird calls 113   The cardueline finches 114   Powerful beaks 114   The vireos 120   Social mimicry in vireos 122   Mystery birds 123   The wood warblers 124   How they compete 128 The tanagers, cardinal-grosbeaks and New World sparrows 134 A note about feeders 137   Why are some birds brightly colored and others dull? 143   Other common sparrows 144   Bathing 146 All of one kind, but so different 149   The blackbirds 150   Some western blackbirds 155   What to do with a foreign egg in the nest! 158   How birds show their age 160   How long do birds live? 161   How do birds die? 161   Song dialects and communication 163   Audubon and conservation 165 Glossary 166   Bibliography 173   Index 174   About the maps 176

Introduction

There are many good guides to bird identification and many handsome books of photographs and paintings showing birds in natural settings. But few books offer insight into the habits of birds—how they live and die and why they behave as they do. Yet the number of people interested in "knowing more" seems to increase every year. We have written this book to provide these readers with accurate and interesting information much of which has up to now been restricted to scientific journals and textbooks.

In 1976 a small book *Songbirds of Eastern Canada* and a parallel volume *Songbirds of the Eastern and Central States* were published; they were written by Trudy L. Rising and illustrated by Kathryn DeVos-Miller. It was the kind reception accorded them that encouraged us to revise and enlarge our study. Those little books discussed some of the commonest songbirds of the northeastern part of the North American continent. In expanding on this, we have added common species from across the continent so that people anywhere in Canada and the United States will be able to read about species familiar to them.

The present work is divided into three sections. The first consists of information on the biology of birds. How did they come to be? How are they different from other animals? How do they fly? And so forth. The second section describes the annual cycle of typical North American songbirds, their mating, nesting, migration and wintering habits. Kathryn produced many new illustrations to decorate these sections and to emphasize points made in the text. The third section introduces the major groups, or families, of North American songbirds, with descriptions of representative and widespread species in each. Here we discuss the characteristics of each family: how does a wren differ from a warbler, or a thrush from a thrasher? We then go on to describe the specific habits of the commonest and most widely distributed North American representatives. Where interesting variations exist west of the Rockies, these have also been included. Each species account contains "factual" data on the bird, its nest and eggs, a map showing its geographic distribution, and a color illustration of the species in typical pose and habitat. Throughout we strive to ask and answer the questions "why?" and "how?" Why do birds sing? Why are some birds brightly colored and others dull? Why do birds migrate and how do they do it? How long do birds live? How do they die?

The Latin ("scientific") names of animals and plants might seem an attempt to create a jargon that only experts can understand. Consider the problem they have tried to solve. People use different names in different languages for most species, and a single species may be known by many different names even within a single country. In North America, for example, the White-breasted Nuthatch is called the "white-bellied nuthatch," "Carolina nuthatch," "common nuthatch," "tree-mouse" and "devil downhead," just to mention the English names. It is therefore necessary to have an internationally recognized name for each kind of plant and animal. It was

decided long ago that these international names should be Latin names, or names written as though they were Latin. Until the nineteenth century most scientific writing in Europe was done in Latin, so it was logical that the scientific names would be Latin words. Some of these names in translation are much like our English common names: the Latin names *Parus atricapillus* means "black-capped chickadee," *Sturnus vulgaris* is the "common starling" and *Passer domesticus* is the "domestic sparrow." Some of the other names are more fun. *Troglodytes* (wren) is a "cave dweller"; *Tyrannus* (kingbird), "a tyrant"; *Dolichonyx oryzivorus* (Bobolink), a "long-clawed rice-eater." One of our favorites is the name of the Cactus Wren—*Campylorhynchus brunneicapillus*—a name nearly as long as the bird itself. It means the "brown-capped curve-nose," not a bad description! Lastly, the cowbird, *Molothrus ater*—the "black vagabond." What a value judgment!

In this book we have in general used English common names proposed by the American Birding Association, and have capitalized them when the full name is used. For example, we refer to the Brown-headed Cowbird (capitalized full name), or the cowbird (any of several cowbirds, though in this book always the Brown-headed Cowbird). With each description of the life of a species in Part III, the currently accepted Latin name is cited and the widely used French common name from W. E. Godfrey's *Birds of Canada* (1966) is given.

Some readers may wonder about the arrangement of families. We have presented them in a sequence that, as nearly as possible, puts closely related birds together. We followed the classification of Dr. R. W. Storer (1971), a system we find reasonable and one that will probably become generally used in North America in the near future, although at present not all authorities agree with this sequence.

No good book on a topic such as this is written without the use of the ideas and research of many people. The "ways" of birds we describe are known only because countless researchers have spent hundreds of hours in the field gathering data. We have used their published research extensively to write this book. We particularly want to thank Dr. R. D. Montgomerie of Queen's University (Kingston, Ontario) and Dr. D. M. Niles of the Delaware Natural History Museum (Greenville, Delaware) for reading drafts of the manuscript and offering helpful suggestions and criticisms, many of which led to changes or amplifications. Others who shared their knowledge of songbirds with us are Jon Barlow, David Broughton, Jim Dick, Nancy Flood, Richard Knapton and Tom Parsons. We alone, of course, take responsibility for accuracy.

We also want to thank the Royal Ontario Museum, Department of Ornithology, for the use of specimens for the illustrations, and Dr. Ross James of the ROM for lending his slide of the Evening Grosbeak which we used for our illustration of that species. May Cutler and Jane Moore of Tundra Books gave much help and repeated encouragement. We especially thank our children for their patience. All too often they had to defer some family activity while their parents worked on the "bird book."

Trudy L. Rising
James D. Rising

· PART ONE ·

AN INTRODUCTION TO SONGBIRDS

AN OPEN WOODLAND IN WINTER
Here are some of the birds you will see in open
woodlands in winter. The chickadee, creeper
and White-breasted Nuthatch are among the
songbirds that stay around trees, picking insects
and insect eggs from the bark. Birds other than
songbirds like the small Downy Woodpecker
shown here and its larger relative, the Hairy
Woodpecker, will often be with them.

Birds

The only feature that clearly separates birds from all other forms of life is the presence of feathers. Otherwise, birds are so similar to certain reptiles that scientists have called them, half seriously, "glorified reptiles," or "reptiles with feathers." Certainly it is agreed that birds originated from reptiles, and their closest living relatives are alligators. In fact, alligators, in features other than feathers, are more like birds than like other reptiles (such as snakes and lizards, and turtles).

All birds and most reptiles lay eggs, and both groups are well adapted to live on land. As all terrestrial animals are in constant danger of drying out, those that have succeeded in living on land have adaptations to prevent water loss. The eggs of reptiles and birds are similar and they are remarkably adapted to prevent this desiccation—the developing embryos within the eggs are well protected by a membrane called the *amnion.*

Also, like their close relatives the reptiles, birds possess "scales" that cover their legs and beaks. (They are different from the *scales* of fishes and are more properly called *scutes.*)

Birds are also similar to mammals. For example, both groups are warm-blooded; this permits them to be active at a broad range of temperatures. So-called cold-blooded animals—like insects and reptiles—have to warm up by basking in the sun or by moving slowly before they can become normally active.

Why birds are able to fly

The sight of a soaring hawk or a flurry of migrating blackbirds never fails to be exciting. Most birds are excellent flyers, with many adaptations reducing their weight to make flight possible.

Birds' bones are hollow, making them lighter than the bones of other animals; a bird bone may weigh half as much as a mammal bone of the same length. This means that a bird weighs less than a reptile or mammal of

A typical songbird, a White-crowned Sparrow, seen in flight.

comparable size, and this reduced weight makes flight easier. Though hollow, birds' bones are nonetheless strong. The long bones of the wings and legs are tubes further supported by bony cross struts. The skulls of adult songbirds are also "hollow"; they are composed of two thin layers of bone connected by many bony spicules—again strength is obtained with minimal weight. Adaptations for flight have led to much fusion in birds' skeletons, reducing many bones to highly specialized, but light complexes or elements. The pelvic bones are fused to the vertebrae in the lower back, giving light, but strong support for the hind legs. Many of the tail vertebrae are fused to a single element, the pygostyle, that serves as a place of attachment for the tail feathers, which are used for steering and breaking during flight. The clavicles ("collarbones") of birds are fused to form the "wishbone," which increases the strength of the shoulder region and serves as a place of attachment for flight muscles. Bones of the "hand" and "fingers" are fused to form a rigid place of attachment for the outer wing feathers.

A lengthwise section of the humerus (a wing bone) of the Common Raven illustrates the typical hollow design of bird bones, with cross struts at each end for added strength. Similar bones of reptiles and mammals are nearly solid.

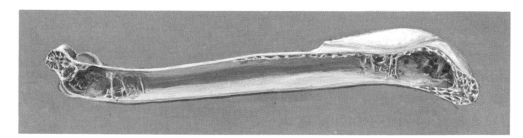

Birds have no teeth or heavy jaws to weight down the head. The gizzard, an internal organ that frequently holds gravel the bird has swallowed, grinds the food and mostly takes over the function of teeth. This means the bird's weight is centrally located in the stomach. Although some birds have enormous beaks—toucans, for example—these beaks are extremely light.

Ovaries, testes, and the ducts to them, though very large in the breeding season, are tiny at other times. Unlike mammals, birds have no ear flaps—they would cause resistance during flight. Even their legs, their "landing gear," are normally retracted while they fly.

Birds excrete wastes in the form of a compound (uric acid) that does not dissolve in water, and thus they do not need to carry extra—and heavy—water to flush away their urine. (The uric acid from their kidneys empties into a chamber called the *cloaca* where it is mixed with the feces; the kidney waste, often called *guano,* is the whitish part of bird droppings.)

Birds have a four-chambered heart which ensures that only well-oxygenated blood is sent out to the flight muscles. (This especially helps them to keep up sustained flight.) Their lungs are extremely efficient and they connect with a system of air sacs that often enter the hollow bones. The lungs and air sacs serve as a cooling system as water evaporates from their moist surfaces when air passes through.

And the feathers? Besides making up the light, but strong, wings and tail and providing a warm coat, feathers also help streamline the bird for efficient movement through the air.

All these features make birds extremely competent fliers.

How do songbirds differ from other birds?

Passeriformes	59.2%
most are songbirds	
Hummingbirds & Swifts	4.4
Woodpeckers	4.3
Parrots	3.6
Waders, etc.	3.6
Pigeons & relatives	3.6
Hawks	3.1
Chicken-like Birds	3.1
Kingfishers, etc.	2.2
Cranes & Rails	2.1
Ducks, Geese, Swans	1.7
Owls	1.5
Cuckoos	1.5
Others	5.8

Some readers will be surprised to see such birds as crows in a book about songbirds. The crow's caw can hardly be called a song. If birds need not be gifted singers to qualify as songbirds, what are the criteria? Here are the most obvious features that unite the more than 5000 species of songbirds of the world.

All have more than four pairs of muscles (syrinx muscles) controlling voice production. This means that they are potentially capable of more elaborate song than are other birds, even though not all live up to their anatomical capabilities.

Their feet have four unwebbed toes that are specialized for perching. There are no muscles in the feet; thus, foot movements are controlled by tendons attached to muscles in the legs. This essentially limits their action to opening and closing their toes.

They produce young that are hatched naked and helpless, requiring intensive parental care.

All are land birds.

All songbird species are fairly small; the raven is by far the largest in North America, and it weighs only about 850 g (30 oz).

Songbirds are neither the largest nor the smallest of birds. Nor are songbirds the fastest fliers. But if numbers count for anything, this group *is* successful. About three-fifths of the approximately 8900 species of birds in the world are classified as perching birds and most of these are songbirds. Of these, about 285 species are regularly found in North America north of Mexico. We have chosen a few of these, which we feel are both familiar and representative of the diversity, to introduce this fascinating group to you.

Records set by birds

The ostrich is the largest bird (150 kg or 330 lb), and the Bee Hummingbird of Cuba is the smallest (2.25 g or 0.08 oz); neither is a songbird. Loons and racing pigeons fly at about 90 km/h (56 mi/h), and Peregrine Falcons may reach 360 km/h (224 mi/h) in a dive. Experts doubt this very great speed of the falcon, recorded only by a World War I aviator, but we are certain that they dive at a speed of at least 240 km/h (150 mi/h). Most songbirds fly at only 40 km/h (25 mi/h).

This graph shows the number of kinds of perching birds relative to other groups of birds. Nearly 60%, or ⅗ of all birds are perching birds, and about 80% of these are songbirds.

When birds came to be

Today

3 million years ago
First human beings

135-65 million years ago
Extinction of dinosaurs

150 million years ago
FIRST BIRDS

200 million years ago
First mammals

210 million years ago
First dinosaurs

325 million years ago
First reptiles

375 million years ago
First land animals—amphibians

450 million years ago
*First animals with backbones,
jawless fish*

600 million years ago
*Hard shelled invertebrates
(trilobites, brachiopods)*

670 million years ago
Soft-bodied worms

1 billion years ago
*First advanced cells
green algae*

2 billion years ago
First well preserved blue-green algae

3.5 billion years ago
*First evidence of life
bacteria and blue-green algae*

Earth's probable beginning
4.6 billion years ago

About 150 million years ago an animal with features of both reptile and bird fell into a body of water in an area today known as Bavaria. This crow-sized, reptilelike bird was buried in silt and became fossilized. In 1861, when people were quarrying the lithographic limestone in which the skeleton had been embedded "high and dry" for thousands of years, this "missing link" was discovered. Six such fossils have now been found in the limestones of West Germany. Named *Archaeopteryx lithographica,* these are the earliest known birds.

One feature of that first fossil made it extraordinarily important—impressions of feathers surrounded the bones. This made scientists of the late 1880s look much more closely at the intriguing new fossils. Otherwise, *Archaeopteryx* resembled some small dinosaurs that had lived at the same time, during the Jurassic Period, from about 190 to 135 million years ago. *Archaeopteryx* had well-developed teeth—no modern bird has teeth—a long bony tail and other features of reptiles. But the feathers made it a bird, and upon closer examination other birdlike features were found.

Except for the teeth, the skull is definitely more like that of a bird than that of a reptile, and the shoulder and pelvic girdles (bones) and the legs are more birdlike as well. However, because of its many reptilian features, *Archaeopteryx* is placed in a subclass separate from all other birds.

Bird fossils — few but fascinating

Little is known of bird life for the first 100 million years that followed *Archaeopteryx's* existence. The next fossils came from the Cretaceous Period, which followed the Jurassic. Some of the best known of these were deposited at the edge of a large inland sea in what is now the western United States; the fossil-rich chalk beds of western Kansas and Montana tell us that marine birds occurred there at that time, about 80 million years ago. The ancient seabirds had few reptilian features. All had a reduced, birdlike tail and a well-developed breastbone *(sternum).* Most had a keel, the broad extension from the sternum to which the large flight muscles are attached.

In the Cretaceous Period, a group of large, flightless, diving birds, generally called *Hesperornis,* were common. The largest of these, *Hesperornis regalis,* were nearly 2 m (about 6½ ft) long. Although fossil feather impressions are rare, they have been found for *Hesperornis.* Birds of the genus *Ichthyornis,* contemporary with *Hesperornis,* were smaller (20 cm or 8 in. long) and had well-developed wings. Unlike any birds living today, *Ichthyornis, Hesperornis* and *Archaeopteryx* had teeth.

The large number of fishbones found with *Ichthyornis* fossils provides good evidence that these birds ate fish. Unfortunately, all the bird fossils from this period seem to be of sea or water birds, but undoubtedly land species existed at that time.

By 65 million years ago many of the modern groups of birds had appeared on earth. Later, giant flightless terrestrial birds emerged; most of these have become extinct. Songbirds appear in the fossil record of 25 million years ago, but they may have existed earlier than that.

The Pleistocene Epoch was a time of widespread glaciation; the last ice receded about 11,000 years ago. Many bird species became extinct during the Pleistocene; but others, such as the flightless emus, cassowaries and moas, expanded their ranges during this time. The moas, giant flightless birds of

Archaeopteryx is the earliest known bird and probably looked much like this. It has features of both reptiles and birds. (This illustration is based on a model in the American Museum of Natural History, N.Y.)

New Zealand which reached heights of over three meters, were extirpated by people less than 1000 years ago.

During the last 11,000 years, the very large group of small perching birds, the Passeriformes, has become dominant. Except for several fairly primitive families, all these are songbirds (Suborder Passeres). Almost all of the familiar birds of woodland and garden are members of this group. (Common birds that look similar but are *not* perching birds are hummingbirds, woodpeckers, doves and pigeons, cuckoos, swifts and kingfishers.)

Although three-fifths of all modern bird species are perching birds and many of them are quite abundant, we have little knowledge of their evolution. The fossil record for all birds is poor when compared with that for reptiles and mammals. Bird bones, often hollow and fragile, do not fossilize well. Teeth of animals are often the only parts that are found, and these give evidence of the place and the time when those animals lived. But since modern birds have no teeth, the evidence is scant.

The fossil record for perching birds is especially poor because they are small, delicate creatures that commonly live in woodlands or grasslands—places where fossilization is always unlikely.

Fossils are formed in several ways. Animals most often become trapped beneath sediments under water and fail to decompose; after a time, the bone (or other tissue) is in part replaced by minerals—the bone becomes fossilized. Much less commonly, animals become trapped in tar pits—places where oil seeps from the earth. Tar pits from southern California have yielded some excellent fossils of birds, including Late Pleistocene blackbirds, not greatly different from some of the present-day blackbirds discussed in this book. Had these not become trapped in the tar, however, we would not have known of their existence.

Were the first birds able to fly?

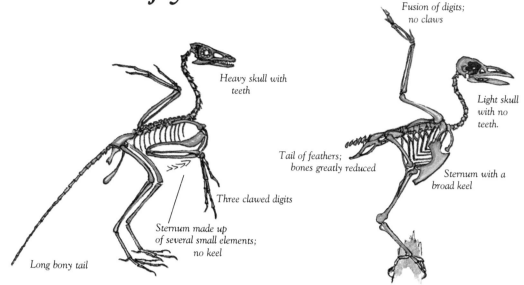

Fusion of digits; no claws

Heavy skull with teeth

Light skull with no teeth.

Tail of feathers; bones greatly reduced

Sternum with a broad keel

Three clawed digits

Sternum made up of several small elements; no keel

Long bony tail

A comparison of the skeleton of Archaeopteryx (left) and that of a modern songbird, the American Crow (right), shows some of the obvious differences between Archaeopteryx and all modern birds. The teeth of Archaeopteryx and its long bony tail are like those of its reptilian ancestors, but its shoulder and pelvic bones are birdlike. The absence of a keel on its sternum (breastbone) shows us that it could not have been a strong flier.

Probably not. It takes large, strong breast muscles to power flight. All modern birds that fly have such muscles, which are attached to the keel on the sternum (breastbone). *Archaeopteryx* did not have such a keel, and could not have been capable of flapping flight. Then why the feathers? We think of feathers as being important to birds for flight, and indeed they are. But at first they must have had other functions. The earliest feathers were probably "scales" (such as occur on the bare part of a bird's leg) with frayed edges—like down feathers (see *Feathers*). These provided the first birds with a downy covering that helped to keep them warm. Different kinds of feathers, like the "flight feathers" of a bird's wing, are specially modified through adaptation for a specific function, such as flight, but are derived from the basic type of feather. The feathers on *Archaeopteryx*'s wings were already modified, so there doubtless existed some bird, an ancestor to *Archaeopteryx*, that had even less well differentiated feathers. Thus, feathers came before flight, and the wing and tail feathers of *Archaeopteryx* represent some intermediate stage in the evolution of flight feathers.

There are two theories of how *Archaeopteryx* used its wing and tail feathers. Though unable to fly, *Archaeopteryx* could have glided from tree to tree as today's flying squirrels "fly." Or, the wings might have been used to catch food, such as flying insects. Proponents of this latter view think that *Archaeopteryx* was primarily a cursorial, that is to say, a running animal, and that it ran along the ground on its hind legs chasing insects and scooping them out of the air, toward its mouth, with its elongated wings of broad, flattened feathers. The legs of *Archaeopteryx* do look well adapted for running, and perhaps one day we will know enough to say that one or the other theory is the more probable.

Many of *Archaeopteryx*'s descendants or cousins *did* use feathers for flying—perhaps first for gliding—and the proliferation of the different sizes, shapes and forms of birds that took place during the 150 million years that have passed since *Archaeopteryx* was based on the new opportunities that flying gave to birds. Only a few have forsaken flight (such as ostriches and kiwis) or have become specialized to fly only underwater (penguins), but we think their ancestors could fly.

Why do birds fly?

Why do birds fly? A popular facetious answer is: "Because it's better than walking." There is an element of truth in that answer. The adaptations that enabled the early birds to fly opened to them ways of living that were not available to most other animals. Flying meant they could escape from predators, and therefore they could wander around during the day looking for food and mates. It meant they could travel great distances with relative ease, thus enabling them to move north in the summer to take advantage of the rich insect and vegetable life there, and south again in the winter when it became cold and inhospitable. They could cross physical barriers such as rivers and mountains that stopped terrestrial cousins. Flying meant that they could catch flying insects, and easily get from one tree to the next. Most of the differences among the groups (families) of modern birds are based on different ways birds have adapted to take advantage of flight; the swallows, flycatchers, blackbirds, warblers and finches all exploit the ability to fly, each in a somewhat different way.

Swifts, swallows and some other birds catch flying insects by searching while in flight for their prey. The kingbird, however, sits quietly on a perch, watching for an insect to fly by. Then it darts out, catches the insect in its beak and returns to its perch to swallow its meal.

Convergence

The beak of the Northern Shrike has a notch behind the tip, which is used for ripping flesh.

The notched beak of the Merlin is similar to that of the shrike.

These footprints in the snow have been made by birds with long hind claws on the back toe of each foot. Convergence has resulted in similarly elongated toes in Horned Larks, pipits and longspurs—all birds that spend much of their time walking on open ground or in short grass, looking for food (see THE LARKS for more about this similarity).

Sometimes two kinds (species) of birds look very much alike. This can occur either because they are closely related to each other—called similarity due to ancestry—*or* because they have adapted to similar ways of living—called similarity due to *convergence*. Convergence means simply that dissimilar things have become similar, either in looks or in behavior.

In several places in this book we point out examples of convergence—such as with swallows and swifts. We can be certain that the similarities between them are due to convergence, for swifts are not songbirds. The two groups must have independently developed their specializations for capturing insects "on the wing."

The bills of hawks, owls and shrikes are another clear case of convergence. They are designed to tear the flesh of the small animals these birds capture for food. The extra projection, or "tooth," on the bills of both falcons and shrikes is particularly striking. Yet hawks and shrikes are not closely related to each other, nor are owls and shrikes. (Scientists disagree about whether or not hawks and owls are closely related.) All have developed certain similarities as a consequence of their similar eating and hunting habits.

Ovenbirds resemble woodland thrushes, such as the Wood Thrush, more than they resemble their much closer relatives, the other warblers. Ovenbirds are primarily brown with spotted bellies, and they walk around on the ground most of the time as thrushes do. Other more specific characteristics show us that they are really warblers. Their ancestors probably flitted about in trees and had shorter legs—they may even have had the green and yellow feathers that are typical of most warblers.

Most sparrows are brown; those that spend much of their time on or near the ground generally have striped or spotted undersides. Is this similarity in coloration among sparrow species due to convergence, or does it exist because they are all closely related? In this case, it is difficult to say. All sparrows (except for the House Sparrow from the Old World) are closely related *and* their dull brown, often striped coloration serves to camouflage them well. Since they are closely related *and* have similar habits, we cannot know which factor led to their looking much the same.

As you can see, the way a bird looks may tell us more about what it does and where it lives than who its cousins are.

Feathers

Down feathers are fluffy and help insulate birds from the cold. They are "downy" because they lack barbules, which connect one feather vane to the next.

Flycatchers and a number of other birds have tiny feathers called rictal bristles around their beaks to funnel in flying insects. Rictal bristles lack vanes.

As feathers start to develop on a young bird, they look very much like the scutes or "scales" of reptiles. While such feathers are growing, they still contain a blood supply, but as they mature, they become hollow and, like hair on mammals, have no living parts.

A bird has different kinds of feathers. Those that cover the body are called *contour* feathers; they give birds their streamlined look. When, as a child, you found a feather, you probably ruffled the *vanes* backward, separating one from the next. Remember how the vanes were hooked together and it required a little effort to pull them apart? But if you stroked them softly downward, they fell back into position and hooked together again. The hooking is done by small *barbs* (too small to see) with even smaller *barbules* all along and on both sides of the vanes. When a bird preens, it is rehooking feather vanes that have become separated. Strong fliers such as swallows have longer, stronger hooks than birds that are not such good fliers.

The uses they serve

Down feathers, which help insulate birds, are fluffy because there are no barbules with tiny hooks to connect one vane to the next; down is especially abundant in birds like ducks and other waterbirds, but even songbirds— especially those that live in cold places—have them. Most of these fluffy feathers also lack the stiff mid-rib called the *rachis* that contour feathers such as flight (wing) feathers have.

The *bristle,* another kind of feather found in some songbirds, is small and has no vanes. Flycatchers and a few songbirds have bristles around their mouths; these funnel flying insects into their beaks. (The "eyelashes" of ostriches are also bristles.)

Feathers protect birds against harsh weather conditions. Birds that stay in the North have denser plumage in winter than in summer. When cold, they fluff up their feathers, increasing the amount of air trapped under the feathers and, thus, their insulative efficiency. It is thought that feathers arose as an adaptation, not for flight, but—like the hair on mammals—for conserving heat. The large, stiff feathers so useful in flight probably evolved from soft feathers that helped to keep out the cold.

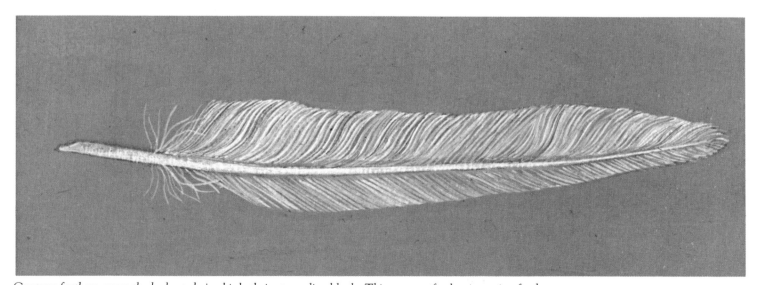

Contour feathers cover the body and give birds their streamlined look. This contour feather is a wing feather.

Feet of birds

HORNED LARK
for walking

AMERICAN ROBIN
for walking and perching

BROWN CREEPER
for climbing

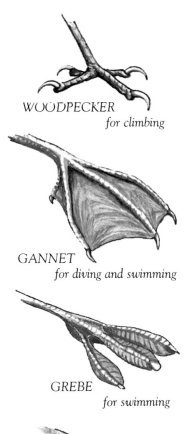

WOODPECKER
for climbing

GANNET
for diving and swimming

GREBE
for swimming

EAGLE
for seizing prey

All songbirds have feet that are specialized for perching, although not all look exactly the same. The Horned Lark has an extra-long back toenail which adapts this bird for walking on sand or snow, while the Brown Creeper has short legs and very long toenails on all its toes that help it in its spiral climb up trees. But in spite of such modifications, both songbirds possess feet that are basically designed for perching.

Many birds have muscles in their feet, but these have apparently been lost in the development of perching birds (although there are vestiges of these muscles in the feet of some primitive species, such as the Eastern Kingbird). The movement of a songbird's feet is controlled by muscles in the "drumstick" part of the leg that are attached to the feet and toes by tendons.

When a perching bird lands, a tendon in each leg tightens, automatically enabling the bird's toes to bend. In this way, its feet grasp the branch or post on which it lands. Tiny projections on the tendons keep the toes "locked" in position so long as the bird's weight is on the foot. Thus, the bird may sit, and even sleep as it sits. This special grasping foot enables the bird to keep its hold.

For perching and hopping

In songbirds and other perching birds, all four toes of each foot extend from the leg at the same level; three are directed forward, one backward. While the feet of shorebirds and woodpeckers look similar, there are distinct differences. In shorebirds, the toe that is directed backward extends from the leg at a higher level than the front three. Most woodpecker feet have two toes forward, one back and one to the side, rather than three forward and one back.

If you see a bird that hops, you will know that it is a passerine—a perching bird. Even the good walkers among the passerines—blackbirds (like the meadowlark and grackle), starlings, thrushes (like the robin) and ground-feeding sparrows (like the Savannah Sparrow)—are able to hop from perch to perch. Why is hopping valuable for perching birds? Probably because it enables them to get around in trees and bushes where a large variety of food exists that simply is not available to other birds. They can hop from branch to branch, drop to lower branches or jump up to higher ones. Those songbirds that spend most of their time in trees, bushes and weeds even hop when they are on the ground.

Other birds

Birds other than perching birds are not able to hop because their feet are adapted for doing other things. For instance, the feet of grebes, gannets and ducks, all in their own way, are excellent for swimming. The feet of predators such as eagles, hawks and owls are specialized for seizing prey; those of woodpeckers are specially adapted for climbing. Other kinds of birds are otherwise modified—ostriches, rails and shorebirds (such as sandpipers and plovers) have feet well adapted for walking.

Beaks of songbirds

Though the feet of all songbirds are much the same, their beaks differ greatly—they are specially adapted to eating particular types of food. For instance, beaks may be specialized for eating seeds, or for picking insects or for catching insects "on the wing," and some are generalized so they can eat a variety of foods.

CLIFF SWALLOW
eats insects on the wing

AMERICAN ROBIN
picks invertebrates and fruit

LOGGERHEAD SHRIKE
tears meat

BLUE JAY
generalized beak

Seed eaters such as finches usually have short, heavy beaks. Warblers and vireos use their narrow, pointed beaks for picking insects from leaves or from between cracks in bark. Swallows have short, wide beaks that, when open, produce a huge gape for catching insects. Shrikes have hawklike beaks that enable them to kill smaller birds and mammals.

Some "generalists" like thrushes, starlings and blackbirds are mainly insect eaters, but they also eat fruit and some eat seeds as well. The beaks of these birds "look" unspecialized: they tend to be long and pointed for catching insects and worms, but they are also fairly heavy, giving the strength needed to crack seeds. Crows and their relatives are even more generalized in their eating habits; they feed on carrion and garbage in dumps as well as other foods, and their beaks are similar to those of other generalists.

BROWN CREEPER
picks insects from bark

RED-BREASTED NUTHATCH
picks insects from bark

MAGNOLIA WARBLER
picks insects

A good look at the shape of a bird's beak will help you identify the bird. For example, two birds may be of similar size and color, but the shape of its beak will help tell you whether the bird is a finch (a seed eater), a warbler (an insect eater), a swallow (an insect catcher) or a blackbird (a generalist).

RED-EYED VIREO
picks insects

WHITE-WINGED CROSSBILL
extracts seeds from cones

AMERICAN GOLDFINCH
picks small seeds

RED-WINGED BLACKBIRD
generalized beak

19

Why birds do what they do

The song of the Cardinal signals other males that a territory is taken.

The shrike often impales its prey on a thorn or barbed wire and returns later to eat it.

We often read statements such as, "The Cardinal sings to welcome another pretty, spring day" or "Waxwings like to eat cherries" or "Shrikes are vicious birds, impaling their prey on thorns." Such statements might be poetically pleasant, or they might describe an activity as we see it. But they are not scientifically acceptable because they ascribe to the birds human emotions, motives or values that the birds probably do not have. We have tried to avoid such anthropocentric (human centered) statements by describing a bird's behavior in terms of the way it lives and the problems it faces.

For example, many experiments have clearly shown us why birds sing—it has nothing to do with welcoming a new day. The Cardinal sings to let other Cardinals know the area is taken! Cardinals that sing have been most successful in defending an area for themselves over the generations; thus, they have come to prevail. (See Part II, *Why do birds sing?* for more on this topic.)

If one says "Waxwings like to eat cherries," what that statement means is that waxwings will eat cherries in preference to other foods. (This is what we usually mean when we say that people like to eat cherries.) But this characteristic in waxwings, just as the previous example of the singing of Cardinals, has arisen as a consequence of selection for a certain diet (waxwings with a preference for cherries are the ones that became most numerous). The availability of cherries, competition with other animals that eat cherries too and, we can be certain, many other factors have been involved in the evolution of this habit in waxwings.

Shrikes, in capturing and eating the foods they are specialized to take—insects and small birds and mammals—are no more "vicious" than are waxwings in capturing their food. Shrikes, like all predators, must kill other animals for their own existence, but (much as it might offend us to see a mouse impaled on a thorn) shrikes cannot be considered "morally inferior" to waxwings and other nonpredatory animals. (Part III, *Loggerhead Shrike*, discusses impaling of prey.)

Learning the right language

Let us explore how another behavioral trait might be interpreted, and how it most likely became characteristic of the species. We know that male birds of many songbird species continue to sing after their offspring have hatched. We also know that baby birds of some species at this time learn or begin to learn to recognize songs—the language of their species. We could say that the father sings the song to teach it to his children, but that probably is not true. The male sings and his offspring hear his song and learn it. If males do not sing to teach their song to their offspring, then why do they sing at this time of year?

Let us speculate that in the past there were some males that continued to sing after their young had hatched, and others that did not. This difference in singing behavior was inherited—passed on from parent to child as are eye color and blood type in humans. Thus, nonsingers would produce male birds that would, as their father, cease singing just after mating, and females that would never hear their father's song. These young birds would be at a disadvantage the following spring when they themselves would be old enough

The Cedar Waxwings shown here are "petal passing," a common practice among waxwings during courtship. Petal passing and berry passing by these gregarious birds are thought to help keep pairs and flocks together.

to mate and raise young because they would not have had an opportunity to learn their species' song. Because of their poor ability to communicate with others of their kind, these would produce fewer offspring than others of their species that had learned the song as chicks. They therefore would pass their "nonsinging" characteristic on to fewer young than would the "singers." In a few generations, all these nonsingers would be gone simply because they would have failed to reproduce as efficiently as the singers. The singers would be prominent because they *had* been successful in producing young—not because they were trying to teach their young the song. Nonsingers would be "weeded out" by natural selection.

Although songs of most birds are "species-specific" (i.e., there are specific songs of each species that differ from the songs of all other species), not all individuals of a species sing exactly the same song. For example, Indigo Buntings sing songs that are made up of several different, somewhat disconnected elements; in a population of these birds studied in Michigan, a total of 98 different elements were found, but individual males used different combinations of about 6 of these to create songs that were unique to them.

· PART TWO ·

ANNUAL CYCLE OF SONGBIRDS

In springtime, you might actually see this spectacular array of warblers in the same tree as they return from the South to their nesting grounds. The singing bird is a Black-throated Blue Warbler; the one in flight is a Magnolia Warbler. The brilliant black and orange warbler is an American Redstart; a Black-throated Green Warbler sits in the bottom center of the picture.

Territory

Most creatures protect their home; birds are no exception. A *territory* is any area that is defended by one bird against other birds mainly of the same kind. All songbirds display territoriality in the breeding season. Usually the male of each species establishes and defends the area. He sets up and maintains the territory by singing, posturing (aggressive displays), chasing and fighting. Once the female lays her eggs and begins to incubate them, the male tends to defend his territory less, so that it becomes somewhat smaller. After nestlings hatch, the male generally chases intruders less vigorously, perhaps because he is so busy helping his mate feed the young that he has little time left over to be on the lookout. A very few songbirds (for example, Florida Scrub Jays and Mexican Jays of southwestern mountains) maintain a familial territory, with young of previous nestings helping. For these species, the territory is a "family affair" and no *one* bird has a territory.

Why do birds have a territory? It guarantees cover, nesting material and sites and, in some cases, food for the young. Also, the ritual fanfare involved in the defense of territory helps the birds recognize a member of the opposite sex and helps to form and maintain a pair bond between male and female. The territory, too, provides a familiar area for the birds so that they have a much better chance of escaping from predators. And when they know their surroundings, it is easier to get a tasty caterpillar just when they "want" one, or to have a dust bath just when they "feel" like it. It is thought that territoriality helps reduce the spread of contagious diseases by limiting the number of birds of each species in any one area.

Large or small, it is defended vigorously

Defense of a territory early in the season probably prevents later intrusions by other birds at more important times—during pairing and nest building. By establishing a territory early, energy is not wasted when the male really needs it to help build the nest, and especially to help feed his young. There is also less chance of his mate copulating with another male—promiscuity is reduced. Males of many species continue territorial defense by singing after nestlings have hatched; this gives their offspring an opportunity to learn songs and postures that are so important for species recognition.

An excellent indication of just how important birds' territories must be to them is the amount of time they spend defending them. Male Black-capped Chickadees spend almost half of their waking hours defending their territories during the prenesting stage, and about a third of their time during the nest-building period!

A territory can be very large, such as that of the Northern Shrike which ranges from about 46 to 98 hectares (1 ha = 1000 m² = 2.47 acres). Or it can be very small, as is the case with the Bank Swallow. The swallow defends an area of only a few centimeters between its particular nesting cavity in the colony and that of adjacent birds. The highly social Cedar Waxwing apparently does not need much space either; often there are many waxwing nests within a small area.

Some White-throated Sparrows have tan stripes on their heads; others have white. When these birds mate, it is nearly always with birds of the other color striping. Birds of each striping have different "personalities." For example, white-stripes are more aggressive and sing a great deal more than tan-striped birds. For defense of the territory, it is probably important that there is a white-striped bird in each pair (see p. 145 for more on this topic).

A male redstart perches on a branch in his territory and sings to an intruding male redstart, then repeatedly flies in circles in front of the intruder if he doesn't go away.

The size of the territory is influenced by the abundance of food on it, and whether it includes a foraging area. While the shrike catches most of its food on its territory, the Bank Swallow maintains only its nest site. Swallows and waxwings do not defend a foraging area. During nesting season swallows eat flying insects which are abundant and which are not defendable because of their rapid movement from place to place. The waxwing's lack of defense of a foraging area during nesting season reflects its year-round feeding behavior. It is to the benefit of each waxwing to travel in flocks with others, foraging for their plentiful, but localized, food supply—berries and other fruit. Several bushes in one area may be covered with berries, while the next "energy depot"—another berry bush or stand of trees, rich with fruit—may be several kilometers away. Though the food is difficult to find, once one waxwing spots a supply, there is plenty for all. Apparently searching with others is so important for this species that they are very social, even at nesting time. (Interestingly, waxwings nest just at the time when many berries are becoming ripe.)

Other factors also influence territory size and are often interrelated. For some species, density of the population and availability of good nesting space are important; if the population is large one year, many songbirds make their territories smaller.

Usually the bigger the bird, the bigger the territory it defends. Carnivorous birds such as eagles and hawks often have a limited food supply, so they need a lot of room to seek it out. (The Golden Eagle's territory is about 9300 ha; the smaller, very common Red-tailed Hawk defends 130 ha.)

Sometimes it is difficult to determine why similar-sized birds with similar habits have such different sizes of territory. The Least Flycatcher is an insect eater that needs only 0.08 ha (⅕ acre), whereas the Black-capped Chickadee, about as big and also an insect eater, has a 5.3 ha (13 acre) territory. Chickadees may need more space in winter when their food, mainly insect eggs in the bark of trees, is not plentiful.

Having a territory of a certain size is apparently very important. One study of Savannah Sparrows showed that males with territories between 0.06 and 0.12 ha (¹⁄₁₀–³⁄₁₀ acre) had nests on them 56–89% of the time, but territories less than 0.06 ha (¹⁄₁₀ acre) had nests on them only 11% of the time.

Even in a marsh with a dense colony of Red-winged Blackbirds, each male has his own territory. He defends this vigorously, and many of the younger or weaker males are unable to hold onto a site that would be suitable for nesting; they are pushed out of the marsh into less suitable places. Therefore, in the best places for nesting there may well be more females than males, and polygamy is fairly common (most songbirds are monogamous). Unlike most female songbirds, the female red-wing is aggressive toward other females (thus, territorial). She, and her young when they are out of the nest, will do a great deal of feeding nearby, so it is probably in her best interests to keep other females and their young as far away as possible.

Migratory songbirds tend to return to their territories or nearby. One study in which adult robins were banded showed that 74% of them returned to within 16 km of their nesting site of the previous year. Studies with Tree Swallows, House Wrens, Baltimore Orioles and Song Sparrows showed similar fidelity.

Probably all reptiles, birds and mammals are to some degree territorial. Wild birds give us the opportunity to look closer at this very interesting behavior.

This marsh looks crowded with Red-winged Blackbirds as do many marshes in spring. Each bird assures itself of a certain amount of space, however, by being territorial.

Some special displays

"Wings out" display. If someone glared at you in the manner this bird is, wouldn't you go away? It usually has that effect on other male Chestnut-sided Warblers. A male Chestnut-sided Warbler gives this "wings out" display after a prolonged encounter with another male intruder on his territory. His singing advertises his presence and usually is sufficient to keep other males of his species off his territory. If his singing does not prevent the intrusion, he gives this display. If both warnings fail, the warbler will attack, snapping his bill as he flies. The intruding bird ordinarily leaves, but if he perches just outside the territory near the boundary line, he will again receive this "wings out" glare until he departs.

"Head-up" or "bill-pointing" display. North American blackbirds have distinctive postures for communication. These postures are usually, but not always, linked with certain songs or calls. The "head-up" or "bill-pointing" display illustrated here is used in threat situations. Though a Common Grackle is shown, you can see the same display performed by male Red-winged Blackbirds, Brewer's Blackbirds and some cowbirds. A bird foraging on the ground gives this display to other birds that land nearby; males also use it as a threat during courtship. This display, along with his song, helps a male establish his territory. If a female approaches, the male changes this threatening "head-up" posture to a "ruff-out" posture, fluffing out his feathers to attract her.

These male Common Grackles are exhibiting an aggressive ("bill-pointing") display.

Why do birds sing?

All vertebrates have some way of recognizing and communicating with others of their species. Since songbirds often live in thick foliage where it is difficult to see one another, sound is an important way for them to reach their own kind.

Songbirds have two types of vocalization—calls and songs. Calls are brief sounds with only one or two syllables, and involve only a few notes. They are usually given to inform nearby birds—mate, offspring or others in the flock—of a situation requiring an immediate response. For example, starlings give different calls to signal distress, escape, feeding and so on.

Songs, on the other hand, are made up of sounds or notes consistently repeated in a specific pattern, and are involved with courtship and mating. Almost always, only the male of a species sings. His song attracts a mate and keeps other males away. Song substitutes for actual fighting in defense of territories; by singing, a male bird "tells" another male that an area is taken. The other male almost always responds by going elsewhere. No battle is usually necessary to establish the territory, though such battles can occur between territorial male songbirds. Song thus helps maintain the pair bond by keeping other males away. It probably also informs the female that the male is still there, reducing the chance that she will abandon her nest or copulate with another male. (See also Part III, *Bird calls.*)

The Painted Bunting: a southern beauty. Though it is not one of the most common North American songbirds, we couldn't bear to exclude this little bunting with tropical colors. It is found in thickets and brushy areas of the South, the same habitat where you'll find its relatives, the Indigo Bunting in the East and the Lazuli Bunting in the West. Colorful males, like the one shown here, have warbling songs and a call note that is a sharp CHIP. Females and young males have green backs, with lighter yellow-green underparts.

Why do birds have color?

Most colors that birds have in their feathers are due to the presence of complex chemicals called pigments; the blues are an exception. Here, special feather structure refracts light in a way that causes the feather to look blue. Besides giving feathers their color, pigments have other important functions such as absorbing heat from the sun and making the feathers stronger so that they will wear longer (that is why so many birds like gulls have black wing tips).

Why do birds come in such a variety of color, some very bright, others dull? For some species, color serves as camouflage. This is probably especially important in defenseless species that live in the open; with some notable exceptions (such as the male Bobolink) most field songbirds are dull and camouflaged. In many species of songbirds, color is an important signal for recognition—to threaten and distract other males of their own kind and (perhaps) to attract females. Birds, unlike many mammals, are not color-blind; they can see bright colors as well as we can.

Several simple experiments have shown the importance of color as signals in some species. In Common Yellowthroats (a warbler), the male has a black mask, which is absent in the female. When a male yellowthroat was presented with a stuffed dummy of a female yellowthroat in his territory, he courted and tried to copulate with the dummy. But when a black mask was painted on its face, he rejected it emphatically.

Many other birds respond in the same way. Male Baltimore Orioles or Red-winged Blackbirds will tear apart dummies of males that are placed in their territories. The little (but aggressive) European Robin responds to the color red, and will even attack a piece of red cloth put in its territory (both males and females do this).

Some experiments with Red-winged Blackbirds show us that males and females of this species respond differently to the male's colors. Male Red-winged Blackbirds are black with a large red epaulet or patch on their shoulder. When males had their bright epaulet feathers blackened during the time they were establishing territories, 64% of them lost their territories. Other males fought them more aggressively and drove them away. To compensate, the blackened birds had to display even more vigorously than usual. The experimentally altered birds, however, experienced no difficulty in attracting females to their territories: the bright epaulets are an important signal to other males, but not to the females. (See also Part III, *Why are some birds brightly colored and others dull?*)

How birds woo

Courtship displays are among the most fascinating displays of complex behavior. Waxwings pass petals to each other, crows stroke each other's feathers, mutually preening, and larks perform aerial antics—all for the sake of securing a nesting partner.

Special features of the courtship displays of common songbirds are described in Part III. But a few displays are discussed here as a sample of the "wooing" that occurs in the spring. It is more likely that you will see the lark or blackbird displays than the vireo display—vireos are rather secretive birds.

The Bell's Vireo shown here is involved in a complicated precopulatory display. The male fans his tail, ruffles his body feathers, withdraws his head and holds it back slightly with his mouth open. Then he begins to sway back and forth before a female. At the low point of his swing, he begins his courtship song. If the female crouches, with body feathers fluffed and tail slightly raised, the male will leap onto the female's back and they will copulate. Since male and female vireos look the same, this elaborate display serves as a signal of recognition. If the other bird responds to the swaying by singing, he will chase it away, for that tells him it is another male.

In a precopulatory display, the male Bell's Vireo sways back and forth before the female, then begins his courtship song.

The male Red-eyed Vireo has a different sort of precopulatory display. After a simple display he vigorously attacks the female, sometimes knocking her to the ground. This is evidently done for sex recognition. If the other bird fights and/or sings, it must be a male. If it does neither, it must be a female. She will show a submissive, crouching posture when attacked. When a tape recording of a Red-eyed Vireo is played and a model set up in a male's territory, he will attack it ferociously until the song is stopped; then he stops attacking.

"Ruff-out" display of a Brown-headed Cowbird.

"Ruff-out" display. This display in which blackbird males fluff out their feathers is sometimes done when they simply perch alone, but more often it is used in aggressive threats and in courtship. The cowbird male uses this display to attract the feeding female. With feathers ruffed out, bill pointed downward, tail widely spread and wings drooped and held out from the body, he displays for her attention. If the female responds by elevating her tail and lowering her wings, it is a signal to the male that she is receptive. Copulation between the two follows.

In mating season, the male Horned Lark performs an aerial display by flying straight up, high into the air, making no sound. Then, spreading his wings and soaring, he sings a lovely, joyful-sounding song. After flapping his wings several times, he soars again and repeats his song. Often a male will fly into a headwind so that rather than moving forward as shown here, he appears to be suspended in one spot over his territory, repeatedly flapping his wings, then soaring and singing. Then, as suddenly and silently as he went up, he plunges to earth. Just as he is about to crash into the ground, he spreads his wings, lands gracefully and struts about with his feathery "horns" held high. Like the blackbirds' "ruff-out" display, this spectacular Horned Lark display probably serves both to attract a mate and to keep other males away.

The Horned Lark puts on a spectacular courtship show. He flies straight up, flaps his wings and sings his song over and over. Then he plunges to earth and lands gracefully.

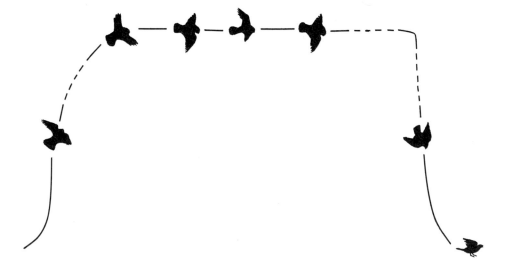

A male goldfinch feeds his mate while she sits on the nest.

Courtship feeding

Many birds "courtship feed." Most often the male feeds his mate during the period of copulation and egg laying, and frequently continues while she is incubating and brooding (in some species the female also "courtship feeds" the male). Courtship feeding, swaying before a mate, and many other small actions of one bird toward the other help them recognize each other and keep the pair bond strong. A strong pair bond ensures that both parents stay at the nest to provide food.

Courtship feeding by the male also demonstrates to the female a "willingness" of the male to help feed. When they become sexually active adults, nestlings will perform the same rituals, having inherited them from their parents. Inheritance of these characteristics in "the wild" might be made clearer by an example: the selective breeding of sheep dogs has resulted in the production of puppies with an inborn tendency toward herding.

Some people believe that kissing in humans originated with courtship feeding. Not very romantic, but possible.

Mating and copulation in songbirds

The mating of birds involves a flurry of activity—males chase each other and display before females who, in turn, signal males of their readiness *or* lack of readiness to mate. After males have established territories and a male and female accept each other and form a "pair bond," the birds are said to have *mated*.

The culmination of the mating process is *copulation* between a male and a female to transmit sperm. To copulate, a male stands on a female's back and by folding his tail to one side and downward, the cloaca of the male comes into contact with the cloaca of the female. (Birds have a single opening called the cloaca for the removal of waste from the digestive system, urinary waste from the kidneys and eggs from the ovary or sperm from the testis. Birds such as ostriches, tinamous, grebes, storks and ducks have a grooved penis which can be erected to direct sperm from the male into the female cloaca during copulation. But songbirds and most other birds such as hawks, owls and woodpeckers have no such intromittent organ.) The contact between cloacas allows large numbers of sperm to pass from male to female. Sperm are briefly stored in a pouch in the lower oviduct of the female; then they swim up the oviduct and fertilize the eggs at its upper end. It may seem an improbable feat but, judging from the great number of songbirds, it must be effective.

To copulate, the male Red-winged Blackbird stands on the female's back and folds his tail to one side until their cloacas meet.

One mate or more?

What determines whether birds mate with only one member of the opposite sex, or with many? We do not know for certain, but we can speculate.

After songbirds form pairs in the spring or early summer, most remain mated to each other for the entire breeding season—they are monogamous. Some kinds of birds mate for life, but few migratory songbirds do. Those that nest in holes or cavities such as Bank Swallows and House Wrens remain united for only one brood. In these species, the male cares for the fledglings of the first brood while the female of the pair seeks a second mate and nests again elsewhere. Generally such polygamy exists in species in which only one parent is necessary to rear the brood.

All birds "try" to be the parent of as many nestlings as possible. Birds of course do not realize that they are trying, but it is perhaps the best way of describing the effect of their behavior.

A brief digression might help explain this difficult concept. In a certain species, bird A lays two eggs and raises two young, and bird B lays four eggs and raises four young. Bird B will give its characteristics to twice as many offspring as bird A, and if the number of eggs laid is a characteristic that is inherited, four of the six young birds produced will be programmed to lay four eggs. Whereas we began with equal numbers of A and B, the proportion of the total that are B increases dramatically with each generation.

As an example, we have invented two different kinds of female birds, Type A and Type B. Type A lays 2 eggs and Type B lays 4. We assume that the number of eggs laid is an inherited feature, passed on from mother to daughter. These two females, then, produce a total of 6 eggs; if all hatch, 2 young are Type A and 4 are Type B, and if all are daughters, 2 of them will be "programmed" to lay 2 eggs and 4 of them

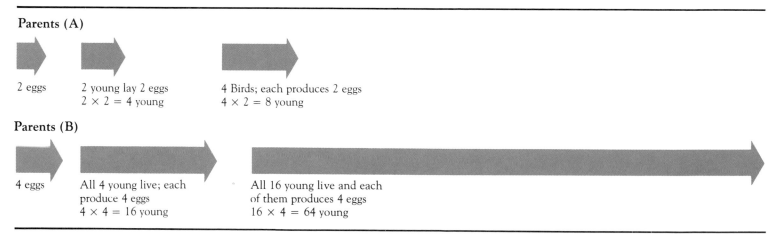

Parents (A)

2 eggs

2 young lay 2 eggs
2 × 2 = 4 young

4 Birds; each produces 2 eggs
4 × 2 = 8 young

Parents (B)

4 eggs

All 4 young live; each produce 4 eggs
4 × 4 = 16 young

All 16 young live and each of them produces 4 eggs
16 × 4 = 64 young

to lay 4. The percentage of birds that will lay 2 will be 33%. If the mothers die, and the daughters all mate, 4 of the daughters (Type A) will lay 2 eggs and produce a total of 8 young, and 16 (Type B) will lay 4 eggs and produce a total of 64 young. On a percentage basis, only 11% of the birds of this generation will be Type A. Through additional generations, this percentage would continue to decrease and become very small. (Of course these parents would produce sons as well as daughters, but this would not influence the percentages of the different types of daughters produced.)

Populations of all animals are checked by death, brought on by disease, starvation and other factors so that the number of individuals in a species approaches a certain upper limit. If the population size of our hypothetical species were at this limit, and the *proportion* of the number of individuals laying four eggs were increasing, in very few generations the *number* of individuals laying only two eggs would be small, perhaps zero. In jargon we say that those laying only two eggs have been selected out of the species in favor of other individuals producing more. Selection generally favors those individuals producing the largest number of offspring possible.

The maximum number of young a bird can raise is limited not just by the quantity of eggs the female is physically capable of producing or incubating but by how many young she alone, or with the help of her mate, can feed. In most songbirds, close cooperation between the male and female of a pair helps them raise as many young as possible. Both help feed and protect the young, although only female songbirds are able to incubate the eggs (the males lack brood patches; although they can sit on the eggs to shelter or hide them, they cannot really impart much of their body heat to them). In some cases, however, it is possible for one parent alone to take care of the brood as well,

Front view of the posture.

Side view of the aggressive posture of a male Red-winged Blackbird toward another male red-wing.

or nearly as well, as the two working together. This can happen if food is abundant and one parent can gather enough for all, or if the nest is so secure that there is little need to guard it. In such cases, one of the parents can mate again—become a polygamist—without jeopardizing its first offspring. In this way the bird can increase its number of young, and in such species polygamists would be selectively favored over monogamous individuals.

For example, nestlings of hole nesters are better protected from heat loss and enemies than are nestlings in open nests. Since such nests are relatively safe and require less attention, a single parent can usually raise the brood. This selects for the other parent to attempt to mate a second time—perhaps with another partner (though commonly the pair remains together and the female starts a second brood while the male feeds the young from the first). Data have been gathered that lend credence to this explanation for why polygamy occurs. About 50% of male Winter Wrens in England and Holland are polygamous. But on the isolated island of St. Kilda, off the west coast of Scotland, where food is scarce and two parents between them have trouble finding enough for their young, the wren is strictly monogamous. Neither the mother nor the father would have more surviving young by taking on a second mate or brood.

Some species that are not hole nesters are polygamous, too. The familiar Red-winged Blackbird is an example. These pugnacious birds nest in colonies in marshes. The males defend territories by aggressive behavior, driving the less successful males from the marsh. This creates a shortage of males and consequently some females, in order to mate at all, must pair with an already mated male. The most successful males hold territories with several mates. The nests are built close together and, being in bushes or cattails over water, they are safe from most predators. The male can help guard them all at the same time, and the females take sole responsibility for feeding the young. This polygamous behavior is advantageous to males that have mates—they father more young than they would if monogamous. The females benefit both by having superior nest sites that are controlled by successful males and by having such a bird as the father of their offspring.

We could, in our minds, design a "more fair" blackbird society that included the less aggressive males—but such a society does not exist because the despotic behavior of the males is selectively favored.

Nest building

Tree Swallows use the hollow cavities in dead trees to make nests of dry grass and straw; these are then lined with feathers.

Almost all songbirds build some sort of nest in which to lay their eggs. (Among the few exceptions is the wily cowbird who dumps her eggs into the nests of other birds for them to incubate and raise.) Nests vary tremendously. Some are sturdy. Others are so flimsy you'd think they would give way under the weight of the young. Some are placed high, others low. Building materials range from mud to snakeskin. Each kind of bird builds a nest that is distinctive.

In North America some of the most interesting nest types you'll see are made by the several species of swallows. Tree Swallows are hole nesters as are bluebirds and most wrens. They make simple nests of dry grass and straw and line them with feathers. Barn Swallows make nests of mud reinforced with straw and lined with feathers. Here we describe the nesting habits of three other swallow species.

By sticking mud to the sheer face of a cliff

Cliff Swallows. The Cliff Swallow breeds from northern Canada and Alaska south to Alabama and central Mexico. Its mud nests look like bottles turned on their sides. In spring, Cliff Swallows can be seen landing on muddy lakeshores, usually in small groups. As they land, they hold their tails high and flutter their wings above their backs, probably to maintain balance and prevent sinking into the mud. They fill their beaks with mud, roll it about to make it compact and fly off to their nest sites. It takes about 1000 mud pellets to make one Cliff Swallow nest. (While mud is being gathered, the male often alights on the back of the female and they copulate.)

Nest sites are sheer cliff faces or, more frequently, eaves of buildings. Using mud pellets, the birds construct the bottom of the nest first, then outline the whole thing on the wall. Soon one bird, assumed to be the female, stays at the nest and welcomes the male with cries and fluttering wings each time he returns with more mud. In about a week the nest foundation is complete. It is then lined with feathers, leaves, rags or similar materials. In the past it was thought that the swallow's saliva (like that of some swifts) held the mud together. Since the nests crumble when wet, as any mud does, it is unlikely that swallows use saliva to paste their mud nests together.

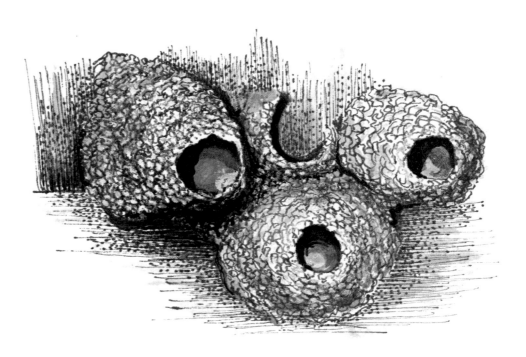

The mud nests of Cliff Swallows clinging to cliffs or the eaves of buildings look like bottles turned on their sides.

If the mud nests crumble easily, how are they successful? One observer tells of seeing a large colony along the cliffs of the Red Deer River in Alberta. He noticed that the mud nests were clumped together in groups, then for no apparent reason there were empty spaces on the cliff side, then more nests clumped together. A closer look told him why. Some areas of the cliff side were darkened where water from past rains had run. Those were precisely the spaces left vacant by Cliff Swallows. It appears they have an uncanny way of knowing just where the water runs that would ruin their nests.

Cliff Swallows hold their tails high and flutter their wings to keep from sinking into the mud they gather for their nests.

By hollowing out chambers a few inches a day

Bank Swallows. Bank Swallows, found almost worldwide, dig chambers into the side of a sandy cliff. After the male bird selects a site, both male and female cling to a slight projection on the bank and peck at the surface. After they have made a depression, they peck out the ceiling and sides of the chamber, clinging to the sides as they hammer and scrape. They kick backward with their claws to dig out the floor and use their wings to rid the chamber of fallen dirt. Progressing about 7 to 10 cm (3–4 in.) a day, they carve out a burrow with arched ceiling and flat floor, about 1 m (40 in.) deep. In spite of the hard work, when Bank and Cliff Swallows are building their nests there is a "holiday atmosphere." Great twittering and flying about are interspersed with periods of work.

After the burrow is completed, the male and female bring in grass stalks and finer materials to build the nest. One person studying these birds found that the depression within the grassy nest at the end of the chamber where the female sat incubating was only 5 cm (2 in.) wide and 1.5 cm (0.5 in.) deep.

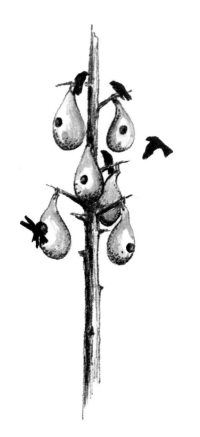

Gourds, once used by Indians to attract Purple Martins, are still popular birdhouses in the southern US.

Purple Martins. Even before Europeans came to America, certain birds were being attracted to nest near people. Indians used dried gourds to attract the Purple Martin. They placed the hollow gourds on posts and small tree branches outside the doors of their homes. This kind of birdhouse is still popular in the southern US though large apartment-type birdhouses are generally used to draw Purple Martins in the North. These large swallows, with rich gurgling calls, are welcomed as harbingers of spring. Once Purple Martins nest in a particular house, they will probably return to it the following year. One man tells the story of taking down his martin house for a paint job and forgetting to replace it on its pole. The loud calls of the martins suddenly back from the South startled him. They kept circling his yard and calling until he got the house back on its pole!

Two other very interesting nest-building habits are described here, that of the orioles and the House Wrens. In Part III, we have discussed nesting habits of a select number of other species.

By weaving a masterpiece

Orioles. The pendulous nests of Baltimore and Bullock's Orioles are perhaps the most elaborate and familiar of all songbird nests. Suspended in trees, usually from near the tips of branches, orioles' nests are inaccessible to most nest predators. But the orioles must work hard for this security. The female builds the nest. She starts construction by loosely wrapping a few long grasses or hairs around the twigs she has selected to support the nest. Over the next few days she continues to add more grasses and fibers, pulling each through others with her bill. Slowly the nest develops, from a tangled ball of grasses to

Female orioles weave their nests from long strands of grass and other fibers such as the long hair from manes and tails of horses; today they sometimes use monofilament fishing line. In the South, they use chiefly Spanish "moss."

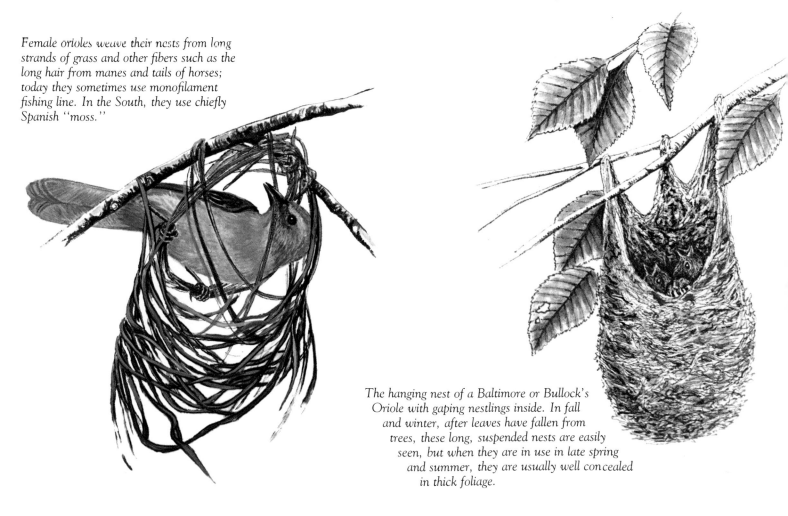

The hanging nest of a Baltimore or Bullock's Oriole with gaping nestlings inside. In fall and winter, after leaves have fallen from trees, these long, suspended nests are easily seen, but when they are in use in late spring and summer, they are usually well concealed in thick foliage.

a loose pendant mass. As the nest grows, the female settles inside it from time to time, using her weight to tighten the weave. When the nest has reached its final proportions, 15 cm (5 to 6 in.) or longer, she lines it with dandelion, willow or cottonwood down. The entire effort takes her at least 4½ days, but she has created a masterpiece, a secure, warm nursery for her nestlings. As elaborate as these nests are, however, the oriole builds a new one each year.

House Wrens are easily attracted to bird-houses. Their beautiful, melodious song makes them popular tenants.

House Wrens. Usually it is only by luck that a songbird chooses to nest in our yard, but a few can be attracted by birdhouses. The House Wren is perhaps the most easily attracted species. For best results, put up several houses—so that the wrens can make their own choice. With luck, a male will establish his territory in your yard, rewarding you with nearly constant song. He lays claim to all suitable nest sites in the area by stuffing coarse twigs into them. When his mate arrives, she selects her favorite site, then commences to rebuild the nest. Often she cleans out the male's work and starts anew. He helps her build, but she does most of the work. He's too busy singing to be efficient. Though wrens readily come to human-made boxes, and even seem to prefer them when available, they will nest in nearly any suitable cavity—even an old oriole nest.

A variety of nests

The Parula Warbler builds an unusual looking nest, hanging lichens from a tree branch and making an entrance to one side.

The Winter Wren may build several nests in the upturned roots of fallen trees; the female chooses one, then builds a roof over it.

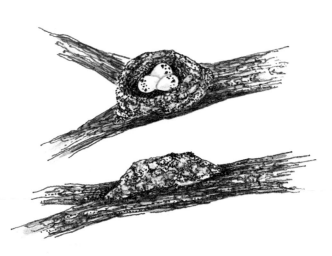

The nest of the Eastern Wood Pewee (or Eastern Pewee) is so tiny and shallow it is almost impossible to find. From a distance, it looks like the knot on a tree branch.

The Great Crested Flycatcher is notorious for stuffing its nest into roadside mailboxes, and using, among other things, snakeskins (or in modern times such synthetic substitutes as cellophane) as filler.

Long-billed Marsh Wrens (sometimes simply called Marsh Wrens) nest in marshes. A male may make as many as 10 unlined nests before the female arrives in the area. The female then lines the nest she chooses. Some males attract several females to their territories.

Egg laying

Some birds lay a set number of eggs, one after the other, and then stop. Others continue to lay eggs until their nest contains a given number, and if an egg is removed, they will lay another to replace the missing one. A female of the latter species is capable of laying a larger number of eggs than she ordinarily incubates in a single clutch (a set of eggs); the chicken is an example of this sort of "indeterminant" layer. How the females "know" when they have laid enough—the right number—is not understood. Somehow, having reached a certain number stimulates hormonal changes that cause the ovary of the female to regress. Then she is ready to start incubating. The fact that most female birds can lay more eggs than they ordinarily do shows us that they do not merely stop because they have "run out."

Each species of bird lays a characteristic number of eggs, although there is some variability among individual females. Young females usually lay fewer eggs than older ones. The time of year may also be a factor: near the end of the season, females of many species lay smaller clutches than usual. The number of eggs laid by the female of a given species may also vary from place to place. For example, in northern Canada, most female Savannah Sparrows lay five eggs; in southern Canada, most lay four; and in western Mexico, most lay three. This pattern seems to be usual for songbirds: they tend to lay larger clutches in the northern parts of their range. Some people think that the longer days in the North give the parents more time to find food for a larger brood. On the other hand, in the South, birds tend to lay more clutches because they have more time—the summers are longer. Perhaps in the North the birds literally put all their eggs in one basket—they produce as many young as possible in a single brood, the only one that they will have time for that year.

The Eastern Bluebird nest, here viewed from above, is placed in a cavity and contains light blue or white eggs.

The eggs of the American Redstart have a wreath of speckles around the large end.

The nest of a Wood Thrush contains brilliant blue eggs. (See WHY ARE BIRD EGGS DIFFERENT COLORS?)

When eggs are being produced, the ovarian follicles grow large and secrete hormones that cause an increased absorption by the intestine of calcium from the foods eaten; to a certain extent, also, the female "takes" calcium from her bones to deposit in the shells of her eggs. This calcium is important for the shells of the eggs. It is believed that the female eats the shells after her nestlings have hatched to replenish her low calcium level—as well as to destroy this evidence of a nest location that predators may be watching for.

Perhaps you have heard of "egg shell thinning" that results from DDT poisoning. This has not been described in songbirds, but is a known problem in pelicans, Peregrine Falcons and many other birds. When a certain level of DDT is reached in the tissues of these species, below the level directly lethal to them, the hormonal system that normally controls the female's calcium metabolism is affected, and she is no longer able to deposit sufficient calcium in the shells of her eggs. Often such eggs are broken when she sits on them to incubate or tries to turn them. The birds become extinct in some areas simply because they have failed to reproduce.

Incubation

If you asked a child what incubation is, he or she would probably answer, "That's when birds sit on their eggs." That is basically correct, of course, but it is not the whole story. For a complete understanding of this process there are more facts one needs to know.

No incubation takes place unless heat is supplied to the eggs, and male songbirds cannot supply that heat. The reason? They do not have feather-free areas on their bellies through which heat passes easily from their bodies to the eggs. Of the passerines found north of Mexico, only in some flycatchers—not true songbirds—do males have these *incubation* or *brood patches*. A male songbird will sometimes sit on the eggs while the mother is out searching for food (or stretching her wings). In doing so, he protects them from predators and keeps the eggs from getting cold quickly, but he does not "incubate" them.

If you happen to be involved in a bird-banding program, or if for some other reason you're able to hold an adult female bird in your hands during the spring, you'll probably be able to see the brood patch. Hold her on her back against the palm of your hand so that you can see her belly, and gently blow the feathers on the belly toward her head. You will see a bare area where the skin is thick, spongy and richly supplied with blood vessels that allow an efficient transfer of heat from the mother to the eggs, and later to the nestlings.

Feathers on the female's belly are lost just before egg laying (in Song Sparrows, four to six days before the first egg is laid); these feathers grow back during the general replacement of feathers that takes place in late summer, before the onset of cold weather. It has been found that eggs incubated by a female House Wren with an incubation patch have a 6°C higher temperature than when a male sits on them. For most songbirds, the incubation period—the time between the laying of the last egg to the hatching of the last egg—is 12 to 14 days. It's interesting to note that brightly colored males (except for the Rose-breasted Grosbeak) rarely sit on the eggs; but if the male and female are similar in color, they share the nest-sitting task.

Will the embryos in the eggs die if they get cold? Embryos are more sensitive to cold later in incubation than earlier, but at any time it will slow down their development so that nestlings will not hatch as soon. All songbirds leave their nests on occasion while they are incubating, but unless it is extremely cold, embryos in eggs or small nestlings will not die on brief exposure to cold. Some adults, like the female Cedar Waxwing, stay on their nests almost constantly because the male partners feed them. But in other species, the female must go out for her own food. Some females fast for part of the incubation period.

All incubating birds look restless. They change sitting position, then rise, sometimes turning the eggs with their bill, and settle again. They tamper with the nesting material and poke around on the bottom of the nest.

It is not true that birds always abandon their nests if you touch or even handle their eggs. They might, however, abandon their nests if they are disturbed too frequently, or for too long a time.

Many birds do not recognize their own eggs and will accept any that are the same size. The fact that so many tiny birds accept the larger eggs of the cowbird shows that even size is not always important. The robin and catbird, which regularly throw cowbird eggs out of their nests, both lay plain blue eggs; this doubtless makes it easier for them to spot the speckled cowbird's egg.

Hatching

Chicks hatch by pipping the shell with their "egg tooth." For most species it takes from 5 to 22 hours to emerge from their little prisons.

Chicks hatch themselves! Even songbird nestlings, although blind, helpless and hungry after hatching, can get themselves out of the egg. The embryos develop a special muscle in the neck, the *hatching muscle,* and even a special structure, the *egg tooth,* to help them do this. When the muscle (in the back of the hatchling's neck) contracts, it pulls the bird's head up, forcing the egg tooth against the shell. The egg tooth, a short, pointed, horny projection on the top of the bill, "pips" the egg in this way. The one tiny crack where the egg is pipped permits fresh air to enter. Wood Thrush nestlings free themselves from 5 to 22 hours after pipping the egg; other species take about this amount of time or a little longer. Within a few days the egg tooth falls off the little beak and the hatching muscle begins to shrink.

It is now known that the clicking sound made by some chicks one to two days before hatching acts as a signal to others of the clutch. This synchronizes the hatching of the clutch, especially in birds with precocial young, that is, birds that do not require much care upon hatching, such as quail and ducks. Amazingly, there is a standard number of clicks per minute for each species. Tree Sparrow nestlings click at the rate of 60 clicks per minute. It has been shown that when all the eggs in the nest are in contact with each other, the hatching of the clutch is well synchronized, probably because the vibrations are transmitted better.

Here we see the brightly colored male Rufous-sided Towhee perching nearby while the female builds their nest. The towhee gets its name from one of its song, TOW-HEEEE, though in most parts of its range it more commonly sings DRINK-YOUR-TEA. The towhee is a New World sparrow, but unlike most male and female sparrows who look alike, the towhee sexes have noticeably different plumages.

Nest sanitation

As soon as young birds hatch, their parents rid the nest of the fragments of eggshell. There is some evidence that predators spot nests more easily when the shells are left. Removing the shells thus makes nests less conspicuous.

Sometimes the female does the work alone; sometimes both parents help. Some birds carry the shells away from the nest and drop them, but the instinct of some females is to eat them. This probably helps her replenish the calcium in her body that was used in producing the egg. Shells are not merely dropped over the side of the nest; they are carried some distance.

To keep the nest clean and free of parasites the parents also remove the nestlings' wastes. Nestlings produce envelopes of thick mucous, called fecal sacs, that contain whitish semisolid urine and dark feces. The parents either eat these sacs or carry them away. Swallows drop them into water; wrens and nuthatches find branches far from the nest and leave them there. Some parents remove the sacs throughout the nesting period, while others stop

(Left) Nestlings produce waste inside fecal sacs. To keep the nest clean, the parents either eat the sacs or carry them away as this Gray Jay is doing.

(Right) When her chicks have hatched, this Blue-gray Gnatcatcher cleans the nest of eggshells. Some birds eat the shells; others carry the shells far away and drop them.

about three-quarters of the way through the period and just let waste accumulate from then on. Interestingly, after they reach a certain age, young swallows, along with most cavity-nesting birds, will back up to the edge of the nest before defecating. When we tried to act as parents for a young starling recently, we noticed that when it was about seven to nine days old, it no longer just sat wherever it was to release waste, but turned around and backed up before doing so. It is also interesting that the material did not simply fall from the young bird, but was propelled forcefully. Starlings nest in cavities and had this young bird been in a nest cavity, its inherited tendency to turn around and forcefully eject its waste would have helped keep the nest clean.

Birds with nest-cleaning tendencies have been more successful over the years, and as a consequence have come to predominate in nature.

Keeping the nestlings warm

Some songbirds of the northern woods are such early nesters that it is difficult to imagine how their young nestlings can survive the cold. Gray Jays start nest building while snow is still deep, and the young hatch when temperatures are well below freezing. Crossbills are known to nest at any time of the year, and they too may have young in the nest when temperatures are extremely low. The reason that the young of these species survive is, of course, that they are *not* exposed to low temperatures except when they are being fed. The female broods them while the male brings in food. All songbirds, in fact, brood their young. The female sits on the nestlings just as she did on her eggs, transmitting her body heat to them through her brood patch. The body temperature of adult birds, like that of mammals, is regulated at a certain level: the "normal" body temperature for people is about 37°C (98.6°F), and the normal temperature of most birds is somewhat higher. (Just how body temperature is controlled is not fully understood.)

When songbirds are newly hatched, they are "cold-blooded." It takes anywhere from 5 to 12 days for the nestling songbirds to be able to regulate their own body temperature. During this time the parents must brood them, but they do so less and less as the days after hatching go by. In one study, workers found that Carolina Wrens brooded 68% of the time on the hatching day, 65% the next day, 15% on the third day and by the sixth day they no longer brooded at all. During the nights, however, the wrens brooded constantly.

A Canada Warbler broods her young. Even on a hot day, the mother needs to continue brooding. She pants and spreads her wings both to keep cool and to shade her young so they do not overheat.

Just how long baby songbirds remain in the nest after hatching seems to depend mainly on whether they are nestlings of open-nesting species or of hole nesters. The young of open-nesting species generally leave the nest about 11 days after they have hatched, whereas the young of birds hatching in nests in holes leave after about 18 days. (Bank Swallow nestlings do not leave until they are about 23 days old; once they leave, the parents no longer feed them.)

Development of the young among shorebirds and ducks contrasts sharply with that of songbird nestlings. For details see p. 50.

How birds respond to intruders

Two Eastern Kingbirds mob a much larger crow who has come too close to their nest. Such a sight—small songbirds attacking a large predator—is not uncommon!

Birds have several ways of responding to predators and other intruders near their nests. Those having nests that are well camouflaged, covered or inside cavities, usually "freeze" when an intruder comes near. Those with open nests in trees and bushes fly away. Those with nests on the ground, like the Horned Lark or Savannah Sparrow, usually run for some distance away from the nest and then take off. Generally, birds will "sit tighter" near to hatching time than early in incubation.

Some birds make a great deal of noise when a predator comes near their nests. If the Blue Jay has young in its nest, for example, it squawks and screams, often attracting other Blue Jays. Together they mob the intruder by flying just above its head. Red-winged Blackbirds, grackles and Mockingbirds will scold and mob a predator. Most will not actually strike an intruder, but red-wings and kingbirds commonly do; they will attack a passing crow or hawk, picking feathers from it, sometimes even landing on its back. Large birds of prey on occasion attack people, and many an eager photographer or egg collector has felt their talons. (Egg collecting is illegal today.)

Some songbirds give a warning call to their nesting partners, who respond by remaining very still. Others, like the redstart male illustrated here, fly away from their nests to another branch, make a great deal of noise and display their bright plumage in a threatening way. This "distraction" display calls attention away from the nest and toward themselves.

Many ground-nesting species have yet another approach to intruders. Sometimes sparrows give a "rodent run" display—they run off through the grass away from the nest, running like a small rodent, enticing the predator to chase them. Others, like the female Ovenbird illustrated here, fan out their tail, spread and vibrate their wings and move along the ground in such a peculiar way that it looks as if a wing is broken. This "broken wing" display makes the bird look like an easy victim to predators, and they chase the female who leads them away from the nest before flying into a thicket to hide. Unlike other birds using this display, the Ovenbird adds a little flair by ruffling her back and rump feathers while limping away.

Interestingly, wood warblers that do not nest on the ground also have been seen giving this broken wing display. Since, apart from them, only ground nesters give this distraction display, their use of the display suggests that these particular tree nesters descended from a ground-nesting ancestor.

Is the broken wing display a sign of birds' intelligence? Probably not. Researchers have seen birds use it at other times such as when they find another bird's egg in their nest. This response to a strange egg does not indicate ability to think, since a distraction display will obviously have no effect in this case. Undoubtedly, birds have inherited the tendency to use the broken wing display. Those of a certain species using the display have been more successful than those who have not and, thus, this behavior has become predominant in the species.

To a predator, this female Ovenbird appears to have a broken wing. This "broken wing" display often lures predators away from Ovenbirds' nests.

The male American Redstart is displaying his colorful plumage. By using this "distraction" display, he draws a predator's attention from his nest to himself.

Who does the feeding – and how?

In most songbirds both parents feed their nestlings, but there is great variety in how they do it. In Red-eyed Vireos, the female feeds the young about 75% of the time; in Arctic Warblers, the female feeds about the same amount of time, *but* the male brings more food on each feeding trip than the female does. House Wren females may leave their young after a few days and begin laying eggs for a second brood; then the male alone is left to care for the first brood.

No matter what adult songbirds eat in their own diets, they feed their nestlings mainly insects. This food is high in protein and provides for rapid growth and development. Adult finches, such as the goldfinch, crossbill and redpoll, swallow the food they eat, and regurgitate it into the beaks of their nestlings. But most other songbirds simply feed the young soft-bodied animals (insects, worms) or small fruit.

The feeding instinct is very strong; if parents lose a nest to predators or foul weather, they often try to feed nestlings of other birds in the vicinity. Extreme examples have been observed such as that of a Cardinal who adopted goldfish in a pool for several days, feeding them at its edge! Birds sometimes acquire the "feeding" drive before they "should" so that there are many reports of adults songbirds, especially males, trying to feed *eggs* days before they have hatched! And the opposite extreme has occurred; sometimes it seems the migration drive becomes stronger than the feeding drive, and the birds abandon their nestlings before they have fledged.

How nestlings get their parents to feed them

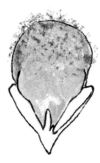

(a) *This head of a starling nestling shows the soft, swollen flanges on the sides of the nestling's beak that parent birds tap to cause the beak to spring open. Food is then shoved in.*

(b) *The Horned Lark nestling has an orange mouth with contrasting black bars on its tongue and spots on the roof of the mouth, all of which—when it gapes— stimulates the parent birds to feed it.*

Usually, songbird nestlings stimulate their parents to feed them. They give "begging" cries and wave their heads vigorously with their mouths open wide. Most nestlings have feeding targets; these are markings within their mouths which the parents see and toward which they direct the food. The mouth of a Horned Lark nestling has black spots, a bright orange roof and bars on its tongue! Nestlings hatched in nests within cavities usually have flanges at the edges of their beaks that are bright yellow or white, making it easier for the parents to see the wide-open gaping mouths in the dark recesses; those that are hatched in open nests almost always have a bright red or orange mouth. These colorful markings usually fade as the nestlings mature. These are some of the stimuli to which parents respond.

But some nestlings seem to need stimuli from the adults as well. The starling nestling has a swollen, sensitive mouth edge that is highly supplied with nerve endings; when this edge is touched by a parent, the mouth springs open. Sometimes parents shake the nest; this signal, especially after the first few days, causes most nestlings to open their beaks—to gape. Bank Swallow parents give high-pitched notes when they come to the nest; if the nestlings don't open their mouths, the parents gently trample them until they do!

Equal food for all? When we see songbirds busily feeding their young, devoting almost all their waking hours to them, we tend to think, "Ah, what marvelous parents these are, making certain their young are well fed." In fact, the process seems to be entirely instinctive. Birds do *not* consciously make certain that each nestling is well fed. Adult songbirds simply thrust food into the closest, widest open, gaping beak.

Nestlings have a special swallowing reflex; after a nestling has swallowed, it is physically incapable of swallowing again for a short time. This means that if it gapes after just having swallowed food and a parent sticks more food into its mouth, it cannot swallow it. When this happens, the parent simply plucks out the morsel and puts it into another gaping beak.

Helpless or independent at hatching?

A 15-day-old Eastern Bluebird nestling waits inside a cavity for a parent to bring food. Nestlings of such hole-nesting songbirds remain in the nest much longer than nestlings of open nesters, whose young fledge within 11 to 13 days.

Songbird nestlings hatch with their eyes closed; they are naked except for a few downy feathers. Cold-blooded and completely helpless, they depend entirely upon the constant brooding and feeding of their parents to survive. Just after hatching, the body temperature of the House Wren is 37°C (98.6°F); it gradually increases until after 15 days it is about 41.5°C (106.7°F)—approximately the normal body temperature of an adult House Wren at rest. Only after nestlings have been kept warm for several days (about six for most species) by parental brooding can their bodies maintain the temperature they need, that is, they become "warm-blooded." The terms "warm-blooded" and "cold-blooded" are used to distinguish animals that are able to regulate body temperature internally from those that regulate their body by sitting in the sun or shade, or some other method. The body temperature of many "cold-blooded" animals can be quite warm, depending upon whether they are out in the sun or resting in the shade.

Three-day-old Cardinal nestlings.

Five-day-old Cardinal nestlings.

Woodpeckers, hawks and owls also produce nestlings that require a great deal of care upon hatching. Such nestlings are said to be *altricial.* The opposite term, *precocial,* applies to the many young birds that are able to get along with little or no help from their parents. Shorebirds, such as the common Killdeer, plovers and sandpipers of various sorts, as well as ducks, chickens and quail, are precocial when hatched. These babies have a complete covering of downy feathers, their body temperature is almost as high as their parents' and they can regulate it without much brooding. Their eyes are not closed and they are virtually "ready to go" from the moment they hatch. Many start getting their own food the first day out of the egg. Most birds with precocial young are ground nesters. The adults are good runners or swimmers, and feed on the ground or in water.

These illustrations show the rapid development of typical songbird nestlings. Although they are helpless and their eyes are closed when hatched, most songbirds are able to leave the nest within 14 days.

Eleven-day-old Cardinal fledglings.

The Eastern Meadowlark chick depends entirely on the constant feeding and brooding by its parents to survive for several days after hatching. This altricial development is typical of songbirds, woodpeckers, hawks, owls and some other kinds of birds.

The plover egg has over four times the volume of the meadowlark egg, although the adult birds are almost the same size. The incubation period of the plover is almost twice that of the meadowlark so the young bird emerging from the hatched egg is much more mature.

These two ways of nesting work equally well, it seems, for the particular birds using them. The differences are nonetheless fascinating. The Golden Plover and meadowlark, for example, are birds of about the same size, but the plover's young are precocial and the meadowlark's altricial. The plover's egg has over four times the volume of the meadowlark's, and the developing young spend a longer period of time in the egg. There is much more yolk in a precocial bird's egg and not all of it is used up before hatching; with about one-seventh to one-third of the yolk remaining in the belly of the young bird, it continues to receive nourishment while it begins to forage for itself. Altricial chicks like those of the meadowlark who have no such food storage system must be fed very soon after hatching; a young Wood Thrush will call and gape as early as four minutes after it has wriggled out of its shell.

The Golden Plover chick is "ready to go" from the moment it hatches, needing little help from its parents. All shorebird chicks, as well as ducklings, goslings and the young of some other birds, exhibit this precocial development.

Feathers and molting

A bird's feather covering is called its plumage. Periodically all birds shed their plumage by molting. The very first occurs when the young are still in their nests. Born with little bits of fuzzy down, nestlings change their appearance within just a few days. The fuzzy down is attached to the tips of the next set of feathers that are just under the skin. These feathers push the down out so that it soon drops off. In late summer or fall of the bird's first year, this set of feathers is lost in another molt. All the feathers or only a part of them may be involved in this second molt. Now the bird has its first winter plumage which lasts through the winter and may be retained as its first spring breeding or "nuptial" plumage. But some species molt yet again before their first spring. Almost all species have a complete molt after the nesting season—July through early September. That's why you don't see many birds about at this time; they're quiet and still. Those you do manage to see will appear scraggly.

Songbirds do not lose all their feathers at once so they are still able to fly while molting. (Many ducks, grebes, loons and some other waterbirds, on the other hand, *do* molt all their wing feathers at once and cannot fly for a while.)

In order to understand the sequence of feather molting in a songbird's wing, it is necessary to name the feathers. The outermost nine or ten wing feathers are called "primaries"; those closer to the bird's body are called "secondaries." (Sometimes the feathers closest to the body are called "tertials," but many people simply call them secondaries.)

Orderly and precisely timed

When songbirds molt, the innermost secondary flight feathers—the tertials—of each wing are the first to go. It usually takes over a week for each feather to be replaced; the growth rate is several millimeters a day. By the time the three innermost secondary feathers are grown, the innermost primary falls out. This continues until all have been replaced. Typically after a few primary feathers are out, the outermost of the secondary wing feathers goes.

With tail feathers, molting starts in the middle and goes outward. Interestingly, creepers, who need their tail to climb, lose their two innermost feathers last. In these birds, the molt begins with the second from innermost tail feathers. Last of all, the two innermost ones fall out. As you can see, the molt of the wing and tail feathers of each species is an orderly process, precisely timed. For flying animals like birds it is especially important that these feathers are lost in a symmetrical way. In most species the flight feathers are replaced only once a year.

Birds look as if they have feathers over their entire bodies, but in fact they are concentrated in "feather tracts." During body molts, birds do not lose all the feathers out of a tract at the same time, but rather lose some, then others, while the first are being replaced. During some molts, only feathers in certain tracts are lost. For example, many songbirds replace only the winter feathers in their head region before their spring migration. Many other species have two complete sets of body feathers in a single year.

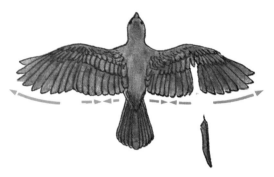

The sequence of wing feather loss during molt illustrated here is nearly universal in songbirds. First the three innermost feathers (secondaries) are lost, then the innermost primary feathers (at the bend of the wing). The molt of the primaries proceeds outward to the tip of the wing, and the remaining secondaries are lost from the bend of the wing inward. Thus there is never a gap of more than two feathers in the bird's wing during the molt.

In late summer, the male Scarlet Tanager's red plumage is mixed with patches of green. This molting male will soon be entirely green, with black wings and tail, and will look like the female tanager does year round.

Why do birds molt? Animals probably use energy only for those acts that are important to their survival and reproduction. It takes a great deal of energy to grow a new set of feathers—and during that time birds have reduced insulation and flying abilities. For example, cowbirds have been found to use up 13% more oxygen when molting. The more energy an animal uses, the more oxygen it consumes; hence, molting birds are using a lot more energy and require more food during their molt.

Why do they do it? The main reason birds molt is simply because their feathers get worn and broken. But it may also be a means of sanitation: it has been shown that certain sparrows that molt once a year have higher infestations of lice than others living in the same places that molt twice a year.

Also, birds that molt twice a year often acquire brighter feathers during their molt in late winter than they do during the late summer molt. These "nuptial" feathers may be important for courtship and mating. Many species, though, acquire their bright summer colors merely by wearing off the dull tips of their winter feathers.

The mystery of migration

Most songbirds migrate to and from their northern breeding grounds at night.

Many kinds of animals migrate. This regular movement from one place to another, and back, occurs among bats, fishes, squids, whales, butterflies, as well as birds. But it is birds we think of first when we hear the word, for their migration is most obvious to us.

Of all birds, the migration of the Arctic Tern is the most awesome. They breed in the Arctic; then they fly south for the winter, stopping not in Central or South America as do many other migratory birds, but going all the way to the Antarctic. (Only a few stop at the very tips of South America and South Africa.) From the frozen Antarctic, they fly out to sea, foraging there on the very plentiful floating plankton (consisting mostly of small shrimplike animals called krill) in oceanic upwellings. The next spring they fly back to the Arctic to breed. This round trip may cover over 40,000 km (25,000 mi) in a single year!

No songbird migrates as far as the Arctic Tern, but many do go very great distances. For example, the Bobolink breeds in the northern half of the United States and in southern Canada. It flies along two major routes to the pampas in Argentina and Brazil where it spends the winter. It must pass over mountain ranges and, along its eastern route, it crosses some 800 km (500 mi) of ocean. The Scarlet Tanager is another long-distance migrator among songbirds.

Where do they get the energy?

During migration, songbirds will also often fly great distances in a single flight—without stopping for food. Where do they get the energy required for such flights? The answer is from fat. Usually, only about 5% of a bird's total body weight is fat, but just prior to migration it stores tremendous extra amounts of fat and this serves as an energy supply for use in flight. For example, Blackpoll Warblers weigh about 12 g. But when blackpolls are about to embark on a long migratory flight, they can weigh as much as 22 g! Fat makes up half the total body weight.

The importance of this fat reserve was shown in an interesting study made of a large number of birds that were killed when they accidentally flew against a TV tower near Tallahassee, Florida (see *Migration kills* for more information on such accidents). Among the birds that still had a very long distance to travel, a large proportion of their body weight was made up of fat; on the other hand, the fat content of birds that had almost reached their destination was much less. The following table lists some examples. The long-distance

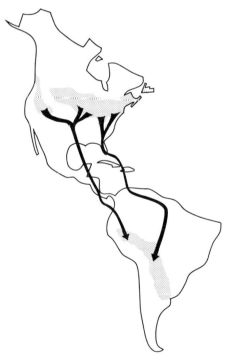

On its migration route, the Bobolink flies from its breeding grounds in the northern US and southern Canada to Argentina and Brazil to spend the winter.

Male Bobolink seen in spring migration. Before the fall migration, males lose these bright feathers and grow a plumage like the females' for winter (see Part III, BOBOLINK, for a picture of the female).

The Blackpoll Warbler migrates slowly at first, then speeds up to about 300 km per day as it moves north.

54

The Importance of Fat Reserves for Migration		
Species	Estimated average distance left to migrate	Percentage of body weight that was fat
Scarlet Tanager	2360 km (1465 mi)	Approximately 42%
Bobolink	2340 km (1454 mi)	Approximately 42%
Summer Tanager	250 km (155 mi)	Approximately 19%
White-throated Sparrow	180 km (112 mi)	Approximately 6%

migrants, those that were going to fly south into South America, had nearly half of their total body weight still in fat; all birds that had almost reached their destinations had very little stored energy left in their bodies.

Not all of the migratory fat laid down, however, is used for the flight. Especially in spring, some songbirds return to their breeding grounds early with some fat still left. They arrive early to claim good breeding territories, and this leftover "Florida fat" helps tide them through any late cold weather when food may be scarce.

Time, speed and routes

By day or by night? Whether birds migrate by day or by night depends on their need to feed, their method of feeding and how strongly they fly. Most warblers, vireos, sparrows, orioles, flycatchers and tanagers migrate at night; gulls, loons, some ducks and geese, hawks and—among songbirds—swallows, robins, blackbirds and others generally migrate by day; robins will migrate either by day or by night, but more often by day.

Flocks of migrating warblers and other small songbirds that migrate by night can be seen en route during the daytime where they have stopped to rest and eat. Many of these birds fly across the Gulf of Mexico and Caribbean Sea to reach their winter grounds; of course, when over these large bodies of water they must continue their flight into the daylight hours and many are captured by predators.

Cliff Swallows are known to fly along the shoreline of eastern Mexico rather than out over the Gulf (see map). With their wide, gaping beaks, they eat flying insects as they migrate by day. Although this route is longer, they always have a ready food supply of insects along the shore. Many Purple Martins and Barn Swallows, however, do take the shortcut across the Gulf; they do with less food, but arrive more quickly. All swallows can "outfly" most birds of prey such as hawks or gulls. (In daylight these predators can pick a flying sparrow or vireo out of the air.) Other daytime migrators like robins and blackbirds are also strong fliers and are too large for many predators to attack easily.

Speed of migration. The time it takes different species to migrate varies greatly. The Black-and-white Warbler is a slow migrator, advancing about 30 km (19 mi) a day toward its northern breeding grounds in spring, while the Gray-cheeked Thrush (a bird that breeds in Alaska and northern Canada) goes about 250 km (over 150 mi) a day. The Blackpoll Warbler travels slowly at first (about 45 km or 28 mi a day) as it travels across Florida and the Southeast, then speeds up to about 300 km (186 mi) a day as it moves north and the season advances; it, too, breeds in northern Canada and Alaska. On

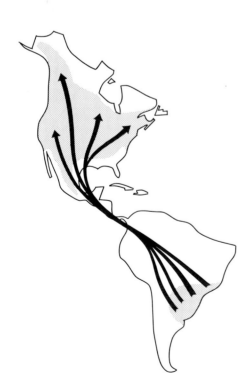

Unlike most songbirds, Cliff Swallows fly by day. Their migration route keeps them over land where they can catch insects while in flight.

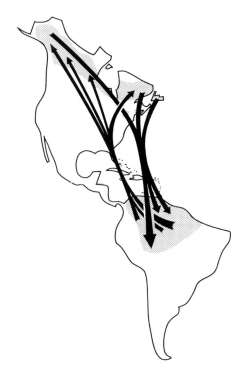

The migration route of the Blackpoll Warbler is different in spring and fall.

the return trip in fall, most blackpolls move to the Atlantic Coast, north of Virginia, and then fly nonstop over the Atlantic Ocean to the Lesser Antilles and northern South America. The migratory paths of the Blackpoll Warbler are illustrated on the map here.

The routes birds take. Each species of bird follows its own migratory path, and generally follows the same one year after year. Some species, however, follow one path in the spring and another in the fall (see the Blackpoll Warbler again). Though many birds have started to breed in new regions, their migratory paths seem to be "conservative," that is, they use the same routes as their ancestors. Notice on the Bobolink map that though these birds have begun breeding in the West, they still fly eastward until they reach their probable ancestral flyway; then they head south. The Wheatear, a thrush that breeds in Alaska and northwest Canada on the west side of the continent, and in Greenland on the east side, is another species that uses its ancestral migratory route. These Wheatears, widespread in Eurasia, probably immigrated to Alaska and western Canada from northern Asia and to Greenland from northern Europe. Today, all but a few stragglers return to the Old World before flying south. The western Wheatears fly across the Bering Strait to Asia, then south to Africa to spend the winter; the Greenland Wheatears fly southward through Europe to Africa.

When do they migrate, and why?

When do they leave? By responding to the changing day lengths in spring and fall, birds are able to "anticipate" climatic changes that are important to them. Thus, they generally leave in the fall before their food becomes scarce, and arrive in the spring after the winter weather has ended. Some birds, however, seem to respond more directly to the abundance or shortage of food. This is especially true of species that do not always face a shortage of food every year such as Blue Jays, nuthatches, chickadees, crossbills and redpolls. Many robins, too, seem to tempt fate by staying north after the ground is covered by snow—especially if there are many berries on trees and bushes.

Some songbirds do not leave at all—Boreal Chickadees, Gray Jays and ravens rarely migrate. Other species always migrate and spend their winters in the same location each year. A major study of Song Sparrows in Ohio showed that even birds of the same species may vary in their migratory tendencies. Individual birds were banded so that each could be identified. One year about half the male and two-thirds of the female Song Sparrows migrated in the fall; the rest stayed in Ohio for the winter. The following year, of the birds that had migrated the previous year, some did not migrate again, while others did. Evidently the tendency—the "urge"—to migrate varies from year to year and is stronger in some of these birds than in others.

We know that the tendency to migrate is inherited in some species and that, potentially, "migrators" and "nonmigrators" occur in all species. In regions where food is scarce or hard to find during one season, the nonmigrators often die, whereas in regions where food is available year round the migrators are at a disadvantage (at best migration is a risky business). Although many species live only in regions that always favor either migrators or nonmigrators, the Song Sparrow lives in many places—such as Ohio—where neither strategy is clearly favored: the risk of a bad winter is equal to the risks of migration.

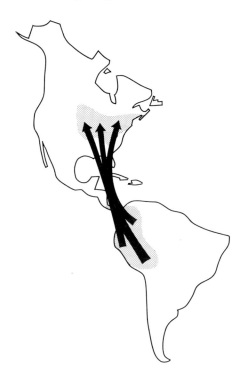

Scarlet Tanager migration route.

Migration of North American birds—going south. Migratory flight exposes birds to great dangers and uses an enormous amount of their energy. Surely, then, birds migrate only if a great advantage is gained by doing so.

Generally, insect eaters (especially birds that eat flying insects) leave early in the fall and go farther south than most seed eaters. (Seed eaters tend to be less migratory.) Not only is more food available in the South in winter, but the greater variety undoubtedly provides a more nutritious diet. The question then arises: why don't they simply live in the South? Why do the birds bother to return to the North in spring?

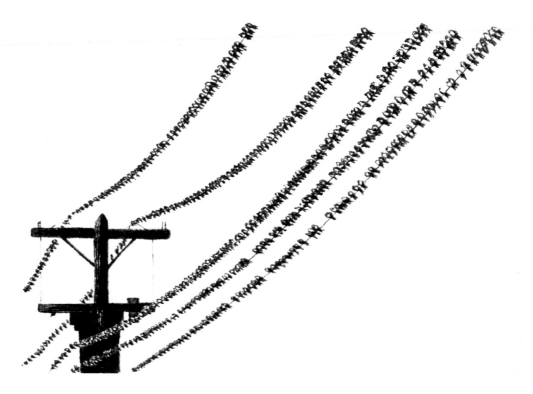

In August, swallows begin to migrate southward. As evening approaches, huge numbers line up on fences and wires.

Migration of North American birds—going north. There are several reasons why it is important for some species to return to the North to breed and why it has become an established pattern. This northern movement reduces competition with other birds for food and nest sites. Since the days are longer in the North than in the South, there is more time to get food for developing nestlings. As any northern camper knows, insects are extremely abundant in late spring and summer. It is probably important, too, that there are far fewer predators in the North. And birds that migrate in the spring move to areas that are less crowded and, thus, are less likely to be attacked by parasites or become diseased.

Swallows in bad weather

The northern flight of swallows in spring depends on movement of warm air masses that bring out insects. Prolonged cold or rainy weather forces insects into shelter; then young or weak birds have trouble surviving. The Tree Swallow manages better than other swallows at such times. If a cold snap occurs and insects disappear during their migration, Tree Swallows will eat berries and can be seen hovering about bushes such as the waxy-fruited bayberry bush found along the eastern coast.

How did this migratory pattern begin? There is one generally accepted theory explaining why breeding northern birds migrate to and from southern wintering grounds. This theory says that birds originated in the tropics. Moving northward became a set pattern when population expansion drove more and more birds to seek new nest and foraging sites—especially during the breeding season. As glaciers receded, birds of certain habitat types could occupy the many available areas in the North. Now these birds breed and forage in the North during spring and summer, and those whose food supply is not available in winter return to the South.

Orientation and navigation

How do birds "know" where to fly? For hundreds of years people have noticed the departure of birds and their return. More recently, researchers have tried to discover how birds know where to go and how they get back. Look at what is involved. Birds must be able to tell direction, "know" which direction they must fly and "know" when to stop. Many questions remain, but a great deal of information about how birds orient themselves in the right direction and how they navigate is now available.

We know, for example, that most birds that migrate do not learn to do so from their parents; they have inherited the tendency—it is innate. It is also known that they use natural landmarks as guides; birds migrating during the day use the sun to determine direction; those that travel at night use the stars. It has been established, as well, that birds have a magnetic sense, that they migrate with the wind, and that some have the ability to use olfactory (smelling) cues. Most recently, there is evidence that they can hear such low intensity sounds that they might be able to detect wave action or thunder several hundred kilometers away. It is possible that some birds have the ability to use clues for orientation that earthbound animals do not have.

For more details about how birds migrate, a summary of a number of experiments follows. The Bibliography lists several books and journal articles that explain these fascinating experiments in even greater depth.

1. *The "urge" to migrate.* We have already mentioned that the "urge" to migrate is innate. What evidence do we have for this? One experiment done with gulls showed interesting results. Two species were used—one that migrated and another that did not. The eggs of these two kinds were switched from one nest to the other. When the eggs hatched, those chicks of the nonmigratory gulls left with their foster parents when the time for migration came. They simply followed their foster parents to their migratory destination. But the nestlings of the migratory gulls who were raised by nonmigratory gulls *also migrated* when the time came, although their foster parents did not! They had inherited the ability to migrate and the urge to do so.

In another study, nestling crows were captured in central Alberta and raised in captivity, away from their parents. Then after their parents and other crows had migrated to areas previous studies had shown to be their wintering range, to the southeast in Kansas and Oklahoma, the hand-raised crows were released. In response to an intensive publicity campaign to get local support, several of these young crows were recaptured; most were heading southeast, in the appropriate direction even though they could not possibly have learned to do so from adult birds that had made the journey in previous years.

Normal migratory route of a population of starlings in Europe from breeding grounds to wintering grounds.

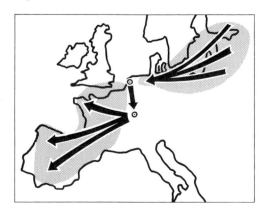

Starlings were caught and banded as they migrated through Holland (upper dot on these two maps) and were released in Switzerland (lower dot). The map above shows that adults redirected themselves and flew to their normal wintering grounds. The map below shows the path taken by young, inexperienced birds. They simply continued to fly in the direction they were going when captured.

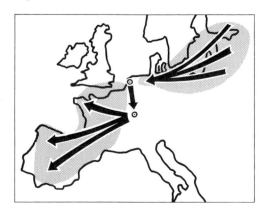

Cliff Swallows at the Mission

Cliff Swallows arrive from their wintering grounds on almost the same day each year. Their punctuality has inspired a popular song and the belief that Cliff Swallows breeding at the Mission of San Juan Capistrano in southern California return on exactly the same day, but close observation has shown that this is not quite true. The dates are fairly regular, but they do vary depending on weather conditions along the birds' migratory route from the south.

2. *How do birds find their way home?* Over the years, a great deal of work has been done with *homing* among different kinds of birds. To learn about birds' homing abilities, they are taken certain distances from their territories and released to discover if they can find their way home again. Other animals such as turtles, fishes, bats, squids and even pet dogs and cats can home, too. Certain birds seem to be the masters of this art, though not all birds. Some titmice and wrens cannot find their way back home even if they are taken only a few kilometers away.

Birds find their way home in many ways. Most simply look for familiar landmarks. In one experiment, Herring Gulls were released at a point away from their nests for two consecutive years. The second year they returned home in one-sixth the time that it took the first year. Therefore, they must have learned the route.

Pigeons learn landmarks quickly, after just a few releases. However, one experiment showed a perplexing aspect: pigeons released from distances up to 15 km or over 80 km away found their way home easily, but between those distances they had difficulty. It is likely that at short distances these birds simply use landmarks, and at long distances they have different special systems of navigation (doubtless using some of the senses discussed later). At the intermediate distances, their "instruments" seem to work less efficiently. People have used the pigeon's homing ability to advantage: carrier pigeons have long been dependable carriers of messages.

3. *How good is a bird's sense of direction?* The first major experiment on birds' sense of direction was done with the Common Starling in Europe. Some starlings that breed in the Baltic countries pass through Holland on their way southwest to wintering grounds on both sides of the English Channel. Both juveniles and adults, caught as they migrated through Holland, were banded. Then they were released, not in Holland, but in Switzerland. The result? Adult birds corrected for the change in position and ended up at their proper wintering grounds, but not the juveniles. The maps illustrate these differences. The young, inexperienced birds kept going southwest and ended up in Spain and southern France; they continued going to their adopted wintering grounds year after year. This experiment showed that the young birds had only an inherited sense *of which direction* to migrate *and of how far* they should migrate before stopping. Knowledge of the landmarks gained from previous migratory trips enabled the adults to compensate for the experimental displacement, and to return to their "proper" wintering areas; but the inexperienced, young birds simply continued moving southwestward until "it was time to stop."

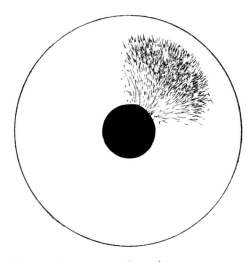

Dr. Stephen Emlen of Cornell University devised this ingenious apparatus for his experiments with Indigo Bunting orientation. First the bird lands on the ink pad at the bottom of the cone-shaped cage. As the bird tries to fly away, its feet leave ink prints at each point where they touch the absorbent paper lining the inside of the cage.

Viewing the apparatus from above, we see the pattern of footprints Dr. Emlen obtained when a bird was exposed to a planetarium sky that simulated a normal star pattern in the night sky. The tracks point northeast, the direction this bird would normally migrate in spring.

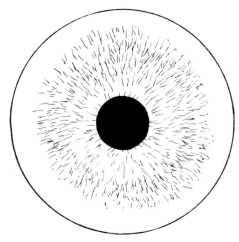

This view of the apparatus from above shows a lack of orientation by the bird that left the ink prints. This random array of tracks is the kind of result Dr. Emlen obtained when there were no stars shown in the planetarium sky, representing a cloudy night.

4. *A magnetic sense.* Migratory European Robins in one experiment were kept in circular cages with no view of the sky to give them a directional cue, but they faced northeast, the direction of their migration. When these cages were enclosed in a steel chamber so that the magnetism of the earth would not affect them, the birds' directional orientation disappeared. Conversely, when the birds were subjected to artificial magnetic fields, they again oriented but in the direction of the new magnetic field.

In another experiment, these same birds were allowed to see the sky, but with a magnetic field inside the cage that was 115 degrees different from that of the earth. They oriented according to where the field was, *not* by what they saw in the sky. Interestingly, the strength of the field had to be comparable to that of the part of the world where they lived; otherwise, the birds moved randomly rather than in a set direction, apparently ignoring the magnetic field. But given magnetic fields of natural strength, the birds got accurate information about the proper direction in which to migrate.

This raises another interesting question. How do birds sense these magnetic fields? Recently, a concentration of cells with many iron-containing molecules has been located in the brain of pigeons. Perhaps this is the "mystery" magnetic sense organ. There is increasing evidence that other animals also have a magnetic sense.

5. *The sun as a compass.* Many experiments also have been done to discover if birds use the sun to help them keep direction. In one of these, Common Starlings were put in individual circular cages, open at the top so that they could see the sky. If the sun was out, the birds fluttered on perches in the direction of their normal migration, indicating an inclination to fly in that direction. But on cloudy days when they could not see the sun, these birds fluttered randomly. When mirrors were used to make it seem that the sun was in a different place, the birds fluttered in the direction of its apparent position. In these experiments the birds seemed to respond to one cue only—the position of the sun; the fact that they changed their orientation when they were shown the reflection of the sun in mirrors ruled out the possibility that they were using other cues, such as magnetic fields.

To be certain that this conclusion was correct, a second set of experiments, involving something called "clock-shifting," was devised. Animals, including people, become used to having a certain number of hours of light per day; this adjustment of our bodies to a certain "photoperiod" is often referred to as a biological or internal "clock." For example, it can be shown that an animal's metabolism starts speeding up before it actually awakens from sleep—its body anticipates the coming of day. In these studies, birds were put in cages they could not see out of. Lights in the cages were set so that when it was dawn for the birds, it was actually midnight outside. After they had become used to the shift in photoperiod, they were released. The released birds flew off in the direction that was appropriate for their internal clock, but not appropriate for the actual time of day. Because their clocks had been "reset," their orientation was off. They were, in fact, off course by precisely the amount (number of degrees the angle of the sun would have changed) that their clocks were off time. No other factor would have left them disoriented in just this way.

An example might help explain the preceding experiments. If the time period that light was allowed to shine in the cages was advanced by 12 hours, and the birds were released at 7:00 a.m., they would "think" it was 7:00 p.m.

If these birds lived in the North, the sun would be in the south*east* at 7:00 a.m., but because it would seem like 7:00 p.m. to them, they would respond as if the sun were in the south*west!*

It is probably important for birds to be able to use the sun as a compass when they are away from home and unaware of their location. In other words, they must get positional as well as directional information. Just how they can determine this is unknown. Some people think that vision alone is not adequate—the birds must have a way of checking latitude as well as being able to use the sun for orienting, and they need exceptionally accurate internal clocks. For example, a displaced bird may look at the sun and by knowing the time of day, it can determine direction. But how can it know if it is north or south of home? The bird could do this by knowing where the sun would be if it were at home. In the northern hemisphere, if a bird is moved north of its home the sun appears lower in the sky than it would appear at its home *at that same time of day.* If birds are moved small distances, these differences in the apparent position of the sun are very slight, and it is difficult to believe that their perception is that precise. Thus, for short-distance migration, birds probably do not use the sun as an aid in orientation.

6. *Navigating by the stars.* Similar experiments revealed that if European warblers that migrate at night were kept in circular cages and could see the stars, they sat and fluttered on their perches in the direction of normal migration; on overcast nights they did not. These birds were then put in cages in a planetarium. It was found that when the stars were correctly positioned, as they appear outside, the birds oriented in the direction for normal migration. When the sky was shifted, they shifted accordingly. Another experiment with White-throated Sparrows at spring migration time showed that as long as the North Star in the planetarium sky was in the north, they oriented north, but if it was shifted to the south, they oriented south.

Because of such findings, people began to think that birds that migrate at night have inherited the ability to recognize the stars and fly according to the direction that a pattern "told them was home." A Cornell scientist, Dr. Stephen Emlen, however, conducted some experiments that questioned that thesis. First he found that Indigo Buntings also reversed their path if the planetarium sky was reversed with the North Star in the south. He then hand-raised three groups of Indigo Bunting nestlings and tested their orientation in the fall. The first group was raised indoors seeing no sky or planetarium stars. When tested with a static star pattern in the sky, these birds could not orient correctly. The second group was exposed to a normal, rotating planetarium sky, and did orient correctly. The third group was exposed to a planetarium sky with stars that rotated around a fictitious axis, with a different star of about the same brightness chosen as the "north star," the central star about which the others revolve. Remarkably, these birds oriented the "correct" direction in the fall relative to the new axis of rotation.

So Indigo Buntings must *learn* the night sky to orient properly; they are not born with a "map" of it. Dr. Emlen thinks that the axis of rotation gives a reference system and that fledglings respond to the stars' movement in the night sky. Since stars located near the axis of the earth's rotation seem to move more slowly than those over the earth's equator, this allows birds to locate a north-south directional axis.

Night sky. On clear nights in the spring, it appears that birds orient toward Polaris, the North Star, as they migrate northward toward their nesting grounds.

7. *Can birds smell "home"?* The sense of smell is poorly developed in most birds, but recent studies have shown that some species are able to home using odors—they fly toward the "smell of home." This has been demonstrated only in pigeons and petrels (small seabirds that fly to their nesting burrows on islands only at night), however, and may play no part in songbird navigation or homing. Interestingly, though they nest in dense colonies, the petrels can apparently tell their own burrow by its odor.

The mystery remains. Can these tiny, feathered, winged creatures really do all of this? It would seem to take a computer to analyze all the different types of information relative to the position of the stars and the sun, the earth's magnetic field and rotation, the time of day, the local landmarks—perhaps even the odors and who knows what else. But information that could be useful for navigation and homing is present in these clues, and experiments have shown that birds are sensitive to the clues.

The birds probably do not use all of them at once. They doubtless home by local landmarks if they recognize any. If these fail, perhaps they search for celestial clues. Those that migrate at night must get a basic north-south orientation from the stars; those that move by day, must get the same information from the sun. They have a great capacity to learn routes and to remember them for a very long time. Do they have a great refinement of the senses that we do know about? Do they possess other senses that we have yet to discover? We may never have all the answers to the mystery. Each new discovery seems to make migration more complex rather than easier to understand, but each new discovery also makes migration that much more fascinating.

Migration kills

The skyscrapers of our modern cities have meant death to many small birds. Literally truckloads have been found dead at the base of buildings and towers after a cloudy night.

Warblers, vireos, tanagers, thrushes, sparrows and many other songbirds migrate mainly at night. When low clouds force them to fly close to the ground, lights from tall buildings, towers and very high airport ceilometers attract and confuse them. Thousands collide with the building and are killed every migration season. More die this way in the autumn than in the spring because there are more birds in existence following the summer reproductive season and nights are cloudiest at that time of the year. After one overcast October night in a southern state of the US, 50,000 birds were found at the base of an airport ceilometer. In an 11-year study of birds that were killed at a TV tower near Tallahassee, Florida, 44% of the total were warblers (7% of the total were "Myrtle" Warblers), 23% vireos (18% Red-eyed Vireos), 5% thrushes and 9% sparrows. At a tower near Topeka, Kansas, 54% of the birds killed were warblers, 15% vireos and 13% sparrows.

The only way to prevent these deaths is to turn off as many lights as possible in tall buildings, particularly on the north side during the fall season. The current campaign to shut off lights may help conserve some of our songbirds as well as our energy.

The swallow myth

Swallows were well known to medieval European farmers who saw the birds swoop over the fields as they worked. Because swallows suddenly disappeared each fall and returned each spring, people once believed that they slept in mud during the winter. The Greek philosophers, especially Aristotle, recognized over 2000 years ago that other birds moved to and from areas at different times of year; they knew that migration occurred. But Aristotle thought that swallows hibernated in mud. That myth began with his writings. The swallow eventually became a Christian symbol for the resurrection of Christ because of the notion that it emerges in spring from a winter's sleep. As people began to travel more, it became apparent that swallows did not hibernate in the winter but, like many other birds, migrated to other parts of the world.

A flock of birds migrating by day. Only larger, stronger flying species risk daytime migratory flight.

Irruptions: The unpredictable birds

Clark's Nutcracker is a bird of western evergreen forests where it frequently appears around campsites to beg for a handout or steal a bite to eat. In winter nutcrackers depend extensively on stored pine seeds for food, and when there is a poor crop of these, nutcrackers irrupt, often wandering into the Great Plains and to the Pacific Coast.

While many North American birds are migratory—they move from a particular breeding area to a particular wintering area and back, once each year—some species are quite unpredictable in their movements. They may be common in an area one year, then absent for several. These irregular movements are called *irruptions*. Birds that show irruptive movements generally have less predictable food supplies than those that migrate. The insects upon which "regular" migrators, such as warblers, swallows and vireos, depend for food become available every spring after a few warm days—and disappear again each fall after a hard frost. But some species depend on foods that are available only during some years.

Crossbills are the most notorious of all irruptive birds. Their appearance in most areas seems to be completely unpredictable, but when they appear, they can be very common. Between 1800 and 1965 there were at least 67 invasions or irruptions of Red Crossbills into southern Europe from the north (in England this bird is called the "common crossbill"). Similar irruptions have occurred in North America but have not been so thoroughly documented. (A crossbill invasion into England was reported as early as 1251!)

Crossbill irruptions from an area often occur after a poor cone crop, leading some biologists to conclude that crossbills move in search of areas where food is plentiful. Sometimes, however, there is little crossbill movement even though the cone crop is poor and, in some years, the irruption from one area to another occurs *before* the effects of a poor crop are felt. This suggests that the birds, in some way, are able to assess the richness of the forthcoming crop. It seems that several factors, perhaps working together, may trigger an irruption: high population levels may be one and a poor cone crop, or even an "anticipated" poor cone crop, another.

If crossbills find a place with a good cone crop, they will sometimes breed during an irruption. Irruptions thus differ from migratory movements—migratory birds do not breed in their wintering grounds, whereas irruptive birds will at times stay at a new locality to breed.

The unpredictability of irruptions is another difference to migration. In North America, Red Crossbills have been known to breed during some years south to Kansas, North Carolina, Georgia and Pennsylvania—far south of their usual breeding range in the East. There is one isolated resident population of White-winged Crossbills on the Caribbean island of Hispaniola; their ancestors probably settled there during a crossbill invasion in some time past.

Other North American birds that are irruptive seem to be the kinds that depend on foods that are common some years, uncommon others. Several northern owls (not songbirds, of course) are irruptive. The most famous, the Snowy Owl, depends to a great extent on lemmings for food. The population of these little rodents varies in cycles, and when they are scarce, Snowy Owls move south, regularly to the Great Lakes, and occasionally into the central states.

The Pinyon Jay of the West feeds primarily on the nuts of the Pinyon Pine (people who live in that region eat these flavorful nuts too). Like the seeds in pine and spruce cones that crossbills eat, pinyon nuts are plentiful only during some years. Therefore, the number of Pinyon Jays varies from year to year. Waxwings, too, are unpredictable. Doubtless their berry food varies from year to year.

Many other species show irruptions on occasion. Black-capped Chickadees, Blue Jays and White-breasted Nuthatches are found throughout most of their breeding range during the year, but some individuals move south each fall and every once in a while they move south in great numbers. The cause of this movement must be high populations—not enough food to go around during the winter—but little is really known about it. Irruptions are still something of an enigma.

Crossbills are other "irrupting" birds, leaving an area with a poor cone crop, and sometimes remaining to breed in a new area with a good cone crop.

Birds in winter

Songbirds foraging in a field in winter. The two birds above are Horned Larks, the one in the middle is a Lapland Longspur and the other three are Snow Buntings.

Many birds avoid cold and lack of food in winter by leaving, by migrating. But what about those birds that stay? What do they do on very cold days?

Birds that stay north in winter are those that are able to find food—like the wily chickadee who busily flits to and fro digging insect larvae from tree bark and picking seeds off plants that protrude through the snow. Others, who also stay north, like the Gray Jay and nuthatch, store caches of food for these leaner times and move closer to human habitations. Grassland birds, such as Snow Buntings and Horned Larks, find seeds of grasses and weeds in fields and along shores of lakes. And everyone knows what the House Sparrow does; it comes to neighborhood feeders, stealing all that expensive bird food we put out to attract other less common and "more desirable" birds.

The intense cold does take its toll on large numbers of birds, but most have found ways of protecting themselves. Snow Buntings sink themselves as low as possible into snow on extremely cold nights so that their legs and feet, body parts from which heat is easily lost, are not exposed to the air. (Though winter air temperatures may fall to −30°C or lower, at these very low temperatures snow provides insulation.)

Songbirds that stay north often stick together in small loose flocks, fluff up their feathers to keep warm and roost in little groups at night. At night chickadees let their body temperature drop if it is cold. This conserves energy. Since their food supply is available year round, they don't migrate.

As mentioned previously, the amount of oxygen an animal breathes gives a good indication of its rate of metabolism, which in turn reflects how much energy is being used. One experiment showed that a single starling has to use a huge amount of energy to keep warm at low temperatures. At a roosting temperature of 2°–4°C, a single starling consumes 92% more oxygen than those huddled in groups of four.

In Europe, Tree Creepers huddle together on the trunks of trees during extreme cold, their heads all pointed inward. They look like one fluffy brown ball with ten or so tiny tails sticking out from the central ball.

Other small woodland birds find cavities and huddle together inside.

Birds such as Evening Grosbeaks are well adapted for cold weather, with body feathers covering a soft, fluffy, gray down that keeps them warm. Their short feet can be tucked under their feathers and the ridged, cornified cushions on the bottom of their feet are good for gripping icy branches.

When snow is heavy, Evening Grosbeaks congregate at feeders and pack in tightly, pushing each other off and chasing away other kinds of birds. (Put out sunflowers seeds for them. After a while, they will become less wary of you and will even eat from your hand. But be careful—their beaks are powerful.)

As it becomes warmer, Evening Grosbeaks leave the feeders in favor of tender maple buds. They can be seen, along with many other birds, sipping the maple sap as soon as it starts to run. You might see them drinking melted snow from rooftops, or water from cold northern streams. People have seen these hardy birds bathing even while streams are half frozen!

Amazing survival

Songbirds may appear fragile with their thin, delicate legs and small bodies, but nearly everyone who has ever watched birds has a story to tell about their toughness. Our favorite story concerns a male Cardinal. This special bird has come and gone from our feeders for two winters, and has flown in and out of bushes and trees with his less spectacular, duller mate for two breeding seasons. This is extraordinary only because he has only one leg! (He probably lost the other in an escape from a cat.) His life depends on his ability to perch on that one leg while eating, guarding his territory and feeding his young. Yet he has successfully mated for two years and hasn't been replaced by a younger, stronger male. That he has retained his territory and has survived two harsh winters in this condition is amazing.

· PART THREE ·

FAMILIES OF NORTH AMERICAN SONGBIRDS

A WOODLAND EDGE IN WINTER

Look low among the brown, dry weeds of the past summer's growth for
small birds that gather the seeds from asters, Queen Anne's Lace, grasses
and many other weeds. Close to the woodland protection, you'll see birds
like those shown here (junco, lower left; Tree Sparrow, lower right;
redpoll, center; goldfinches, top). They are dull in their winter dress but
easy to spot. (Look, too, for black and white Downy Woodpeckers that
might be there, along with chickadees, knocking on goldenrod galls for
the insect larvae inside. Streaked, delicate Pine Siskins sometimes join all
these birds at woodland edges to fortify themselves on seeds for the long,
cold winter nights.)

How to identify songbirds

To be able to identify birds, you need a good field guide. If you live east of the Rockies, you might use Roger Tory Peterson's *A Field Guide to the Birds*; if west, then his book *A Field Guide to Western Birds*. Another very popular guide is *Birds of North America* by Robbins, Bruun and Zim. All fit into the pocket and are available in soft cover—which reduces their weight as well as their cost.

Almost as important as having a good guide is finding other people who already know birds fairly well and are willing to go with you into the field. There are many naturalist clubs that you can join for such companionship. Birdwatchers are generally so enthusiastic that they welcome newcomers and are usually helpful and patient.

After a very few sessions out with field guide in hand and a good pair of binoculars—the only major expense of the pastime—you will start to learn the most common birds and where to find them. Knowing where to look is often as important as knowing what to look for. For instance, look for birds such as Common Yellowthroats and Red-winged Blackbirds in or near marshes; vireos, tanagers and most warblers, high in trees; thrushes, the Ovenbird and White-throated Sparrow, low in woodland thickets; Song Sparrows and Yellow Warblers, in bushes and small trees at the edge of a woodland. Horned Larks, meadowlarks, Bobolinks and Savannah Sparrows can be seen in open fields and pastures.

It is not as difficult as it may seem to become good at identifying birds. Most birds are easily recognized if you look and listen carefully. The few look-alikes and sound-alikes of the bird world give an added challenge.

The species illustrated in this book are among the most common and conspicuous. You might start by familiarizing yourself with these. Even if you never learn to recognize them all, birdwatching makes every walk in the outdoors more exciting.

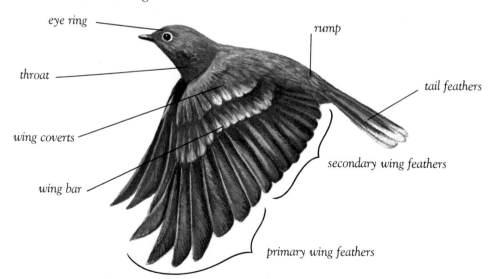

eye ring

rump

throat

tail feathers

wing coverts

secondary wing feathers

wing bar

primary wing feathers

(a) Look for identifying marks on the birds, like stripes on the head or through the eyes, or patches of white on the wings, or a ring around each eye (an "eye ring"). Note the size of the bird, the shape of the beak and the length of its tail. Notice, too, how the bird behaves. Does it hop like a sparrow or walk like a lark? Does it flit nervously like a kinglet or warbler or deliberately pick insects from a leaf like a vireo? Does it fly straight like most birds or undulate and sing while it flies like a goldfinch?

(b) Listen to the songs. Some birds are so secretive you will hear them before you see them. This is especially true of dull woodland-dwelling birds such as the thrushes and Ovenbird, the Winter Wren and small marsh birds. Some, like the catbird or Red-eyed Vireo, sing so persistently that it would be difficult to see them before hearing them; their songs will lead you to them. But, of course, birds do not sing very much in winter or when they are migrating, so then you must depend on just watching.

How to identify a bird by its song

The only way to identify a bird's song is to listen intently. Some songs are difficult; others are easy. The songs of some wood warblers can take a long time to learn, while the songs of many other birds like the White-throated Sparrow, robin and Red-eyed Vireo can be learned quickly because they are sung so persistently and are so distinctive.

The best way to start learning the songs is to go walking with a patient person who knows a lot about birds. The next best way is to take along a handy field guide which will give you a bird's markings and briefly describe how its song sounds. If you don't happen to have a field guide with you, write down what the bird looks like and how you think it sounds. As soon as you return home, check your guide or play a record of the songs you think you heard. (Many stores and nature centers carry these records.) The easy songs will get you started. The more difficult ones will give the challenge you are looking for. For complete descriptions of songs of eastern birds, use A. A. Saunders' *A Guide to Bird Songs.* You might like to carry it with you in the field.

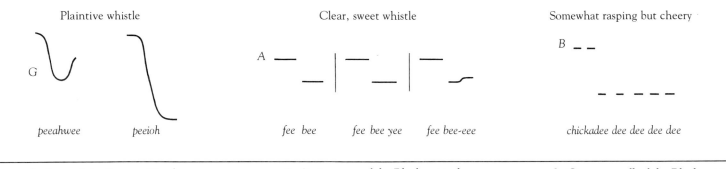

Plaintive whistle	Clear, sweet whistle	Somewhat rasping but cheery
peeahwee peeioh	fee bee fee bee yee fee bee-eee	chickadee dee dee dee dee

1 Song of the Eastern Wood Pewee.

2 Spring song of the Black-capped Chickadee.

3 Common call of the Black-capped Chickadee.

The two most accepted ways that songs have been represented in books are by verbal description and by phonetic rendering of the song. To show how you will most often see song described, four examples are given here. (1) is the simple song of a flycatcher, the Eastern Wood Pewee, (2) shows the Black-capped Chickadee's spring song *and* (3) its very commonly given call *chicka dee dee dee dee dee,* and (4) shows the very complex song of the Wood Thrush (from Saunders, *A Guide to Bird Songs,* 1951).

Loud central portion of each phrase, clear, melodious, and flute-like.   Introductory notes guttural.   Terminations sibilant.

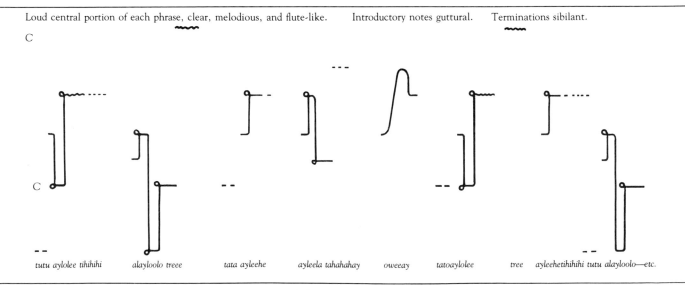

tutu aylolee tihihihi   alayloolo treee   tata ayleehe   ayleela tahahahay   oweeay   tatoaylolee   tree   ayleehetihihihi tutu alayloolo—etc.

4 Portion of the song of the Wood Thrush.

An identification quiz

If you see a stubby-bodied, short-tailed black bird, you will know that it is a starling, not a grackle.

The Common Grackle has a long, sleek body and struts majestically.

Compare a grackle (lower left) and starling in flight. The starling is shorter and its wings are pointed.

If you look at the two birds pictured here and immediately identify one as a starling and the other as a grackle, you are well on your way to recognizing birds, and may find this section a waste of time. But if you are one of the many people who know only very common birds like the robin, Blue Jay and House Sparrow and perhaps lump all black birds under the name "blackbird," please read on.

Here you can see that though both birds are black and similar in size, they are different. Looking at them together on the page, however, is easier than focusing on a bird as it flies past or walks along looking for food in your local park.

Both birds are "robin sized" and iridescent black, both form flocks and forage on the ground and both walk rather than hop. In these ways, they are similar. But by knowing just two or three ways they are different, you can easily tell them apart. Here is a list to help you identify them, beginning with the most obvious differences. For example, if you see a stubby-bodied, short-tailed black bird, you will know that it is a starling, not a blackbird such as the grackle. Using just two major differences—body shape and tail length—you can easily distinguish them.

Common Grackle	Starling
long tail	short tail
body has a long, sleek look	body has a stocky, stubby look
iridescent black all year round	brown wings and white spots covering its black coat in fall
black, slightly down-curved beak	yellow, pointed beak (except in fall and winter when it is brown)
black legs and feet	pinkish legs and feet
"majestic," strutting walk	waddles as it walks
in flight, body looks long	in flight, body short and stubby; wings pointed
eyes have a yellow iris	eyes have a brown iris

The tyrant flycatchers — Family Tyrannidae

Most passerine birds (perching birds) are constantly on the move. They flit from place to place in search of insects lodged between leaves and under bark, or for seeds on the heads of plants. But not the North American flycatchers; they sit quietly on a perch, motionless and alert, watching. When an insect flies past, the flycatcher darts out, snaps at it with a quick click of the bill, returns to its perch and waits for the next unwary fly or mosquito. You will rarely see flycatchers walk or hop. Their thin, spindly legs and delicate toes probably make them weak footed, so they fly from perch to perch.

Technically flycatchers are not songbirds. Their vocal organs are less well developed than those of songbirds and they belong to a more primitive group of perching birds. Most scream or shriek rather than sing, but some do have pleasant, simple songs. Since they are common and are "almost" songbirds, they're included here.

This family of birds belongs strictly to North and South America, and most of its 367 species live in tropical areas. The group of birds in Europe that are also called flycatchers are not closely related to these New World, or "tyrant," flycatchers, but belong to the same family as thrushes. Birds in both groups, however, "flycatch" so they have been given the same English common name. (See Part I, *Convergence*, for more on this topic.)

Many kinds of flycatchers are secretive and inconspicuous; some species are so similar in appearance that individuals can be identified as to kind only by their different songs.

Often only the sad-sounding song of the Eastern Wood Pewee, a small, common bird, lets you know it is present; it sings *pee-a-wee* over and over. Its nest is tiny and shallow and is built far out on a tree limb so high off the ground that it is almost impossible to find. When viewed from the side or from below, the nest looks like just one more knot on the branch of a tree. The pewee uses grass, weeds, spiderwebs and hair to weave its dainty nest; then it decorates the outside with lichens—small "plants" that are part algae and part fungi. Sticky spiderwebs are woven into the nest to glue the lichens to the sides.

Another species, the Great Crested Flycatcher, nests in cavities and can be attracted to birdhouses. This bird was especially notorious in the old days for stuffing its nest into large, roadside mailboxes. It has a curious habit of using castoff snakeskins in the walls of its nest. Today one might also find cellophane or some other material that is superficially like snakeskin in the nest cavity. (See Part II, *A variety of nests.*)

The most spectacular North American flycatcher, the Scissor-tailed Flycatcher, nests commonly from Nebraska south to Texas. In mating season it opens and shuts its tail feathers when "excited" and performs whirling flights. There's a Mexican myth that this bird eats the brains of other birds. Like its aggressive relative, the kingbird, the scissor-tail attacks large predatory birds such as hawks and crows, alighting on their backs and stabbing at them with its beak; probably the Mexican myth originated with this habit.

The Scissor-tailed Flycatcher is the most spectacular North American flycatcher.

Eastern Kingbird

Tyrannus tyrannus

Le Tyran tritri

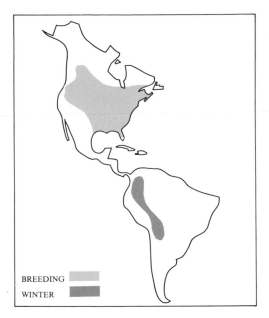

Eastern Kingbird 20–22 cm, 7.8–8.7″; 3–5 eggs, creamy white, with brownish splotches; cup-shaped nest of twigs, grasses and weeds, lined with finer materials of the same kind; placed 1–13 m (3–42′) high in tree, in orchards, open woods, roadsides. *

*The brief paragraph of facts about each bird in this section is self explanatory except for two sets of figures directly following the bird's name. These numbers give the bird's length in centimeters and in inches from the tip of its bill to the tip of its tail.

Although the kingbird is smaller than a robin, it does not hesitate to attack larger birds like crows, vultures and even hawks. The unsuspecting bird is suddenly met by a kingbird diving out at it while uttering a torrent of harsh, staccato notes. Kingbirds have been known to go after birdwatchers who come too close with their cameras. One was even seen chasing a low-flying airplane! No wonder Indians called this bird "little chief" and its Latin name is *Tyrannus tyrannus*.

The kingbird has also been called "bee martin" or "bee bird" because of its habit of seeking out honeybee hives. For this reason it was considered a pest and shot. But now, like all songbirds, it is protected by law. Are kingbirds really a problem for apiarists? One study, which involved looking at the stomachs of 281 of these birds, showed that only 14 contained honeybees. Of the total of 50 bees found in the stomachs, 40 were drones, 4 were workers and the other 6 could not be identified. Honeybee drones (males) have no function other than to breed with the queen bees; it is the workers (females) that gather the pollen and make the honey. Thus, this study showed that kingbirds probably do much less damage to beehives than had been thought.

The mating song of the kingbird is a simple dry cry. The courtship that follows is often dramatic, as the male swoops and dives near a female. Male and female look alike: plain colored, except for the reddish-orange crown on their heads which is visible only when they are alarmed. Their noisy, aggressive habits make them one of the most commonly seen birds of open country.

From the Great Plains westward, you will find the Western Kingbird as well as the Eastern Kingbird. It is a very different looking bird, with a bright yellow belly, a white throat and white along the sides of its tail, not on the tip.

The larks – Family Alaudidae

Of the 75 species of larks in the world, few live outside of Africa. Only one, the Horned Lark, spread to North America where it became widely established. Larks are birds of open areas; almost all are ground nesters and all have long hind claws on the back toe of each foot. Prints on snow or muddy shores, which show this elongated hind toe, are a sign of the recent presence of larks or of similarly long-clawed pipits and longspurs.

The most famous lark, the Skylark, is a common bird in Europe and has inspired many poets over the centuries with its spectacular song and courtship flight. We recently lived in Nottingham, England, for several months. The sight of a male Skylark ascending toward the sky from a meadow just one block from our house was common, but always exciting. Sometimes he would climb so high that he could no longer be seen, but still his beautiful song would float down to the ground. Because of their great love for the bird, European immigrants attempted to introduce the Skylark to North America a number of times, but it has become established only on the southern part of Vancouver Island. In spite of the admiration held by the British for this bird, they widely shot and netted it for food during the last century. Even today in other parts of Europe it is killed in large numbers for the table as are many other songbirds including the Horned Lark (called the Shore Lark in England).

Though nineteenth-century poets found the Skylark song variously "joyful" or "cheerful," its song, like that of other birds, serves as a stern proclamation to other males that an area is taken. While the song also helps to attract a mate—a joyful enough function—its primary function is to keep other male Skylarks off his territory. (See Part II, *Territory.*)

We should point out that the Eastern Meadowlark shown elsewhere in this book is not a lark. It was called that by immigrants because, like most larks of Europe, it lives in meadows and fields, it resembles a lark and perhaps because it, too, has a beautiful song. The meadowlark is really related to orioles, grackles and cowbirds—a group we commonly know as blackbirds.

The spectacular song and courtship flight of the male Skylark have made it the most famous of all songbirds.

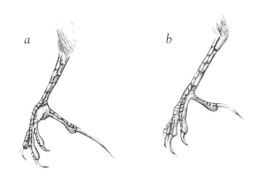

a　　　　　*b*

Foot of the Horned Lark (A) and Chestnut-collared Longspur (B). Both birds forage in fields for food. They are not closely related but, having similar habits, have developed similar feet with long back claws. This is an example of convergence.

The Chestnut-collared Longspur, a sparrow (Family Emberizidae) of plains and prairies, and the Horned Lark (Family Alaudidae), shown on the opposite page lead similar lives, though they are unrelated.

Horned Lark

Eremophila alpestris

L'Alouette cornue

BREEDING

Horned Lark 17–20 cm, 6.8–8″; 3–5 eggs, grayish, speckled with pale brown; nest a shallow cup of stems, leaves, lined with fine grasses, thistledown, feathers; placed in a hollow in ground, in short grass fields, grasslands, golf courses, airports.

Horned Larks, common in North America from northern Canada to Mexico, are most conspicuous during the mating season. In the air, the male puts on a spectacular show. (See Part II, *How birds woo.*)

On the ground, following his courtship flight, he struts around with his wings drooping and the black feather "horns" on his head sticking up; this both attracts a mate and keeps other males away. His strutting and pecking at the ground create an imaginary boundary line between his territory and the next male's. The Horned Lark's "horns" are merely tufts of dark feathers which it can raise.

The female does the work of building the nest and incubating the eggs. She builds a simple nest on the ground, using any handy materials. In the North the nest may be sunk into reindeer moss and lined with ptarmigan feathers and caribou hair. The female often lays her first eggs before all the snow has melted.

When the eggs hatch, the male becomes about as active as the female in feeding the young. One birdwatcher noted that a pair of Horned Larks fed their nestlings 108 times in one day. (Baby birds of most species have to be fed so frequently that they rarely survive when people try to look after them.)

Look for Horned Larks walking, not hopping, along the ground in any open place with short grass—prairies, airports, shores, Arctic tundra, cultivated fields. You'll have to look closely. Their dull brown color and black-and-white striped heads camouflage them well, even though you might not think it from the illustration. The black stripes tend to break the bird into separate pieces so that from a distance it merges into the background. Shorebirds, such as the Killdeer and Semipalmated Plover, have similar bands of black going around or bibbing their necks, and across the front of their faces, then running back through their eyes. Birds with these so-called "disruptive" patterns about the head and neck are often not seen by a predator (or a human) looking across a shoreline or field.

The swallows — Family Hirundinidae

Here are six kinds of swallows commonly found in most of North America. From left to right they are: Barn Swallow, Cliff Swallow, Bank Swallow, Rough-winged Swallow, Tree Swallow and Purple Martin. In the West, you might also see the Violet-green Swallow.

In August swallows begin to form loose flocks for their migratory flight southward. You might see hundreds or even thousands in flight. As evening approaches, watch for them along roadsides where huge numbers line up on fences and wires. When the largest of the North American swallows, the Purple Martins, abandon their colonial nesting houses in July and August, they roost in flocks so large that branches have been known to snap under their weight.

Swallows spend more time in flight than any other songbird. The exceptionally long primary feathers of their wings give them a great wing span.

Swallows feed as they fly, making sweeps over fields and marshes picking insects out of the air with their large mouths. Rictal bristles (stiff hairlike feathers) around the beak help funnel flying insects into their gape. (Flycatchers, too, have these specialized feathers around their beaks.) Purple Martins are touted as being important predators of mosquitoes, but a study in southern Canada showed that they generally eat larger insects; 90% of the diet of the smaller Barn and Tree Swallows, however, is small flies such as midges, houseflies and mosquitoes.

Swallows are the most widespread of all songbirds, absent only in the Antarctic and the coldest areas of the Arctic. Otherwise they can be found in almost every habitat clear of forests. Of the 79 species most have probably benefited from people. Our buildings have given them nesting places, and many of our activities have encouraged the insects they need for food.

The six kinds of swallows commonly found in most of North America are pictured here sitting together on a wire as you might see them during their fall migration. With a little practice, you will be able to distinguish one from the other. The Barn Swallow and Purple Martin on each end are easy to identify. The four in the middle are somewhat more difficult, but look carefully for different markings on each.

You will know a swallow by its swooping flight, long wings and forked tail. If it has a deeply forked tail, you need not check further—that alone tells you it is a Barn Swallow. If its tail is squared off at the tip, the bird is a Cliff Swallow. Like the Barn Swallow, it has a dark throat. When it veers to the side so that you can see its upper parts, a pale rump and a light area just above its bill will tell you for certain that you're seeing a Cliff Swallow.

If it has a brown back it is either a Bank or a Rough-winged Swallow: a dark brown breast band tells you it is a Bank Swallow, and if it has a buffy throat, it is a Rough-winged Swallow.

Tree Swallows are iridescent green-blue on the upper parts, with snowy white underparts. In the fall young birds may be brown backed, but are pure white below.

The Purple Martin is conspicuously larger than you'd expect a swallow to be. As shown here, adult males are deep iridescent blue-black, but females and young males have a grayish belly.

When you are trying to identify swallows, don't confuse them with the Chimney Swift. Swifts are not songbirds; they are more closely related to hummingbirds. But both swifts and swallows have long wings and both catch insects from the air. This is an example of "convergent evolution" where two different kinds of animals become more similar through time because they are increasingly specialized to do similar things. In the case of swifts and swallows, both catch their prey in the same way. (See Part I for a discussion of *Convergence*.)

On closer look, you will see that the wings of swifts are much longer for their body size than are swallow wings. Also, the swift's body is stubbier; it is cigar shaped with a short, stiff, squared tail. The flight of swifts is powerful, direct and less erratic than that of swallows which tend to dip and course. Swifts give a "twittering" call while in flight. They also have shorter beaks and no rictal bristles, but you won't see this from a distance. They have such wide gapes they evidently have no need for stiff funneling bristles. Another difference you won't see—they have 10 instead of 12 tail feathers.

You'll always see swifts flying, never perched on wires or in trees the way swallows rest, and when swifts land, it is always on a vertical surface such as the inside of a chimney.

With binoculars in hand, you're now ready to solve some problems of swallow identification!

When you are trying to identify swallows, don't confuse them with the Chimney Swift, which is not a songbird. The wings of the swift are much longer and its body is stubbier. Shown here are the Barn Swallow, above, and the Chimney Swift, below.

Tree Swallow

Iridoprocne bicolor
L'Hirondelle bicolore

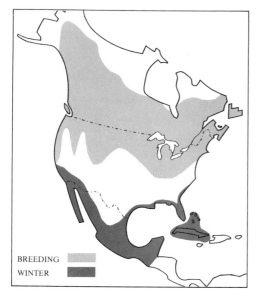

Tree Swallow 13–16 cm, 5–6.2"; 4–6 eggs, white; nest a cup of grasses, lined with feathers; placed in abandoned woodpecker holes, bird-houses, other cavities.

BREEDING
WINTER

The Tree Swallow can be distinguished from other swallows by its white underparts. It is the last swallow to leave in fall and the first to return in spring.

Tree Swallows are easily attracted to birdhouses, so you might get a family of them to nest in your backyard by putting out wooden nest boxes. (Make the entrance hole less than 3.8 cm (1½ in.) wide if you wish to keep starlings out.) Once you have attracted them, they are likely to nest with you year after year. Tree Swallows also build nests in old woodpecker holes and in dead trees in flooded areas.

Human activity does not seem to disturb these birds. One year a colony of Tree Swallows nested in the train station of a busy island amusement park in Lake Ontario. (The site was used by House Sparrows and Purple Martins the next year.) These little birds and their relatives, the Barn Swallows, have even been known to build nests in moving boats!

Violet-green Swallow

Tachycineta thalassina
L'Hirondelle à face blanche

Only in the West is there another swallow you might confuse with the Tree Swallow. Especially in the mountains, another green-backed swallow occurs, the Violet-green Swallow. This swallow resembles the Tree Swallow, but has patches of white where the Tree Swallow is dark—above and behind each eye and on the sides of its rump. The large white patches on the sides of its rump almost join, making the entire rump appear white. The back of the Violet-green Swallow is iridescent green while that of the Tree Swallow is more blue-green, but from a distance this is hard to see! Look, instead, for the white patches to tell these two swallows apart.

Barn Swallow

Hirundo rustica

L'Hirondelle des granges

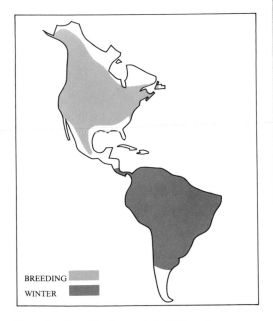

Barn Swallow 15–20 cm, 5.8–7.7″; 4–6 eggs, white, speckled with reddish brown; nest of mud mixed with straw, lined with feathers; placed on a flat surface, on rafters in buildings, under bridges, culverts.

The Barn Swallow is the most widespread songbird in the world. In England the Barn Swallow is known simply as The Swallow. It is said to be one of the most domesticated of wild animals because it is so often found associated with people and shows little fear of us. Barn Swallows sometimes build their nests in cliff holes or on rocky ledges where they probably nested before the advent of human beings, but more often now they choose the eaves of buildings, the undersides of bridges and, of course, the rough beams of old-fashioned North American barns. Farmers welcome these birds as insect eaters.

When Barn Swallows return to their breeding grounds in spring, courtship begins. You'll see two swallows swiftly and gracefully flying to and fro, occasionally interlocking bills.

To build their nest, both the male and female bring pellets of mud in their bills, plaster it in place with grass and straw, then line the nest, usually with feathers. In a farmyard, don't be too surprised to see a swallow swoop after a feather caught in an updraft—for its nest lining. Sometimes the birds find an old nest and repair it, since a new one takes so much time and energy. One birdwatcher saw a pair of Barn Swallows work on their new nest 14 hours a day for eight days, bringing a load of straw, grass or pellets of mud every two to three minutes.

Fortunately the days are long gone when Barn Swallow feathers were used for women's hats. A massive slaughter of swallows went on for several years in the 1880s but was finally stopped as a result of publicity by naturalists. The Audubon Society was formed shortly after, in part as a response to this killing.

It is difficult to describe in words the songs of swallows. Termed variously as "light," "bubbling," "trilling," the Barn Swallow song is a welcome one for all who know it.

The shrikes — Family Laniidae

A small mouse or grasshopper impaled on barbed wire or on a thorn is an unpleasant sight. It is also the sign of a shrike. Shrikes often kill more than they can eat at one time and leave a number of creatures impaled for future food. The habit of impaling probably evolved because of the difficulty shrikes have holding and manipulating prey with their feet, which, like those of all songbirds, lack "intrinsic" muscles—muscles in the toes. The movement of the feet is controlled by muscles in the legs which are connected to the toes by tendons. This restricts shrikes simply to grasping a perch or a food item. Other predators, such as hawks and owls, do have muscles in their toes which give their feet more strength and greater maneuverability to hold their prey. Shrikes are often called "butcher birds" because of the way they kill their prey. They are among the least loved of all songbirds. (Their scientific name, *Lanius*, comes from the Latin word for "butcher.")

Shrikes are of Old World origin; the greatest number are found in Africa. Many are beautifully colored and all are predators. Like hawks, shrikes perch alone at the top of a tree, telephone pole or fence post. They sit erect and watchful as they quietly wait for prey. The Red-backed Shrike of Africa was depicted on Egyptian tombs standing guard.

Only two species of shrikes are found in North America; none occur in South America. The two North American species look almost identical except that the Northern Shrike (found also in the Old World) is larger than the southern Loggerhead Shrike discussed here, and has light gray bars on the breast. Both are birds of open country. Shrikes can be confused with Mockingbirds because both species have white patches on their wings, but the shrikes have much stockier bodies, larger heads and shorter tails.

These ever-watchful birds are always on the lookout not only for prey but also for larger predators that prey upon *them*. The shrike is often pursued by hawks.

To find out what shrikes eat researchers either find the "larder," the favorite tree, bush or fence where a shrike impales its prey, or study the pellets it regurgitates. Like other predators such as owls, hawks and gulls, shrikes regurgitate small compact pellets that contain fur, feathers and bones—the indigestible remains of food they have eaten. A researcher who has worked extensively with both hawks and shrikes, Dr. Tom Cade, calculated the amount of food necessary for a family of two Northern Shrike adults and seven nestlings to survive for the 60 days of the nesting season—the period of time from the parents' arrival on the nesting grounds until the young become independent. He estimated they would need about 9000 g of food. Based on percentages of several types of food typically eaten by these shrikes, this amount equals a total of approximately 75 songbirds, 222 small rodents, 394 bumblebees and a few other insects.

The Mockingbird is the only bird that might be confused with the shrike. Both have gray bodies with white wing patches and white outer tail feathers.

Shrikes have much stockier bodies than Mockingbirds, larger heads and shorter tails. Close up, one can also see that the patches of white differ and only shrikes have black on their heads.

Loggerhead Shrike

Lanius ludovicianus

La Pie-grièche migratrice

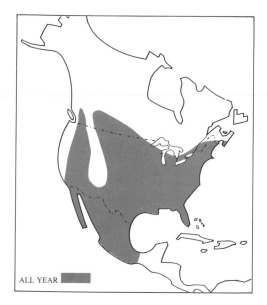

ALL YEAR

Loggerhead Shrike 22–23 cm, 8.6–9.2″; 4–6 eggs, grayish white, spotted with gray and brown; bulky nest of woven sticks, weeds, rootlets, coarse grass, lined with finer materials; placed 2–9 m (5–30′) high, in thorny trees, hedgerows, orchards, mistletoe in open country.

Both the common Loggerhead Shrike shown here and its close relative, the Northern Shrike, very rarely sing their lively, varied songs. Usually, when you hear them, they are emitting a shrieking cry, so it is easy to understand why they were given the name "shrike," which comes from the same Old English root as the word "shriek." These hawklike birds, nevertheless, have syringeal (voice box) muscles and other internal features that are typical of songbirds.

In courtship the male Loggerhead Shrike flutters his wings and spreads his tail in display, but if he displays for too long the female chases him away. (The solitary nature of these birds ensures that each has a large foraging territory. This is necessary because, as predators, their food is often scarce, but it also results in less social behavior even at mating time.) The male stands guard at the nest and brings food to the female while she incubates the eggs. Often the male is still feeding the first set of nestlings when the female is laying her second batch of eggs.

Although we may be offended at seeing a Loggerhead Shrike take a small bird, shrikes are beneficial to us as voracious eaters of large insects, such as grasshoppers. They also capture small rodents.

In the southern part of their range Loggerhead Shrikes are present year round, but they move south from northern parts in winter. At that season they are fairly common along southern roadsides, and in the Southeast have become familiar winter residents in large cities. In the Northeast they have recently decreased in numbers, but they are still prevalent in parts of their range, especially in the Southwest.

The Northern Shrike breeds in coniferous bogs and cool, open woods of northern Canada and Alaska (north to the limit of spruce trees). They move south in winter, however, to southern Canada and the northern states. They are larger than their Loggerhead cousins (though that can be difficult to tell in the field), and eat more birds and mammals.

The waxwings — Family Bombycillidae

Waxwings—so named for the bright red, waxy droplets on the tips of their wings—are gregarious birds. They have sleek, velvetlike, brown plumage, crests on their heads (like Cardinals and jays) and a yellow band at the tips of their tails.

They are an enigma among songbirds. While other male birds watch over their territories during the breeding season and are aggressive toward other males of their species, waxwings remain placid and "friendly." Other birds tend to return to the vicinity of past nest sites each year to breed, but you never know where—or when!—waxwings may turn up. And they may go to different places to nest each year. In winter, they may stay north in Canada at least until all the berries on the trees have been eaten; thus their migration time varies from year to year.

Two of the three kinds of waxwings in the world occur in North America. The Bohemian Waxwing, a northwestern bird, is larger than the more widespread Cedar Waxwing. Of these two species, only the Bohemian is found in Europe. It has white on its wings while the Cedar Waxwing does not, and its undertail coverts (small feathers that cover the bases of the larger feathers of the wings and tail) are rusty instead of white. In both species, male and female look alike, and immature birds are duller in color.

Look for flocks of waxwings. They'll often be faintly warbling a high *zsee*. (Some people refuse to call this a song.)

Waxwings are so gregarious all year round that it is hard to tell when courtship begins. It seems to begin when one bird acts as if it wishes to be fed. Its wings tremble and whirl, and it emits rattlelike sounds. It rushes to another bird and rubs against its breast, then returns to its perch. The other bird reciprocates, and they often offer petals to each other. Also, one bird sometimes sits high in a tree while the other, presumably the male, flies around slowly in an arc overhead.

Like all songbirds, the waxwings feed their nestlings insects (high protein food). But after fledging, the young eat primarily berries.

As soon as nesting is over, the family joins other waxwings, forming a flock of 30 to 60 birds. These flocks behave remarkably as a unit, suddenly darting downward, then alighting in a tree all at the same moment. Even when wintering, they can be found in flocks of up to 100 or so.

Both the small territories of waxwings and their flocking behavior are doubtless due to their fruit diet. When fruit is available, it is extremely abundant, but fruiting trees are spread over a wide area. A flock can search out this plentiful, but localized, food source better than one individual. One of the waxwing's most distinctive habits, "berry passing," may help to keep the flocks together. Two to several waxwings will sit in a row on a branch; at one end, one of the birds will pluck a berry from the tree and pass it to the waxwing next to it. It, in turn, will pass the berry up the line. The berry may be passed from one end of the row to the other and back several times before one of the birds eats it. Often their crests are highly erected while this is going on. Symbolically these actions may signal a willingness to share food. Petal passing described earlier may represent a ritualization of this tendency to pass food to one another. (See Part I, *Why birds do what they do.*)

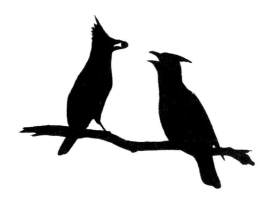

The waxwings shown here are "berry passing."

Cedar Waxwing

Bombycilla cedrorum

Le Jaseur des cèdres

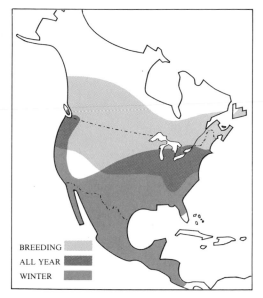

Cedar Waxwing 17–20 cm, 6.5–8″; 3–5 eggs, pale bluish gray or greenish blue, with spots or dots of black or dark brown; nest of loosely woven grasses, twigs, leaves, rootlets, lined with finer materials; placed 1.5–12 m (4–40′) high in tree, in orchards, open woods.

Cedar Waxwings have another name, "cherry bird," because of their love of cherries. Early in this century, Vermont fruit growers tried to make it legal to shoot waxwings because of the damage large flocks did to their crops. It is said that state senators voted against the action after seeing the bird: they thought it too beautiful to kill.

Cedar Waxwings also eat wild fruit. When the blue berries of cedars are ripe, they gorge themselves to such an extent that they are sometimes unable to fly afterward. One birdwatcher reported seeing a flock of Cedar Waxwings tumbling around in such an unnatural way that he concluded the fermented juices from overripe berries had made them drunk. (Robins have also been seen in this condition.) Waxwings also "flycatch" and are sometimes called "cankerbirds" because they eat many destructive caterpillars, or cankerworms.

Cedar Waxwings take their time in forming pairs and mating. Nesting often begins as late as mid-summer; by the time the young are ready to leave the nests fruit will be abundant on the trees. When they are building their nests, they often steal materials from the nearby nests of other birds such as kingbirds and vireos. Although waxwings are not colonial nesters like Bank Swallows and some other birds, several nests are frequently found in a small area. They show almost no "territoriality." (See Part II, *Territory.*)

In the mid-1800s, Cedar Waxwings were considered a table delicacy, and they were killed in great numbers for food. As songbirds, they are now protected by law.

The wrens — Family Troglodytidae

These tiny, brown birds skulk in low, tangled underbrush, picking off their insect prey. Watch for birds with short, stubby tails held high. The Winter Wren and House Wren (and Carolina Wren in the South) live mainly in bushes and shrubs. The Long-billed Marsh Wren nests and forages in cattail marshes. Wherever they are found, wrens can always be recognized by their busy manner, bobbing bodies and cocked-up short tails.

Wrens are hard to spot because they hunt in underbrush and seldom fly in long spurts (except for the House Wren), but their beautifully melodious songs and loud, harsh, chattering calls announce their presence. The translation of the Chippewa Indian word for the House Wren means "big noise for its size."

The House Wren frequently makes its home near people and is easily attracted to birdhouses. Besides nesting in birdhouses and cavities in trees, it chooses all sorts of strange places to live. House Wrens have been found nesting in tin cans in piles of garbage, old boots, open-ended pipes, pockets of scarecrows in fields and various handy spots in farm machinery and cars. Whatever size container they select, wrens will pack it full of nesting material, leaving only a small passage to a tiny cavity within. Often thorned rose twigs are among the materials used!

If you wish to prevent House Sparrows from nesting in your wren house, keep the entrance hole no larger than 2.5 cm (1 in.) wide—about the size of a quarter. You may still have to put up with fights between wrens and Tree Swallows before one of them gains ownership. House Wrens are very aggressive while trying to establish a nest site and have been known to destroy nests of other birds—and even their eggs or young.

Long-billed Marsh Wrens nest in marshes, but build their nests in a variety of plants 30 to 90 cm (1–3 ft) above the water; small trees such as alders or reeds, rushes and cattails are used. Males build the nests and, like the Winter Wren described in the next section, they make several "dummy nests" (sometimes as many as 10) in addition to the one chosen by females. Often male Long-billed Marsh Wrens have several mates.

In the Southwest, look for the Cactus Wren in arid brushland. This is the largest of all North American wrens (20 cm or 8 in. long) and resembles a small thrasher. (Their similar appearance is one reason many experts think wrens and thrashers are closely related.) The nest, like the bird itself, is conspicuous: it is a large ball-shaped mass of sticks built in a cactus with an entrance at the side.

The Wrentit

Along the West Coast, from Oregon south to Mexico, you'll see a wrenlike bird, the Wrentit. The Wrentit is not a wren, but a member of a large, diverse group of Old World songbirds, the Babblers. It is, in fact, the only New World representative of this group, and is related to our thrushes and kinglets. It is a common but secretive bird that would rather "run than fly." The Wrentit occurs in dense coastal chaparral (a unique habitat of low, evergreen shrubs); more recently it has moved into the gardens and parks of cities.

Winter Wren

Troglodytes troglodytes
Le Troglodyte des forêts

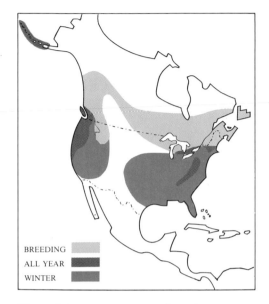

Winter Wren 10–11 cm, 4–4.5″; 4–7 eggs, white, dotted with reddish brown; nest a bulky, ball-like structure with opening in one side, of moss, twigs, weeds, rootlets, lined with fur, feathers, fine grasses; placed in roots of an overturned tree, cavity in a stump or low in a tree, in boreal coniferous forests, heavily wooded swamps.

The American Dipper is a bird of the West that resembles a wren. Dippers are the only songbirds that walk or "fly" underwater in quest of food. They hunt for aquatic insects in fast-flowing streams.

Wrens of many kinds are found in North and South America, but only one, the Winter Wren, seems to have successfully made the trip to another continent. The Winter Wren probably emigrated via the Bering Strait and, long before such events were recorded, became well established in the Old World.

This common northern wren is well known in England as the "Jenny Wren"; its German name means "king of the hedges." Wherever it is found, the Winter Wren is a popular bird.

Like most wrens, the Winter Wren sings an amazing song. Full and rich, it lasts only six to nine seconds, but contains 106–113 separate notes!

Winter Wrens usually build their nests in the upturned roots of fallen trees. The male will build several large bulky nests of moss, grass and roots within different cavities. The female chooses the best-constructed and best-concealed of these, lines it with hair and feathers, then builds a roof over it, leaving a small round entrance hole. While the female incubates the eggs in this nest, the male sleeps at night in one of the "dummy nests." Many Winter Wrens move south in the winter, but they are back in their breeding grounds in April—often while snow is still on the ground.

The Dipper. Another strange, wrenlike bird is the Dipper. Dippers, like Wrentits, belong to a group (Family Cinclidae) different from that of the wrens, but they probably are closely related to wrens. Only four species of dippers exist in the world. All are found in and near clear, fast-flowing streams. Yes, they literally are found *in* such streams as they walk or "fly" underwater in quest of their food—mainly aquatic insect larvae. The American Dipper (or "Water Ouzel") is the only dipper found in North America. It is a slate gray bird about 20 cm (8 in.) long, and is found only west of the Great Plains.

The mockingbirds and thrashers — Family Mimidae

The male Mockingbird can take off into the air without interrupting his song, which may be his own or an imitation of as many as 39 other bird songs.

The Brown Thrasher is popular for its spectacular song and its tendency to nest near our homes.

Mockingbirds act like wrens. They even look like big wrens as they cock their tails in the air and flit busily about. They also skulk in shrubs and brush as wrens do. But unlike wrens, they build open cup-shaped nests and eat both fruit and insects; in these ways, they resemble thrushes.

The family name, Mimidae, reflects a fascinating feature of this group. Most of its members mimic, but none so well as the Mockingbird. One researcher found that, besides the Mockingbird's own song, it has been known to imitate the songs of 39 kinds of birds, the calls of 50 birds and even the call notes of a kind of frog and a cricket. There's an often-told story of a man in Florida who imported several Nightingales from Europe and confined them in cages as an attraction (before that was prohibited by law). Before many days had passed, the Nightingale's song was heard throughout the countryside, sung by mimicking Mockingbirds that had heard the caged Nightingales!

Though we think of the Mockingbird as living mainly in the South, it is found as far north as southern Canada. No book on songbirds would be complete without it. The "mocker" is a bit of a rascal, rivaling the kingbird in its tendency to attack anything that comes into its territory during breeding season—including dogs that innocently wander in.

East of the prairies lives a large, rusty-backed bird, the Brown Thrasher. Along with the Mockingbird and the catbird, it is found in lilac bushes and hedgerows close to our homes. Though most male songbirds sing immediately on their return from the South, the male Brown Thrasher is quiet and sings only after it has been back on its nesting grounds for about two weeks. It sings loudly only until it has mated; then its song becomes softer. Perhaps, in this case, song is used more to attract a mate than to keep other males away.

The courtship behavior of the Brown Thrasher was first described in 1841 by Audubon. The male struts in front of the female with tail dragging behind on the ground; he then perches and vibrates his body in this attraction display.

In sagebrush deserts of the West you will find the grayish-brown Sage Thrasher, which is similar to the catbird in size and bill shape. Of the several species of thrashers found in the southwestern deserts, the well-named Curve-billed Thrasher is the most common. Its distinctive *whit-whit* call (reminding some of the human "wolf whistle") is one of the most characteristic sounds of the thorn shrub of west Texas, New Mexico and Arizona. Its nest is placed in a seemingly impenetrable cactus—commonly a cholla. The ominous thorns of these plants give the bird great protection—but it is a wonder that the nestlings survive their first few runs through the spiny gauntlet to and from their nest! Like most thrashers, they feed primarily on the ground.

The large California Thrasher is one of the birds characteristic of chaparral that grows along the hot, dry, windswept coast of California. The California Thrasher has a dark brown back, an unstreaked gray-brown breast and a deeply curved bill. All of the western thrashers, like their eastern counterparts, are gifted songsters.

Gray Catbird

Dumetella carolinensis

Le Moqueur-chat

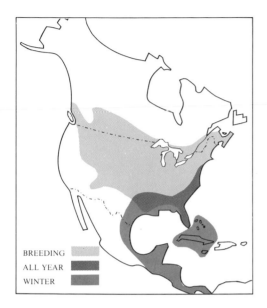

Gray Catbird 21–24 cm, 8.4–9.4″; 3–5 eggs, glossy, deep greenish blue; bulky cup-shaped nest of sticks, twigs, grasses, leaves, lined with finer materials, hair, cotton; placed 0.5–3 m (2–10′) high in dense deciduous thickets, shrubs, hedges, low trees, at woodland edge.

Most people recognize the Gray Catbird by its rattling, catlike, mewing call. It also has a pleasant song which can last as long as five minutes. Though not as clever a mimic as its relative the Mockingbird, the catbird is quick to pick up other birds' songs—especially those of other catbirds. Like each person's language pattern, each catbird's song, though characteristic of the species, is unique. Typically, every male songbird has his own song pattern by which he can be recognized by his mate and neighboring males (and often by a human listener).

While the female builds her nest, the male sings almost continuously, often late into the night. The female makes a nest of twigs, grasses and leaves so deeply cupped that when she sits on it, her tail is thrust up high and her head is thrown back—an extremely uncomfortable-looking position to sit in for 12 to 13 days.

Catbirds have a very strong feeding drive; they often feed the brood of a different kind of bird, especially if their own young have been killed. On the other hand, they have been seen eating the eggs of other species.

Because their nests are usually in dense thickets near the ground, catbirds fall prey to foxes, cats and snakes. But one blacksnake met its match when it came too close to a catbird nest—it was violently attacked by four catbirds, two kingbirds, an oriole and a wren. Sadly, the person who saw this happen shot the snake as it was driven away from the catbird's nest. Increasingly, we are beginning to realize that preservation of snakes is also important. Indeed, it is primarily the destruction of the environment, not natural predators, that ultimately threatens wildlife.

Catbirds forage on or near the ground, gleaning insects and eating fallen berries. Watch for them in gardens where you'll see them poking around with their bills, turning leaves and small branches to find insects in the litter, never far from cover. Look, too, on low branches.

The thrushes – Family Muscicapidae

The only thing the European Blackbird has in common with our blackbirds is its color. It is a thrush, closely related to the American Robin, and is quite unlike North American blackbirds, the Icteridae.

The European Robin, which the British call "Robin Redbreast," is a warbler-sized thrush—much smaller than our robin.

This is the largest family of songbirds, containing 1250 species—nearly one-quarter of the total. In North America, however, only 21 species are found north of Mexico, and these fall into two distinct groups, the "thrushes," and the "kinglets and gnatcatchers." We discuss them separately.

One of the most familiar North American birds, the robin, is a thrush. Interestingly its closest relatives are *not* found here. Some are in Central and South America, but most live across the Atlantic. The European Blackbird—of "four-and-twenty blackbirds" fame—is, in fact, a thrush, much like our robin. This pretty, black bird with the yellow beak and his brown mate are common on lawns and in open country in England and other parts of Europe. Blackbirds reinforce their nests with mud as our robin does and generally lead a similar life. Both the blackbird and the American Robin used to suffer the unfortunate problem of being "good eating"; the blackbird was still sold in European markets early in this century.

The bird the British call "Robin Redbreast," a bird that has inspired children's stories and poetry for centuries, is one of several small, delicate thrushes found in Europe, but it is not related to our North American robin. Early English settlers in North America gave our robin the name of one of their favorites at home. They also gave the name "blackbird" to our New World blackbirds—only in color are these birds like the European Blackbird (see *Blackbirds* for more about these birds).

All thrushes, large and small, have certain similarities. They all have long legs for their size, a robust body and large eyes. Their nests are similar and most feed in the same way. If you've ever watched a robin search for food, you know this technique: it runs across the lawn, stops, looks around, tilts its head from side to side, then plunges its bill into the grass. People used to think the bird was listening for sounds from under the ground. Now we know that it is looking, not listening, for what's below. Songbirds see monocularly, that is, they use one eye at a time.

This family includes some of the best-known singers, like the Nightingale of Europe and the Wood and Hermit Thrushes of North America. We hope that you get to know the thrushes, common birds with beautiful voices.

American Robin

Turdus migratorius

Le Merle américain

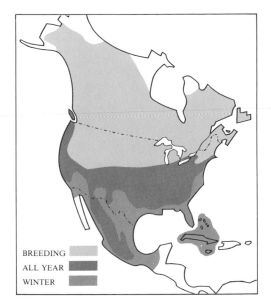

BREEDING

ALL YEAR

WINTER

American Robin 23–27 cm, 9–10.8″; 3–5 (usually 4) eggs, plain blue; cup-shaped nest, firm, compact, of grasses, weeds, leaves, twigs, lined with mud, finer materials, paper, cellophane; placed 2–15 m (5–50′) high in tree fork, horizontal branch, on ledge, in cities, parks, farmlands, open woods, meadows.

Though robins migrate, some go no farther south than New England or southern Ontario for the winter. So if you see a robin in February, it isn't necessarily a sign that spring is on the way.

In most places, males return in small flocks and are back in their nesting areas by March; the females return a little later. Robins proclaim and defend their territories aggressively. You might see one male run at another and bump him. Both may then leap into the air and lunge at each other. All the while they give screams of attack, and when the fight is over, the winner—almost always the original owner of the territory—chases the rival away with ringing calls. Both go back to their pleasant, long-continued "cheerily, cheerily" song. Robins are early risers and often begin singing well before daybreak. If you are up at that hour, they are among the first birds that you'll hear on a spring morning.

Try watching a female build the family nest. First she lays a foundation of twigs and grasses, then finer grasses. While standing in the center, she draws the grasses around one another. Next she brings mud in her bill for reinforcement. After turning around in the nest and pushing down on it with her breast and wings to shape the cup inside to her satisfaction, she brings finer material for lining.

Around the first of June, you will see fat-bodied, speckled young birds squatting in the grass, waiting to be fed. The male takes complete charge of these fledglings while the female starts another brood.

After the second brood is reared, nesting birds join other robins that have already formed roosting flocks. These gather into still larger flocks to search for berries, sometimes doing damage to orchards. Most robins go south by the end of October. There, the flocks become even larger and the birds stay in woods and moist pastures and fields—not as closely associated with people as they are in the summer.

How do animals recognize one another?

Why is it so important for individuals of a species to be able to recognize others of their kind? If animals of different species mate, very rarely will they produce offspring that are healthy and are themselves able to produce fertile young. Offspring produced by parents of different species are usually sterile. For instance, horse and donkey matings produce sterile mules. More commonly, young aren't even produced from such mixed matings. Many hybrid plants, cultivated for the better quality of fruit they produce, cannot reproduce. To avoid such unsuccessful hybrid matings, each species has developed means to recognize others of its kind.

The problem of look-alikes

It is easy to understand how some animals recognize one another and why mistakes aren't made in mating. Most species, even those that are closely related, look quite different. Some species, however, look much the same. How do these "look-alikes" recognize one another?

Songs are one means by which birds recognize their own kind. A revealing series of experiments was done by Dr. William Dilger in the 1950s to investigate how several species of "look-alike" thrushes recognize others of their kind. He worked with five kinds of medium-sized, brown, woodland thrushes that often breed within a few kilometers of one another—the Wood Thrush, Veery, Swainson's Thrush, Gray-cheeked Thrush and Hermit Thrush. In the experiments, dummies of the five species (mounted museum specimens) were set up in the territories of each kind of thrush. No matter which dummy was set up, all were attacked by the males of each species. The males, by attacking, showed that they were unable to discriminate among these similar thrushes on the basis of external appearance alone. (A good birdwatcher, however, can tell one from the other by their subtly different coloring and markings.)

Next, Dr. Dilger put dummies into the territories and played tape recordings of the songs of the species represented by the dummies. The results were enlightening. Only the males of the species whose song was being played attacked the dummy. Even if the wrong dummy was set up (that is, a model of a different species), males of the species whose song was being played attacked the dummy. For example, if a dummy of a Veery was put into the territory of a Swainson's Thrush, and a tape recording of a Veery's song—or of any thrush song other than a Swainson's Thrush song—was played, the Swainson's Thrush ignored the dummy. But if a dummy of a Veery was put into a Swainson's Thrush's territory and a Swainson's Thrush song played, the dummy was vigorously attacked by the male Swainson's Thrush.

It is apparent that the males of the five species of thrushes cannot tell each other apart by appearance alone. It is the song of each that gives the cue for recognition. By recognizing members of their own species, these males do not waste precious time and energy combating every thrush in the area.

Experiments that try to determine which stimulus, sight or sound, is more important to females in recognizing males of their own kind are more difficult to design because females tend to ignore all songs unless they are "reproductively ready" to mate. Females probably require courtship rituals that vary slightly among the species as well as differences in song as recognition cues.

Example that shows the importance of song in thrush species recognition

TERRITORY OF A MALE HERMIT THRUSH	RESPONSE OF THIS MALE
Dummy of Hermit Thrush	Attacked
Dummy of a Gray-cheeked Thrush	Attacked
Dummy of a Hermit Thrush, song of a Gray-cheeked Thrush played	Ignored
Dummy of a Gray-cheeked Thrush, song of a Gray-cheeked Thrush played	Ignored
Dummy of a Hermit Thrush, song of a Hermit Thrush played	Attacked
Dummy of a Gray-cheeked Thrush, song of a Hermit Thrush played	Attacked

This table shows an example of the kinds of responses obtained from experiments with thrushes described in the text.

Gray-cheeked Thrush. Although male thrushes apparently distinguish one another by song, the species also have different plumages.

Swainson's Thrush. Although very like the Gray-cheeked Thrush in appearance, Swainson's Thrush has a buffy rather than a gray cheek, and a buffy eye ring.

Wood Thrush

Hylocichla mustelina
La Grive des bois

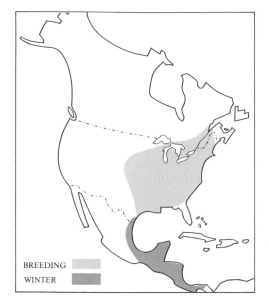

Wood Thrush 19–22 cm, 7.5–8.5″; 3–4 eggs, pale blue or bluish green; bulky nest of grasses, weeds, trash, molded with mud or leaf mold, lined with fine grasses; placed 2–15 m (5–50′) high in tree fork, horizontal branch, in dense, humid deciduous woods.

BREEDING
WINTER

The song of the Wood Thrush is one of the most beautiful among songbirds. It is elaborate and vigorous. Listen for the male's flutelike *ee-o-lay* in low, damp forests early in spring—just after he has returned from Central America. (Unlike many migrants, Wood Thrushes do not form flocks when they winter in the South but remain quiet and solitary.)

Once you've heard the song of the Wood Thrush, you won't be surprised to learn that it is a close relative of that well-known European songster, the Nightingale. Only the males of most species sing elaborate songs. But among Wood Thrushes, the females sing beautifully too, even while incubating their eggs!

After mating, the female chooses a site in the fork of a sapling and begins to build a nest while the male guards the territory. This nest resembles the robin's, but is lined with rootlets instead of dried grass. Wood Thrushes will tolerate many kinds of birds in the area—but violently attack fellow Wood Thrushes and birds like Blue Jays that rob nests of their eggs. The Wood Thrush is a frequent victim of the cowbird; in some areas, over half of the thrushes' nests contain the eggs of this parasite.

Watch for this plump, speckle-breasted, large-eyed bird on the forest floor where it will be searching for insects among the mushrooms and ferns. Don't confuse the Wood Thrush with the Brown Thrasher, a bird with a much longer tail, white wing bars and streaks instead of spots on its breast. (Thrashers tend to be found in brushy areas rather than in damp woodlands.)

Water Pipit

Anthus spinoletta

Le Pipit commun

The Water Pipit is a bird of pastures and meadows. This brown thrushlike bird can be distinguished from thrushes and from similar sparrows by its white outer tail feathers.

Many woodland thrushes are brownish in color. If you see a slender, brownish, thrushlike bird out in the open in a pasture or meadow, it will more likely be a pipit. Pipits are not thrushes but members of another group (Family Motacillidae) found mostly in the Old World. Though it differs from a thrush in several ways, a pipit can be confused with a thrush—or with one of the brownish field birds such as a female Horned Lark or a sparrow. Look for white outer tail feathers—no thrush or similar sparrow has them.

Two kinds of pipits are found in North America. The Water Pipit breeds in tundra and above the timberline in mountains but during migration is found in pastures, meadows and along shores. It is one of several pipits that breeds in northern Europe (where it is called the Rock Pipit). In the northern prairies of North America, you might see the Sprague's Pipit—named by the great naturalist Audubon for his friend Isaac Sprague. Sprague's Pipit rivals the Horned Lark for the most spectacular aerial courtship flight of all North American birds. It circles high overhead—nearly beyond human eyesight—singing its sweet, but thin, descending song. This bird circles and sings, over and over, for perhaps half an hour before coming down to earth.

Attracting bluebirds to birdhouses

Of the birds that can be attracted to nest boxes, the bluebird has the most specific needs. To attract bluebirds, build a birdhouse on a pole, 1.5–3 m (5 to 10 ft) high; the entrance hole should be 3.5–4 cm (1 to 1.5 in.) in diameter to keep starlings out. House Wrens and Tree Swallows also use this size entrance, but bluebirds can hold their own in competition with them. House Sparrows are unavoidable! You can try keeping out sparrows by removing nesting material each day as they put it in. Bluebird houses should be placed in the open, but not far from trees—if possible at the edge of an orchard or wood.

Several books, especially John Terres' *Songbirds in your Garden,* give ideas on houses for various birds and ways to attract them. Terres' book has many enjoyable anecdotes and contains an abundance of good information.

The city bird's worst enemy

The worst enemy of city birds is the domestic cat, estimated to catch an average of 50 birds each per year. Young robins are frequent victims. Wrens and warblers resting in cities during migration are also common catches of our predatory pets.

Eastern Bluebird

Sialia sialis

Le Merle bleu à poitrine rouge

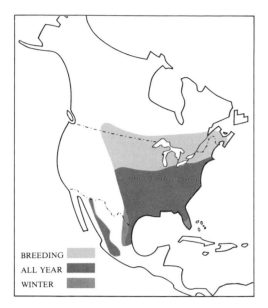

Eastern Bluebird 17–20 cm, 6.5–7.7″; 3–6 eggs, pale blue or bluish white; nest a cup of fine grasses, weed stalks, leaves; placed in cavities, birdhouses, in orchards, woodland edge, open woods.

The Mountain Bluebird is one of the two western bluebirds. Equal in beauty to the much loved Eastern Bluebird, this species and the Western Bluebird replace the Eastern Bluebird in most of the West.

This beautiful blue bird with the soft, warbling voice was once common in eastern North America. But House Sparrows and starlings, introduced from Europe, took many of the nesting cavities that had been used by bluebirds. Now bluebirds can be found only where plenty of birdhouses are available. If you want to attract bluebirds, see *Attracting bluebirds to birdhouses.*

Bluebirds have a beautiful courtship. Fluttering with widespread tail and half-open wings, and singing a soft song, the male perches beside the female, caresses her and brings her food. He often leads her to a cavity or nest box and looks in. The female chooses the nesting site, however, and it isn't always the one the male showed her. Bluebirds are not loyal to their mates and often choose another for the second brood, and still another for the third.

When it's time for nestlings to be fledged, the parents leave the nest and, from a distance, sing for them to come out. When one finally comes tumbling out—probably from hunger—both parents rush to feed it.

Bluebirds hop along the ground or dart among the foliage of trees looking for insects; they also catch insects while in flight. In winter, they can be seen in open places such as the cotton, corn and sugarcane fields of the South searching for insects to augment their winter diet of wild fruit.

Most Eastern Bluebirds that breed in the North move south in the winter, but reappear early in the spring. Look for them in New England, southern Canada and the northern prairies as early as March.

Two species of bluebirds are common in the West—the Western Bluebird and the Mountain Bluebird. The Western Bluebird resembles the Eastern but has a blue rather than orange throat, with some slight reddish on the mid-back. The Mountain Bluebird lacks the rusty color altogether and has a turquoise blue throat and breast. The lovely Mountain Bluebird is found primarily in the mountains east of the Sierras and west of the Great Plains, north into Alaska; the Western Bluebird lives in open coniferous forests and woods from southern British Columbia southward into Mexico.

Why are bird eggs different colors?

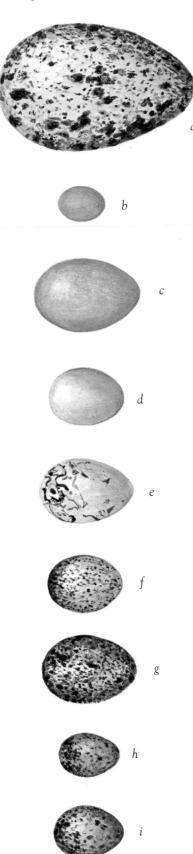

Brown, blue, white. Some are splotched with color; others are speckled or streaked. Some have a wreath of spots concentrated around one end. Some like the eggs of the kingbird have spots of several colors. But eggs laid by the same kind of bird, with rare exceptions, are much the same. Thus, we can usually tell a robin's or cowbird's egg when we see it.

The nesting habits of birds appear to determine the color of eggs they lay. The following paragraph explains how nature has, seemingly, selected for colored eggs in many species.

Reptile eggs are white. Turtles, and snakes that lay eggs (some have live young), tend to bury or hide them under logs and leaves. The color of their eggs is probably unimportant because predators would not use sight to seek them out. Since present-day reptiles generally have white eggs, their ancestors probably did. As birds are derived from reptiles, the "primitive" condition in birds must be to produce white eggs as well. To look at the question another way, one might ask why, if it takes extra energy to produce pigments (and it does), have colored or marked eggs evolved? What is their value? Presumably, birds would continue to produce white eggs unless they were under pressure to do otherwise. Nature can select for egg color just as a poultry farmer can. Chickens originally laid brown eggs, but in many strains breeders have selected for white ones.

It turns out that egg color correlates with nest placement. Most species that nest in cavities produce white or lightly pigmented eggs, whereas those that have open nests produce pigmented eggs. In the open it is harder to see a colored or speckled egg. And where are the most heavily pigmented eggs found? You'll find them in nests built on the ground.

Even in closely related species you'll find that those species with well-concealed sites produce less pigmented eggs than those that nest in the open. For example, among the thrushes, the bluebird nests in cavities and produces light blue or white eggs, whereas the closely related robin and Wood Thrush that nest in the open lay bright blue eggs. One could guess that because nearly all thrushes do nest in the open and lay pigmented eggs, bluebirds have only recently adopted the hole-nesting habit, and, like chickens, they are in the process of having the color selected out of their eggs. If we are right, we might guess that in a few thousand years bluebirds that lay slightly blue eggs will be rare indeed.

How does an egg get its color? Shell pigments come mainly from the blood pigment, hemoglobin, and also from bile pigments. Small pigment glands lining the wall of the oviduct of the mother bird supply the color as the shell is being laid down around the egg. If the egg remains still in an area of the oviduct where there are many of these glands, a ring of pigment will result; so eggs of some birds often have wreathed larger ends. (See the illustrations of the eggs.) If the egg continues to move along, an all blue or all brown egg is produced. And if there are no pigment glands, a white egg is laid. Thus, the presence, distribution and number of pigment glands, plus the rate of movement of the egg through the oviduct, all affect the color of the egg. Perhaps it is not so surprising that birds lay eggs of such a variety of colors.

These are the eggs of some representative North American songbirds. (a) The Common Raven lays the largest, and (b) the Golden-crowned Kinglet, the smallest. (c) The sky-blue egg of the American Robin is known by almost everyone. (d) The white egg of the Purple Martin is typical of eggs laid by hole-nesting species. (e) The streaking on the Baltimore Oriole's egg is characteristic of this species and similar to that of a few other species. (f) The Brown-headed Cowbird lays its eggs in the nests of other species of birds. Though their eggs do not closely resemble, or mimic, those of their hosts, their speckled eggs do look much like those of many songbirds that build open nests, such as the (g) Cardinal, (h) Yellow Warbler and (i) Song Sparrow. These species commonly serve as the foster parents of young cowbirds, so perhaps they find this similarity confusing—as scientists sometimes do.

The kinglets and gnatcatchers — Family Muscicapidae

Golden-crowned Kinglet

American Robin

Common Raven

Here, the smallest North American songbird is compared in size with a common, medium-sized songbird and with the largest North American songbird.

Kinglets are tiny, stubby birds, just bigger than hummingbirds, and smaller than any other North American songbird. All are fairly dull in color except for their brilliant, sometimes partly concealed crowns of yellow, orange or red feathers, and they all have a characteristic jerky, undulating flight.

Regulus, the kinglet's Latin name, means "little king," and these birds do put on regal airs during mating season. The males flash their bright crowns at each other, spread their tail and fluff out their side feathers. They don't fight, but they do follow each other, emitting high shrill calls all the while.

Two of the four kinds of kinglets that exist in the world are found in North America. The others are restricted to the Old World. Kinglets are among the "Old World Warblers," a group of birds that closely resembles our "New World Warblers," though this similarity is only superficial; the two groups are not closely related.

Many birds that spend considerable time in trees are partly or totally green in color. This protective coloring makes it difficult for predators to see them when they are sitting still; it also makes it difficult for us to tell them all apart. We have already mentioned the superficial similarity between the kinglets (Old World Warblers) and New World Warblers—they are all small birds with needlelike bills, and many kinds are green. You can tell them apart by the much stubbier, rounder look and smaller size of the kinglets. Also, kinglets flit and hop around more. In North American woods flycatchers and vireos might also be confused with kinglets. If you see a bird sitting quietly in an upright position, it is probably a flycatcher, not a kinglet. Though green like kinglets, vireos are larger (size can be hard to determine if the bird is high in a tree), and *always* more sluggish, more deliberate in their movement.

One distinctive "subgroup" of these Old World Warblers is found entirely in the New World—the gnatcatchers. Gnatcatchers are tiny, slender, gray birds; the Blue-gray Gnatcatcher found in eastern North America, north just barely into southern Canada, is the most familiar to us. It looks larger than a kinglet because it has such a long tail (nearly half of its 12 cm or 4.8 in. length is tail), but its body is about kinglet sized (they weigh 5–8 g, depending on how fat they are). Although gnatcatchers are not brightly colored birds, they are quite pretty: blue-gray above, white below, with a long dark gray tail edged in white, and a thin, but distinct, ring of white around each eye. They make their nests of plant down (such as dandelion fluff) held together with insect and spider silk. The gnatcatcher's nest is only 4 cm (1½ in.) wide on the inside, befitting such a small bird. Amazingly, however, these tiny nests are often parasitized by the *much* larger cowbird. It is hard to imagine a cowbird egg fitting into the nest, yet sometimes two cowbird eggs have been found with the eggs of the Blue-gray Gnatcatcher. (See *Brown-headed Cowbird* for more on this topic.)

Like kinglets, gnatcatchers are active birds, their long tails constantly in motion as they flit about in trees. In spring they chase each other about the trees, hawk gnats and sing, but the song is so quiet you have to listen carefully to learn it. (The Blue-gray Gnatcatcher is illustrated in Part II, *Nest sanitation.*)

Golden-crowned Kinglet

Regulus satrapa

Le Roitelet à couronne dorée

Ruby-crowned Kinglet

Regulus calendula

Le Roitelet à couronne rubis

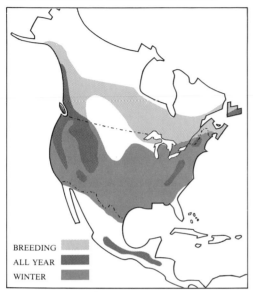

Golden-crowned Kinglet 9–10 cm, 3.5–4″; 5–10 eggs, cream, spotted with browns, grays; globular nest with small opening at top, of *Usnea*, other lichens, bark strips, rootlets; placed 2–18 m (6–60′) high in evergreen, partially suspended from branch, in coniferous forests.

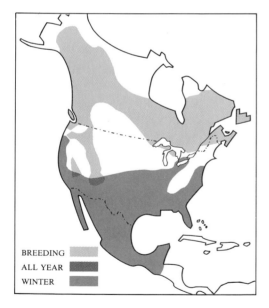

Ruby-crowned Kinglet 9–11 cm, 3.4–4.5″; 5–11 eggs, pale white, with fine reddish-brown dots; nest a deep cup of strips of bark, grasses, moss; suspended 0.5–30 m or 2–100′ (usually less than 8 m or 25′) high from near tip of conifer branch (commonly spruce), in coniferous forests.

The Ruby-crowned Kinglet goes farther north in summer and farther south in winter than the Golden-crowned. Even though its ruby crown doesn't show unless it is excited, the Ruby-crowned Kinglet is a conspicuous bird in spring migration because it frequently sings a pleasant warbling song that is quite melodious and fairly loud—you'd expect it to come from a much bigger bird. The Golden-crowned Kinglet's crown is always visible, and it too is a noisy bird, though its song is so high-pitched that it is difficult for the human ear to detect. Both are noticeable in spring migration because they arrive before the great masses of warblers, and in the fall they pass through later. In migration they are seen in thickets, trees and shrubbery around houses, but they breed in northern coniferous forests.

Kinglets have tiny globular nests that are partly suspended from near the end of a horizontal evergreen bough, such as spruce, fir or hemlock. Even though their nests are tiny, they lay many eggs (5–11) that are often piled in two layers. The newly hatched babies are "bumblebee sized."

Kinglets flit about in constant search for insects. They look through clusters of evergreen needles, peering about the base of each for insects or insect eggs. Sometimes they hover as they search. They catch an insect of some kind—usually a wasp or an ant—every five or six seconds. In winter, insect eggs are an important part of their diet, but they eat small seeds and berries too. They're also expert flycatchers and, like many other small birds, they drink sap that flows from holes drilled in trees by sapsuckers (a kind of woodpecker). As the sap thickens and insects get caught in it, kinglets feed there.

The creepers – Family Certhiidae

This is a small family of birds—there are only six species in the world—but it contains one of the most familiar and distinctive of our songbirds, the Brown Creeper. Creepers fly little except when they are courting; at other times they are much too busy climbing trees in search of insects. Our Brown Creeper is also found in Eurasia (in the British Isles it is called the Tree Creeper), and all other members of this family are restricted to the Old World.

You'll find creepers in forests or in parks that have many trees. They are not generally migratory, but they do move south from the coldest parts of their range in winter and, in mountains, to lower elevations.

Feeding on tree trunks

Creepers and nuthatches are the songbirds most highly specialized for finding food on the trunks of trees, but many others, at least on occasion, search tree trunks for food. For much of the year, chickadees rely on insects and insect eggs that are hidden in the bark of twigs and branches, and the Black-and-white Warbler is almost always seen creeping along a tree trunk in search of food. Another "creeping warbler"—the Pine Warbler—is worth mentioning here. Its old name—"Pine Creeping Warbler"—was appropriate for this species, as they often can be seen creeping along large branches of pine trees. They also pick insects from the pine needles. Pine Warblers are common in coastal pine forests along the Atlantic Coast, from New Jersey to Florida, and they occur locally north to southern Canada.

As a group, woodpeckers are perhaps the best known of birds that feed on tree trunks—and the most specialized. Woodpeckers are a diverse group, some large, some small, but they are not songbirds, not even perching birds. Unlike trunk-feeding songbirds, woodpeckers have a chisel-like bill with which they dig under loose pieces of bark for insects, or into the tissue of a dead tree to find wood-boring insect larvae. As a variation on this, sapsuckers drill holes in living trees, drink sap, then return later to eat insects that have gathered to share in the sap meal. Many other woodpeckers, such as flickers in North America, commonly catch insects on the ground; and still others, such as the Red-headed and Acorn Woodpeckers, augment their insect diets with nuts.

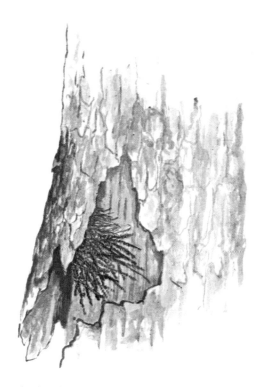

The female creeper builds her nest under a slab of bark that is beginning to peel off.

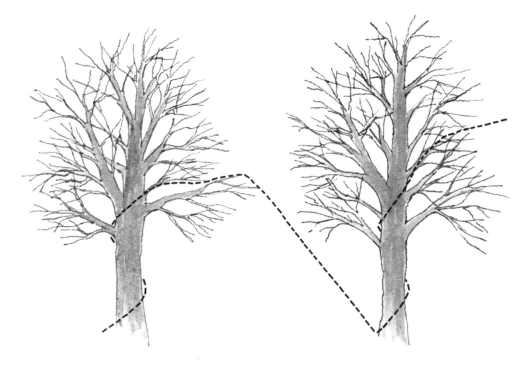

The Brown Creeper usually starts its search for insects at the bottom of a tree, works its way spiral-fashion to the top, then flies to the bottom of the next tree to start another climb.

98

Brown Creeper

Certhia familiaris
Le Grimpereau brun

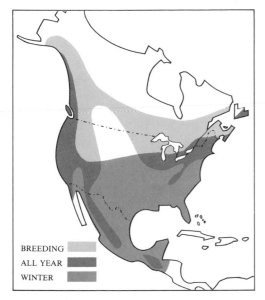

Brown Creeper 13–15 cm, 5–5.75″; 4–8 eggs, white, creamy white, spotted with reddish brown; nest of twigs, bark strips, moss, lined with feathers, spiderwebs; placed behind loose bark 2–4.5 m (5–15′) high, in woods.

This small, brown mouselike bird with long curved beak, long curved toenails and short, stiff tail is not easy to confuse with anything else. The Brown Creeper spends a large part of the day, every day, climbing trees. It starts at the bottom and—using its stiff tail as a prop—it creeps upward making a spiral motion around the tree all the way to the top. It then flies to the base of the next tree and repeats the pattern. One observer counted a Brown Creeper climb 43 trees in one hour in its search for insects. To work branches, creepers usually search to the tip, then fly back to the trunk to continue their upward climb. Sometimes they take short hops back on a branch to reinvestigate crevices in the bark. They can cling to the undersides of branches with no difficulty. On the trunk, they may drop backward, tail first, to check an area again before starting back up. The creeper works alone or in pairs, oblivious to other small birds around it that are also searching for insects in the bark. The creeper seems to see poorly when engrossed in this activity, and occasionally mistakes a pant leg for a tree. As it feeds and flutters from tree to tree, it emits a high-pitched *zi-i-i-it* which is difficult for the human ear to detect. Its spring song is also high-pitched and difficult to hear.

Creepers do fly during courtship—weaving in and out of trees, making wild dashes back and forth, sometimes chasing each other. The female creeper builds the nest, usually behind a slab of bark that is beginning to peel off. She makes a loose, hammock-shaped nest on a foundation of twigs and spider cocoons.

The Brown Creeper is an excellent example of an animal with protective coloration—its plumage closely resembles the bark of the trees it climbs. When pursued by a shrike or hawk, the creeper flattens itself against the tree, wings spread out, and remains completely still. One experienced birdwatcher noted that even he lost sight of creepers when they hid themselves this way.

The titmice – Family Paridae, and The nuthatches – Family Sittidae

The northern Boreal Chickadee has a brown cap, in contrast with the "Black"-capped Chickadee. Songbirds that stay north in the winter puff up their feathers as shown here to provide an insulative coat for warmth.

The gray Tufted Titmouse of southern woodlands is one of only three crested members of this family in North America. The other two, the Plain and Bridled Titmice, are found only in the southwestern US.

In England some years ago there was a great deal of publicity because householders found that milk bottles left at their doors had the metal caps punctured and the cream gone from the top of the milk. The culprits were finally identified. Some innovative titmouse had learned the trick and others learned from it until the countryside had become filled with these early-morning cream thieves!

The titmice are popular birds wherever they live. They look like little balls of fluff and are exceedingly friendly. A few have crests, like the Tufted Titmouse of eastern North America. All are small, active birds, curious and seemingly intelligent, like the jays and crows. Our most popular titmice are called chickadees. The Black-capped Chickadee is the most common; it is found with the Boreal Chickadee (having a brown cap) in the North, and is replaced by the Carolina Chickadee (that looks nearly identical but has a different song) in the Southeast. (You'll find the Black-capped Chickadee, however, on mountaintops in the southern US.) In the West two other chickadees are common: the Mountain Chickadee in mountains, and the Chestnut-backed Chickadee along the Pacific Coast.

The name titmouse can present some confusion. We are still amused when we think of the time one of us pointed out to our brother-in-law the small bird called the Tufted Titmouse. He found it difficult to believe this was the name of a bird. He then went on to tell us of a Scrabble game in which he had played the word "titmouse," having recalled seeing or hearing it. When his opponent challenged the word, he confidently replied that it was "some kind of mouse." The "mouse" part of this word came from the Middle English word "mose," the general name used for these little birds and has nothing to do with mice. ("Tit" is from the Anglo-Saxon word meaning "tiny object.")

Chickadees (and other titmice) cling to branches in every imaginable position—upside down, sideways, right side up—as they search the bark for insect eggs and caterpillars. They also eat bayberries, blueberries, poison ivy berries and seeds. They hold large seeds, like sunflower seeds, between their feet and pound them with their bills in order to break the shell and extract the "meat."

Nuthatches, like titmice, are more numerous in kind in the Old World, but four species live here. Of the two more common ones, the White-breasted Nuthatch is more often seen because it nests in deciduous trees (trees that lose their leaves each autumn) in fairly open woodlands, whereas its close relative, the Red-breasted Nuthatch, prefers conifers in more heavily wooded regions. You may see both in winter, as they move southward. You'll perhaps see them along with chickadees, creepers, small woodpeckers and kinglets. The Red-breasted Nuthatch can be identified by the added black stripe in front of and behind its eyes (it looks as if a stripe goes through each eye), and by its reddish breast. (See Part I, *Beaks of songbirds* for the illustration.)

Nuthatches move, not up, but headfirst down trees—and around limbs—constantly on the watch for insects. They climb downward by anchoring themselves with their foot. With one toe forward and three back—just the opposite of the usual positioning of toes on perching birds—a nuthatch will hang securely while it peers into crevices below for insects. Since they are the only birds that go down trees headfirst, they are probably able to find insects missed by other birds going in the opposite direction.

Black-capped Chickadee

Parus atricapillus
La Mésange à tête noire

White-breasted Nuthatch

Sitta carolinensis
La Sittelle à poitrine blanche

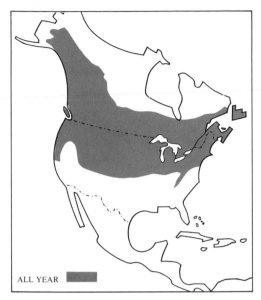

ALL YEAR

Black-capped Chickadee 12–14 cm, 4.8–5.7";
5–10 eggs, white, with small reddish-brown
spots, smooth shell, little gloss; cup-shaped nest
of plant fibers, moss, lined with plant down,
feathers; placed in cavity in tree, 1.5–15 m
(4–50'), in woods.

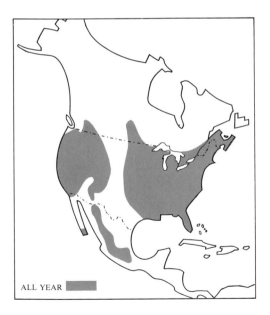

ALL YEAR

White-breasted Nuthatch 13–16 cm, 5.2–6.2";
5–9 eggs, white, spotted with light brown; nest
of bark shreds, twigs, fur; placed in natural
cavity in tree or nest box, 4.5–15 m (15–50'),
in woods.

We are showing and describing the Black-capped Chickadee and the White-breasted Nuthatch together because you'll often see them together, especially in winter, and because it is thought that titmice and nuthatches are closely related.

The small, fluffy Black-capped Chickadee is a common bird of the woodlands and, happily for us, will not hesitate to come into towns if woods are nearby. Its simple, cheerful *chick-a-dee-dee* is heard year round.

While courting in early spring, male chickadees whistle a clear two-noted *fee-bee* which, to some, sounds like "spring time" or "spring's here." The chickadee's nest site is usually a cavity or tree stump. It takes a pair of these birds about 14 days to complete the nest: 10 days to excavate the cavity and carry away the rotten wood, and 4 days to build the nest.

These little birds seem to be quite intelligent. A US government bander noticed that, of the dozen or so species in his traps, only Black-capped Chickadees remembered the way out—and they did it directly, without searching for the exit.

A good way to find nuthatches (and Brown Creepers) is to listen for the easily recognized call of the chickadee. These birds are often found in the same woodland searching for insect food. You'll also hear the distinctive nasal *yank* call of the nuthatches all year round.

White-breasted Nuthatches stick soft-shelled nuts—acorns, pine nuts and chestnuts—into crevices in bark, and peck away at them to crack the shells. Sometimes they take sunflower seeds and little bits of suet and stick these into cracks and crevices elsewhere—storage for a time when food is scarce.

Nuthatches, and many other birds that search for insects in crevices, have white breasts that reflect light, perhaps making it easier for the bird to see inside the dark recesses.

101

The crows, jays and magpies – Family Corvidae

Jays and crows tend to be large, active and noisy, so it's easy to spot them. And because they will eat just about anything, they are found almost everywhere. Everyone knows the crow, and most people know the jays, but not all of us think of them as songbirds. They do not have beautiful songs but, nevertheless, they are perching birds with all the structural features of songbirds.

Crows are large, black (or basically black) birds; but jays are a varied group with an especially great diversity in Central and South America. Almost all crows and jays stay throughout the year near their breeding grounds. The American Crow, however, does migrate from the cold North to warmer places in the fall, as do many Blue Jays.

The word "intelligent" is frequently used to describe jays and crows, and indeed they do seem to be among the smartest of birds. Birds like crows and jays that seek a variety of foods in a variety of ways, appear to show more curiosity and imagination than birds that seek a specific type of food. Thus stories of the clever jay or wily crow abound. A humorous example is Mark Twain's "Jim Baker's Bluejay Yarn" in *A Tramp Abroad:* Jim Baker, a hermetic miner, recalls watching a Blue Jay trying to fill a hole with acorns. But since the apparent hole was, in fact, a knothole in a roof board of a cabin, the acorns fell through into the cabin; the jay's efforts and frustrations in trying to fill up that hole were much like those of a person. "You may call a jay a bird," Jim Baker says. "Well, so he is, in a measure—because he's got feathers on him, and don't belong to no church, perhaps; but otherwise he is just as much a human as you be."

In the West the Blue Jay is replaced by the Steller's Jay—a bird similar in habits, but different in appearance. The beautiful Steller's Jay, like the Blue Jay, has a crest and is basically blue, but it is darker blue than the Blue Jay, and has a grayish hood. This western jay is found almost exclusively in coniferous or mixed forests.

The Black-billed Magpie, closely related to jays, is found in both Eurasia and America, but, curiously, not in eastern North America. In the Great Plains and the West, however, you'll see this handsome bird in farmyards and along roadsides. The bold black, white and green markings make the magpie unmistakable. The nest is similarly distinctive—a large ball of sticks placed in a tree, usually at least three meters off the ground. Like most members of this family, magpies are omnivores—they will eat almost anything—and you'll often see them by a road vying with crows and vultures for remains of a dead animal.

On the next few pages, we describe the habits of a few of the most common and widespread of the jays and crows of North America, beginning with the spunky northern representative of the group—the Gray Jay.

The beautiful, iridescent blue and black Steller's Jay replaces the Blue Jay in the coniferous forests of the West.

The Black-billed Magpie, a bird closely related to jays, is a common bird in the West. Its bold black, white and iridescent green markings make it unmistakable.

Gray (Canada) Jay

Perisoreus canadensis

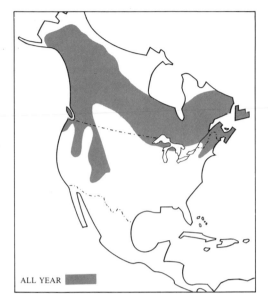

ALL YEAR

Gray (Canada) Jay 27–31 cm, 10.8–12.2″; 2–6 eggs, grayish, with olive spots; bulky nest, neatly built of twigs, bark strips, grasses, lined with lichens, feathers; placed 2–2.5 m (6–8′) high in fork of tree, on horizontal branch against trunk, in dense coniferous woods.

The Gray Jay has been known to grab food right off a camper's plate.

Have you ever felt that you were being watched, even followed, as you walked in northern woods? Perhaps you were—by a Gray Jay. After a silent, inquisitive introduction, the jay usually makes its presence known.

This subtly beautiful bird is so curious and shows so little fear of people that it can be a pest. It is notorious for grabbing food wherever it can and has been reported to enter tents, pry open boxes and carry off anything from soap to tobacco; it will even take food right off a camper's plate! Gray Jays have huge salivary glands which aid them in pasting food in hollows of trees, their storehouses for the winter. But in winter, they also raid cabins and northern settlements for food.

Gray Jays are quiet only during breeding season. Both their quiet manner and clean nesting habits—they keep the ground below their nests free of litter and droppings—are guards against predators finding their nests. The young Gray Jays are among the first birds to fledge in the spruce woods, but they stay with their parents until the next breeding season.

People of the Far North who know this bird best call it "whiskey Jack," which comes from its Indian name, "wiss-ka-chon." Others call it "camp robber," "mouse bird," "moose bird," "venison hawk" and "Hudson Bay bird." Known to mimic hawks and make whistling sounds that aren't usually attributed to jays, the Gray Jay may deceive you if you only hear and do not see it.

Gray Jays tend to stay in fairly thick woods. In their search for food, they sail from high in one tree to lower in another; then they hop up that tree to a height and sail down to the next tree. If you see a large bird behaving this way in northern woods, you'll know it's a Gray Jay.

Blue Jay

Cyanocitta cristata

Le Geai bleu

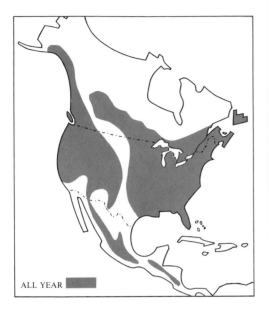

Blue Jay 28–32 cm, 11–12.5″; 3–6 eggs, buff or greenish, with dark brown spots; bulky cup-shaped nest of sticks, bark, lined with finer materials; placed 2–15 m (5–50′) high in tree, in woods, cities, parks. (This map shows the range of the Steller's Jay in the West and the Blue Jay in the East.)

ALL YEAR

Blue Jays are notorious for pestering hawks and owls. If a jay finds an owl perched in a tree, it cries to other jays, and before the poor owl knows what's happening, there's a screaming blue and white feathery mob after it. They chase the owl from tree to tree, diving at it, but rarely actually hitting it.

Though the Blue Jay has beautiful plumage, it usually attracts our attention first by all the noise it makes: calling *jay, jay,* screaming, whistling, chattering and squawking. Blue Jays imitate other birds and have been heard giving the song of the Baltimore Oriole, the cry of the Red-tailed Hawk and the mew of the catbird. The scream of an alarmed Blue Jay is unmistakable. With blue crest erect, it calls loudly and often other jays come flying in to help. Some animals seem to recognize this as a danger signal. A naturalist reported following a porcupine down a forest trail unnoticed by the animal until it was warned of danger by the scream of a jay. Only then did the porcupine put up his quills, sniff around and run into the woods.

Like the Gray Jay, the only time a Blue Jay is quiet is during the nesting season. If you spot a jay during this time and try to follow it back to its nest, you'll almost surely fail. The bird is very wary of danger and careful not to lead an intruder to its young.

Blue Jays eat berries and seeds, catch insects and even hover occasionally to pick acorns from oaks with their beaks. They also rob the nests of other birds, though not to the extent that many people think. In a study of the stomach contents of 292 Blue Jays, eggshells were found in only 3, and the remains of birds in only 2. They eat seeds mainly from wild plants, but sometimes wreak havoc on cornfields.

In summer, these feisty birds are found in cities, fields and mixed woods of beech and oak. In winter, some migrate to where food is plentiful; they do much of their migrating during daylight, and often, in fall, fairly large flocks of Blue Jays can be seen. Those jays that remain in the North are easily attracted to feeders with sunflower seeds and cracked corn.

Anting — The mystery

Why would a robin or Blue Jay pick up an ant, contort itself into all sorts of ridiculous positions and seemingly ecstatically rub the ant along its wing and tail feathers? People have suggested many explanations, but no one knows for certain just why birds do it.

The earliest report of anting (1876) was of a tame crow that appeared to stand quite deliberately on an ant mound and permit ants to crawl over it. (Since then, crows have been seen both inserting ants in their feathers and dust bathing in ant hills.) In another early observation of anting, a pair of starlings almost buried themselves in an ant nest, threw the ants over their feathers and put them under their feathers. Typically, anting birds become so involved with this activity that they are oblivious to what is going on around them. Mr. Roy Ivor, a naturalist who set up a songbird observatory at his home near Erindale, Ontario, found that even a Rose-breasted Grosbeak—usually an irascible species—became so engrossed while anting it barely noticed the 20 or so birds anting around it even though they bumped into one another.

Ivor found that only starlings would ant with more than one ant at a time, grabbing a fairly large ball of them before beginning. Anting birds usually eat the ants after stroking their feathers with them, but may also simply discard them.

Birds in captivity sometimes use the juice of berries to "ant," rubbing the berries on their feathers as they would an ant. There are also reports of birds rubbing beer, orange juice and cigar stubs on their feathers. One captive Blue Jay anted with lighted cigarettes, but did not use unlighted ones.

Not all species ant. For example, the catbird has been seen to ant on many occasions, but the closely related Brown Thrasher—a bird that, like the catbird, lives in thickets—is not known to indulge. Of two related thrushes, the robin and the bluebird, only robins ant. And of birds that do ant, some kinds react almost any time they're near an ant, while others seldom do.

Here are some of the reasons that have been suggested for just why so many songbirds have this peculiar habit: (1) birds secure the ants in their feathers and use them as food when they are migrating (this explanation was never taken seriously—can you imagine a bird trying to fly with a bunch of ants stashed under its wings?), (2) it is a way of removing the formic acid that many ants produce before the bird eats them, (3) the formic acid of the ants somehow benefits the skin, (4) the acid kills parasites in the feathers and (5) the odor or taste of the ant is attractive to the bird. (There is one bit of evidence for this last idea. When an Orchard Oriole's feathers had ants rubbed on them, the oriole grasped the treated feathers and its throat muscles moved as if it were trying to swallow the substance.)

Another researcher reported his experiments in which small amounts of formic acid, vinegar and formalin sprayed on the heads of birds caused the birds to ant. These chemicals are like, or similar to, those emitted by some ants. Thus, he thinks that anting is not a special reaction to the ants themselves, but to the chemicals they produce.

There is perhaps a multiple explanation for this phenomenon.

A catbird here takes part in one of the most mysterious rituals of the bird world: anting. Its translucent eyelid is closed as it ants, preventing the caustic formic acid the ant secretes from getting into its eyes.

American (Common) Crow

Corvus brachyrhynchos

La Corneille américaine

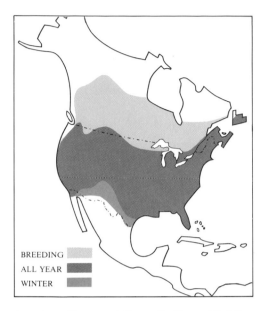

American (Common) Crow 43–53 cm, 17–21″; 3–8 eggs, greenish, spotted with brown; large crude-looking nest of sticks, lined with grasses, finer materials; placed 3–21 m (10–70′) high, generally close to trunk of tree, in woods, parks.

Our family came upon a crow like the one illustrated here in a perfect spot to meet such a symbol of evil. We had stopped to investigate an old, wood-frame church (on a deserted road and in the rain; what could be better?). The crow flew down cawing at us, and blocked our entrance until we fed it some tasty morsels. (A plastic band on one leg of the bird explained its boldness—it was probably someone's pet.)

"If men wore feathers and wings a very few of them would be clever enough to be crows." Henry Ward Beecher's famous quote says well what people have long thought of the crow's intelligence. Crows quickly learn to mimic other birds and human sounds including laughter. They break clamshells by flying high and dropping them on the rocks below; when a group of crows is feeding, one warns the others when intruders approach. Whether these latter acts are signs of learning ability, or are simply habits that were selected through the evolutionary process, is hard to say.

In the spring, crows rattle and coo as they pair up for the nesting season. They have quite a courtship ritual. The male walks toward the female, bows low to her and, with body feathers puffed up, spreads his wings and tail. He sings his rattling song beginning with his head up and finishing with his head even lower than his feet if he is on a branch. This is repeated several times; he then struts around with head held high. Once accepted by a female, the two caress with their beaks and pick gently at each other's heads. The pair selects a nesting spot high in a conifer, or if they are in the southern part of North America, they usually choose an oak and build a big, bulky nest on an upper branch, close to the trunk. Sometimes communal nesting occurs. Two females have been reported to lay eggs in the same nest, and both incubate them— a snug fit!

Crows are omnivores—they eat almost anything. This is why farmers put scarecrows in their fields. How much damage do crows do to crops? One study showed that two-thirds of a crow's diet is insects, most of which are damaging to crops. It has been shown that in some areas where crows were shot, the pasture grass died and the corn yield was poor. The crows may have been eating the young grass and the corn, but they were also eating insects such as wireworms and beetle grubs that fed on the roots of the growing plants. When crows were encouraged to come back to these fields, crop yields improved. Nevertheless, serious damage can be done in large roosting areas such as one in Oklahoma where the winter roosting population has been as high as three to four million birds. (Crows also eat the eggs and young of many smaller songbirds, a habit that does not endear them to birdwatchers.)

Unlike owls and hawks, crows do not have feet that are well adapted for grasping prey, but they are able to carry off small prey. Like all birds that eat small mammals and birds, crows regurgitate what they cannot digest— a compact pellet of bones, fur or other remains. (The only basically predatory songbirds, the shrikes, also do this.)

People have tried to get rid of crows by poisoning, shooting or bombing their roosts, but the species remains and is found almost everywhere. The crow's larger, more magnificent relative, the Common Raven, has not fared so well.

Formerly found south to Alabama and Arkansas, and in the Great Plains to Kansas, ravens are now confined in the East to thinly populated areas on the Canadian Shield and to the more remote parts of the Appalachian Mountains. The raven is found throughout the West in remote areas. Visitors to England may have seen ravens at the Tower of London. These birds are pinioned and cannot fly; but in medieval times, ravens (now confined in the British Isles to remote coastal and mountain areas) were found south to London. They are much more carnivorous than crows, eating mainly carrion and attacking small mammals. The black color, a symbol of evil in many cultures, certainly has not helped crows and ravens in their relations with people.

Crows eat almost anything and have survived in spite of attempts to get rid of them—from bombing to poisoning.

The starlings and mynas — Family Sturnidae

When starlings gather into large flocks in fall, they are considered a nuisance because of the grain they eat, but in spring and summer they benefit farmers because they devour huge numbers of destructive insects.

In the past people liked the starling and the myna so much they introduced these birds almost everywhere. As a result, the starling can now be found on most major landmasses throughout the world. The Crested Myna is also widespread.

In 1889 there were no starlings in North America. Now there are millions. In 1890–91, a British immigrant released about 100 starlings in New York City's Central Park. He, and others who had tried to introduce them, thought the birds were pleasant to have around. At that time, he could not have foreseen the impact of this gesture. The increase in starlings almost certainly led to a decrease in some of our native birds (see *Common Starling*).

The starling is a poor housekeeper; its nest is usually untidy and often foul smelling—quite unpleasant for city dwellers who find starling nests or roosts in their buildings. In fall and winter starlings gather into large flocks that are a nuisance to farmers because of the amount of grain they eat. In spring and summer, however, they are beneficial to farmer and gardener alike because of the large numbers of destructive insects they consume.

The Crested Myna was introduced in the Vancouver area of British Columbia in the 1890s and is now well established there. Fortunately, the myna did not spread across North America the way the starling did (see map); as fruit eaters, flocks of mynas could cause problems in fruit-growing areas of British Columbia and Washington were they to spread from the Vancouver area.

Birds of this family are strong flyers with short tails, pointed wings, long bills and strong legs and feet.

The Common Starling and two of its relatives show us that closely related animals can be very different. The Common Starling is highly adaptable. It can live almost anywhere under a variety of conditions, but two kinds of African starlings, called oxpeckers, are extremely specialized in their requirements. These live only upon large mammals like the rhinoceros and the domestic cow, picking ticks from the hides of these animals. Where cows have been treated to prevent infestation with ticks, oxpeckers are not found because they are totally dependent on ticks for food. They also sip blood from the openings made by the ticks.

Following its introduction to the New World in New York City in 1890, the Common Starling spread rapidly across North America. This map shows the spread that is documented by mid-winter bird counts; by 1940, there were already some records from California, and by 1947 from British Columbia.

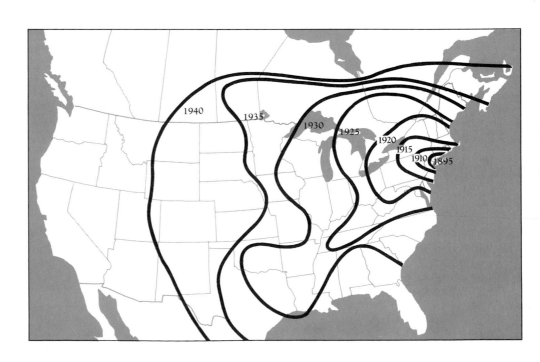

Common (European) Starling

Sturnus vulgaris
L'Étourneau sansonnet

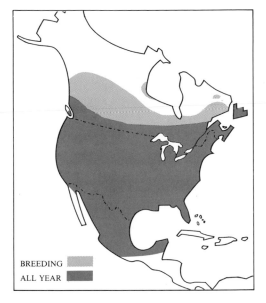

BREEDING
ALL YEAR

Common (European) Starling 19–22 cm, 7.5–8.5″; 4–6 eggs, pale bluish or greenish white, nest loosely built of straw, grass, lined with feathers, finer materials; placed 0.5–18 m (2–60′) high in natural cavity, birdhouse, in cities, open woods.

A common occurrence—a flock of starlings chasing a much larger hawk.

In North America, the introduced starling competes with many native birds such as the Eastern Bluebird, the Tree Swallow and the House Wren (and even some woodpeckers) for nest sites. All are cavity nesters, but starlings are larger and more aggressive than the others. They move into occupied holes and chase the occupant away, sometimes killing the other bird's young or throwing out its eggs. Since the starling has become widespread, the number of Eastern Bluebirds has decreased, in some areas tremendously. Fortunately, recent projects to provide nest boxes with entrance holes too small for starlings to enter have helped bluebirds make a comeback.

Starling means "little star"; the name is apt for in autumn its fresh plumage is dotted with white on a dark background. These whitish or buffy feather tips wear off in winter so that by spring male starlings are usually nearly totally black. The females are generally a little duller than the males, and retain some noticeable speckling on their bellies. Their brown bills change to bright yellow in spring as hormonal levels change, and to brown again in the fall.

Starlings, like their myna relatives, mimic other birds. In some places they sing the Eastern Wood Pewee's *pee-a-wee* so often that birdwatchers used to think that it was the starling's own song, which consists mainly of whistles; it also makes harsh, rasping squeaks and wheezing sounds.

Starlings often form flocks resembling huge black clouds. If a hawk approaches, the flock gathers and chases it, always staying safely above the hawk.

The starling's lack of popularity is not due to its appearance, for though it looks a bit awkward—and "waddles" as it walks—it is a lovely bird, shiny black with purple and green iridescence.

The weaver finches – Family Ploceidae

About 25 million years ago, seed-bearing plants, especially grasses, became abundant on earth. Many kinds of birds then became specialized to eat the plentiful seeds these plants produced. In tropical Africa, one group, the weaverbirds (or weaver finches), became specialized as seed eaters; in the New World, birds unrelated to the African group evolved this habit. Today, many of the descendants of these birds look much the same—in part because they all have cone-shaped bills that are good for cracking seeds. This convergent evolution has made it difficult to know just which birds are closely related.

Some of this confusion about identities is reflected in the English common names that we use. For example, in England the name sparrow is used for the bird that we call the House or "English" Sparrow. This is an Old World bird that has been introduced into North America. (Careful studies of the anatomy and behavior of the House Sparrow show us that its closest relatives are the weaver finches of Africa.) When English settlers came to the New World, they called the small, brownish birds with conical bills they found here "sparrows" because they reminded them of the House Sparrow of their homeland. But the New World sparrows are relatives of tanagers and cardinal-grosbeaks (like the Cardinal and Rose-breasted Grosbeak), not weaverbirds as is the House Sparrow. Confusing? Indeed. The confusion in names mirrors the problems scientists have had in classifying these birds. (We thought you might want to know just why the House Sparrow isn't with the other sparrows in this book.)

The weaver finches are an interesting and varied lot. Many are gregarious. One, the Social Weaver, builds large, globular, apartment nests of woven grass high in the trees of African savannas; these nests can house several families. Another kind, the widow weaver (or widowbird) is a nest parasite like our North American cowbird—it lays its eggs in the nests of other weaverbirds.

Many of the brightly colored, little finches in this group, such as waxbills, cut-throat finches, Java Sparrows and Gouldian Finches, are popular as caged birds. Though not generally good singers, their brilliant coloration and quick, jerky movements make them fascinating to watch.

This map shows the rapid spread of House Sparrows across North America after they became established in the New York City area in the 1850s. People aided their spread by establishing colonies of them in many communities across the continent, and by the early 1900s they were found throughout the 48 states, and across southern Canada and northern Mexico.

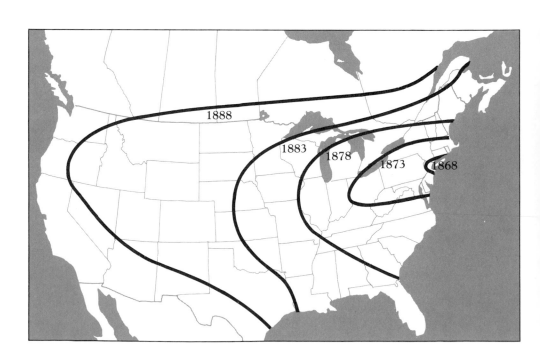

 labels: 1888, 1883, 1878, 1873, 1868

House (English) Sparrow

Passer domesticus

Le Moineau domestique

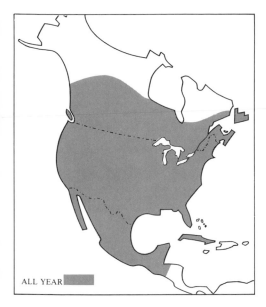

House (English) Sparrow 15–17 cm, 5.8–6.7″; 3–7 eggs, white, greenish white, dotted with grays, browns; nest in cavity of grass, trash, lined with feathers, hair, fine grasses, or large woven ball of grasses, weeds; placed in tree 2–15 m (7–50′) high, in cities, parks, farmyards.

Biologists use the word *commensal* for the relationship that exists between two kinds of animals in which one benefits from the relationship while the other is unharmed by it—"eating at the same table" the dictionary says. The House Sparrow is a commensal of people. It probably first became associated with people in the Tigris and Euphrates region of the Middle East early in the development of agricultural society (about 5000 B.C.). Later, as agriculture moved north into Europe, the House Sparrow followed. Their bones are found in early archeological sites, thus showing a long association with people.

It was not until 1853, however, that House Sparrows made it to this continent. Apparently, several attempts had been made to introduce this familiar bird from Europe, primarily because it was thought that it would keep down the insects associated with horse dung (this was before the automobile was invented). The sparrows that finally became successfully established were the descendants of 50 released in a Brooklyn cemetery in 1853. Impressed by how well these sparrows did, other people who liked the little brown birds brought them to their cities as well. During the next 33 years, House Sparrows expanded on their own, spreading to 35 states in the US and to Canada. At the turn of the century just before horses were replaced by cars, they reached their greatest numbers. By 1915, they spread to the West Coast and became established there. In North America, House Sparrows are now found nearly everywhere people have built cities, even in the Far North at Churchill, Manitoba, on the coast of Hudson Bay where they live near grain elevators, feeding on fallen grain. Since 1800, they have also expanded their range in Europe and have been introduced to places such as South America, New Zealand and Hawaii. Today, the House Sparrow is one of the most widespread species in the world!

Farmers consider House Sparrows a nuisance because of the amount of grain they eat and because they spread pests such as chicken mites. Some city dwellers dislike them because they are noisy, always chirping and chattering, and because they drive away other species from gardens and feeders.

House Sparrows typically stuff their nests into cavities. A missing stone here provides such a cavity.

House Sparrows stuff their nests into any cavity or niche available. Drainpipes are used, as are cracks in walls, nooks under caves and birdhouses set out for wrens, swallows or bluebirds. Making the entrance hole to a birdhouse too small for a starling does not prevent the sparrow from using it; a sparrow can use any house a bluebird or Purple Martin can.

If you wish to keep houses free for other birds, you will probably have to clear out the sparrows' nests. Their nests are made of grasses, feathers, bits of paper and cloth, etc. Sometimes, probably when cavities are in short supply, sparrows weave neat domed nests of grasses, with the opening to one side—reminiscent of the houses constructed by their relative the Social Weaver of Africa. (Most New World sparrows build open, cup nests.)

Full of mischief and fun to watch

House Sparrows are interesting, adaptable, pretty little creatures and it is enjoyable to watch their comings and goings. One observer saw a male House Sparrow bring a goose feather to his nest, lay it there and fly off. A female House Sparrow nesting nearby flew to his nest, took the goose feather and hid it in the fork of a nearby tree. When the male returned and found the feather missing, he immediately flew to the nest of the thief. Not finding the feather, he scolded all the birds in sight and finally flew away. Then the thief flew to the tree, recovered the feather and took it to her own nest.

During breeding, a male hops back and forth in front of a female to attract her. If she ignores him, other males peck at her tail. She doesn't always respond immediately, but she will accept a male within a few days.

House Sparrows are diligent parents who rarely abandon their young. If one falls from the nest, the father or mother feeds and shelters it on the ground until it can fly. These parents form permanent pairs, usually for life.

You'll rarely find neatly woven, domed House Sparrow nests, which have side entrances and are stuck in bushes and shrubs. House Sparrows probably build these nests only when cavities are not available.

Bird calls

The *songs* of birds and the *calls* of birds are quite different. Songs, for most birds, require some learning, are fairly complex and are used primarily to attract mates or intimidate rivals. Calls are apparently entirely inherited, are usually simple in form and are used for general communication among individuals in a group (such as a migratory or a feeding flock).

Experiments indicate that nestlings isolated from their parents shortly after hatching so that they hear no other birds of their own kind, still develop calls that are typical of their species. Most birds have a variety of calls, each with a different meaning. Some show distress, some are used to call other birds to forage and some help coordinate a flock.

The importance of the begging call by the European Bullfinch nestlings was discovered in an experiment in which Bullfinch parents were deafened. Although they could see their nestlings gaping for food, the parents did not feed them adequately because they could not hear the nestlings begging. The begging call of the nestlings in this species is obviously all important. (Adult females of many species use this same begging call later in life as a part of submissive or precopulatory displays.)

Crows have an alarm call. When this call is played to crows on a tape recorder, it causes them to fly away. Similarly, a researcher found that when their "assembly" call was played on the tape recorder, crows gathered from all round the area. There's good evidence that ravens recognize special calls given only by their mates.

Many different meanings

When feeding in dense foliage where it is difficult to see each other, Pine Siskins (little finches related to goldfinches and redpolls) call back and forth; crossbills, too, do this when feeding on cones in a stand of spruce trees. These calls help keep a flock together while the birds are out of each other's sight.

Many species of songbirds have alarm calls; in some there seem to be different calls to indicate degrees of alarm. For example, the Field Sparrow gives a *chip-chip-chip* when a crow or a person is approaching, but a *zeeee* when a hawk is flying over. When the *zeeee* alarm call is given, all small birds in the area seek cover. The alarm calls of most species are short, high-pitched notes, making it difficult for a person or a predator to locate the calling bird.

It is interesting that all of those "chips" and "squawks" and "whistles" we hear in fields and woodlands, in addition to the more melodious songs, are of great importance to the birds. Some may indicate "small talk" among the feathered creatures; but others are a matter of life and death.

The cardueline finches — Family Fringillidae

One spring morning we looked out the window of a home near Ithaca, New York, and saw an amazing sight: an apple tree there looked as if it had sprouted scores of lemons overnight. In a second they were gone. We had just met a flock of goldfinches, one of the many beautiful species of cardueline finches.

Who are the cardueline finches? These generally heavy-beaked finches are thought by many to be a part of the Old World group to which the House Sparrow belongs; others place them close to the New World sparrows. Since experts disagree, we follow a recent classification that places them in a family of their own.

Most male carduelines are brightly colored; yellows and rose-reds are common. It is generally easy to distinguish male from female—males are brighter in color. Species in this group are often among the most common songbirds in the Far North, found either in the dense spruce woods or in the dwarf forests at the edge of the tundra.

Some members of the group not discussed in depth on the following pages are the Pine Grosbeak, a big, chunky bird that breeds in pine and spruce woods of the North, the Chaffinch—one of the most common birds of Europe, the beautiful Bullfinch of British gardens and the Canary, the popular caged bird. Breeding in captivity for song and color for many generations has made caged Canaries different from their wild ancestors, native to the Canary Islands.

Powerful beaks

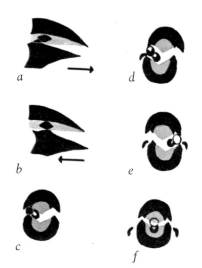

How do birds break cherry stones to get at the seeds within? Only a few do!

The powerful beaks of seed eaters are short, sharp edged and heavy with strong jaw muscles to operate them. Often the tongue is muscular and scoop shaped, like the tongue holding the seed in these diagrams. Try to watch a finch like the Cardinal or Evening Grosbeak handling the problem of shucking off a hard seed covering. Sunflower seeds in a winter feeder should provide you with that opportunity.

a–b: These side views of the beak show how a grosbeak moves its upper jaw forward, then back, holding the seed in a groove in the upper bill, while the sharp-edged lower bill starts slicing off the seed coat.

c: Just left of center is the tongue holding the stone in the groove of the upper jaw. (Orientation of c to f is from inside the bird's beak.)

d–e: The grosbeak moves its jaws to opposite sides to work off the seed coat.

f: Finally, the seed coat is off and falls from the sides of the beak. The tongue now holds the seed, which is ready to be swallowed.

The huge, powerful beak of the European Hawfinch permits it to crack olive pits that should require a force of 48–72 kg (106–160 lb). The bird itself weighs only 55 g (2 oz)!

Evening Grosbeak

Hesperiphona vespertina
Le Gros-bec errant

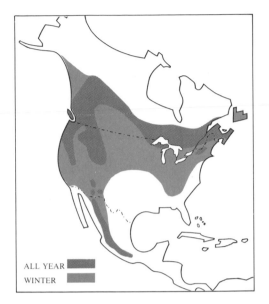

ALL YEAR
WINTER

Evening Grosbeak 18–22 cm, 7–8.5″; 2–5 eggs, blue or blue-green, blotched with shades of brown, gray, purple; oblong cupped nest, loosely woven of small twigs, grass, bark strips; placed 6–18 m (20–60′) high, usually in top of conifer, in coniferous woods.

Both the English and Latin names for this bird are based on a misinterpretation. The Evening Grosbeak or "evening night singer" is really a daytime bird, probably doing its "best" singing in the morning. Their European discoverer first saw these birds at twilight—probably disturbing them from their roost. He mistook their calls for "vespers."

Before the mid-1800s, Evening Grosbeaks were known only in the West to Saskatchewan and Michigan, but then they started to move eastward. The first sighting east of Lake Huron was in Toronto in 1854; in the winter of 1886–1887, they were seen in Missouri, Illinois, Indiana and Kentucky, and, by 1890, in Massachusetts. By 1940, they were breeding in eastern Ontario and New England, and now they are common even in the Maritime Provinces in Canada.

Why did they move east? Probably because of a great increase in the food available to them in winter. Maple seeds are their preferred food, especially Box Elder or "Manitoba Maple" seeds. In the 1800s these trees were commonly planted as shade trees, and since they provided a predictable source of food, grosbeaks apparently followed them eastward. Young maples growing on abandoned marginal farms in New England also provided food. Grosbeaks, of course, eat other things. Like waxwings and crossbills they are opportunistic. Where a spruce budworm outbreak is great, grosbeaks will suddenly appear and breed, feeding their nestlings on the eggs and young of this moth.

The seasonal movements of Evening Grosbeaks are unpredictable. Some years they move far to the south; in others they barely leave their breeding range. In summer and fall, especially in the Northwest, they sometimes gather in great numbers. Unfortunately, automobiles kill many of them while they are picking up gravel from roadsides which they use to grind the seeds. Flocks of Evening Grosbeaks broadcast their presence with their loud, ringing *p-teer, p-teer* flight call.

American (Common) Goldfinch

Carduelis tristis

Le Chardonneret jaune

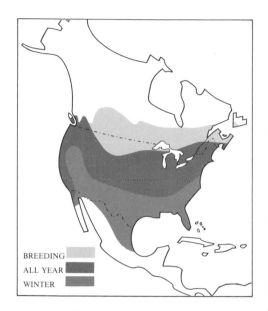

American (Common) Goldfinch 11–14 cm, 4.5–5.5″; 4–6 eggs, pale bluish white, unmarked; nest a compact cup of fine grasses, bark strips, moss; placed 0.3–10 m (1–33′) high in small tree, in old fields, woodland edge.

Compare the undulating flight pattern of the goldfinch with that of a starling, who shows the more typical straight flight of a songbird.

This little, bright yellow bird is sometimes called a "wild canary." More often it is called the "thistle bird." The goldfinch eats the seeds of the thistle, uses thistledown for the lining of its nest and sometimes builds its nest right in the middle of a patch of thistles—or at least not far from a good supply. The nest is so durable it could last several years, but it is only used once.

Goldfinches are late nesters: you will not be able to find their nests until at least July and sometimes only as late as September. Interestingly, nesting begins about the same time composites—the thistles, sunflowers, dandelions and daisies—start to bloom. Although goldfinches eat a few insects, they depend extensively on the seeds of these and other plants for food. Unlike many seed-eating birds that eat large numbers of insects in the summer, the goldfinch's diet includes large numbers of insects only in spring when its favorite seeds are scarce. They apparently postpone nesting until the fall seed crop, which accounts for over 95% of their food intake.

During courtship, the bright yellow male sometimes changes his flight pattern from his usual rapid, undulating flight to a slow flapping of wings, like that of a much larger bird.

When the female goldfinch is on the nest, the male often circles high overhead. Upon hearing her sharp, loud *tee-tee-tee-tee* cry, the male immediately drops to feed her. When she is being fed, she acts just like a nestling: she flutters her wings and gapes like a hungry baby. The male continues to feed both nestlings and the female while she broods the young.

Goldfinches molt in the fall, and in winter the male looks much like the female—a dull olive-yellow. Before the next breeding season, he will molt again to his brighter plumage, like the bird on the sunflower head shown in this illustration. Listen for the goldfinch's call *perchickaree* and watch for its deeply undulating flight when you see flocks of small birds.

Common Redpoll

Carduelis flammea

Le Sizerin à tête rouge

Shown here with the Common Redpoll is a White-winged Crossbill. You may see the two species together, foraging at roadsides.

BREEDING

Common Redpoll 11–15 cm, 4.5–6″; 5–6 eggs, greenish white to pale blue, spotted with reddish brown; cup-shaped nest of grasses, twigs, lined with plant down, feathers, fur; placed on ground, in rock crevice, or 1–2 m (3–6′) high in small tree (willow, birch, spruce), in boreal forests or tundra edge.

Most of us know redpolls only as winter visitors, since they breed in the northern parts of Canada and Alaska. Often several pairs nest near each other in a clump of dwarfed spruce, willows or alders in northern forests or the tundra. At summer's end, some fly south—very rarely as far as South Carolina and other states at this latitude. You may see large flocks of them feeding by roadsides or at the edge of woods, looking for seeds. (They also take in a great deal of gravel, as most seed eaters do.)

A study of captive redpolls revealed a rigid and interesting social hierarchy. They ranked from the most dominant to the least dominant male in the flock, and then down from the most dominant to the least dominant female. As breeding season approached, however, a reversal took place. The females became more aggressive and dominant. Each acted aggressive toward a particular male, and these two eventually formed a pair.

The Far North provides long periods of light—about 20 hours a day—during the breeding season. Females at one locality where they were watched fed their nestlings from 3:00 a.m. to 10:30 p.m. (the period of greatest feeding activity was from 3:00 a.m. to 6:00 a.m.)!

Listen for the redpoll's double-noted *zit, zit* when you see flocks of small birds in flight in winter. Redpolls form large flocks, often with other birds such as their close relatives, the siskins and goldfinches. Goldfinches and redpolls act much the same: they collect in flocks for most of the year and call almost constantly as they fly from place to place. Redpolls undulate slightly as they fly, but not nearly as much as goldfinches.

In winter, if you live in the northern United States or in Canada, you may see paler redpolls with unstreaked, white rumps. These "Hoary Redpolls" breed even farther north than the Common Redpolls—only in the tundra. The two types of redpolls are treated as different species in some books, but mixed pairs of these two similar redpolls are common where the dwarf spruce trees meet the tundra dwarf willows in the Far North. Since the two types interbreed, they can be considered members of the same species.

117

Red Crossbill

Loxia curvirostra

Le Bec-croisé rouge

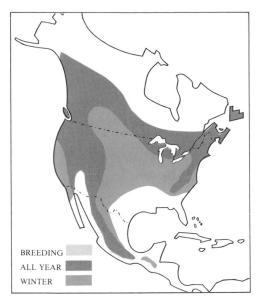

BREEDING
ALL YEAR
WINTER

Red Crossbill 11–16.5 cm, 4.25–6.5″; 3–5 eggs, pale bluish or greenish white, spotted with brown or purple; nest a shallow cup of evergreen twigs, rootlets, bark shreds; often in a dense tuft of needles, 2–24 m (5–80′) high, in coniferous woods.

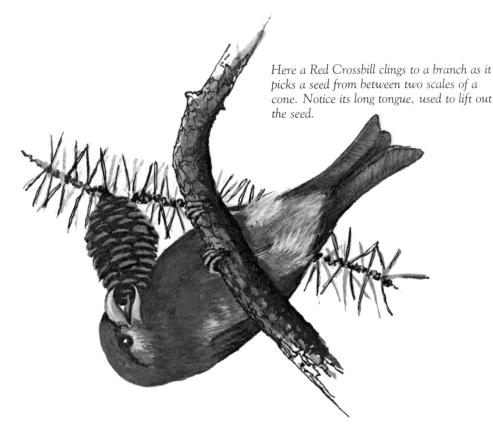

Here a Red Crossbill clings to a branch as it picks a seed from between two scales of a cone. Notice its long tongue, used to lift out the seed.

Those of us who do not live in the mountains or Far North generally see crossbills only in winter when they gather in small flocks near pine or spruce trees. They are often heard before they are seen. As they fly about, they give a staccato *cheet, cheet* call; when seen, their crossed bills and "boxy" body shape make them look more like miniature parrots than finches.

The crossed bill varies a great deal in size. Generally, White-winged Crossbills have smaller bills than Red Crossbills do, and they feed more commonly on smaller cones. In Europe, the White-winged (or "Two-barred") Crossbill feeds primarily on small larch cones; the Red ("Common") Crossbill eats the larger spruce cones. Red Crossbills that live in Scotland have especially large bills; there they eat the seeds from the large cones of the Caledonian Pine. In North America, the bill size of the Red Crossbill differs depending on where they live and how large the common cones are in that place. In the Pacific Northwest, where they primarily eat the seeds of relatively small cones, they have small bills; but in Mexico, where they eat from large-coned pine trees, they have very large bills. In the Northeast, the White-winged Crossbill specializes in tamarack, Black Spruce and hemlock—all species with small cones, whereas the Red Crossbill eats relatively more seeds from the larger pine cones.

Red Crossbills have been known to nest during every month of the year, though they most often breed in late winter. When nesting occurs in late winter, it is especially important for the mother to keep the young closely brooded. The male feeds her on the nest, regurgitating spruce or pine seeds from his crop into her bill—a method that both parents will use later to feed the young when they are out of the nest and learning to fend for themselves. Crossbills are born with uncrossed beaks. The parents continue to feed the nestlings until their beaks become fully crossed; then they are able to attack cones on their own.

White-winged Crossbill

Loxia leucoptera

Le Bec-croisé à ailes blanches

BREEDING

White-winged Crossbill 15–17 cm, 6–6.75"; 3–4 eggs, pale bluish or greenish white, spotted with shades of brown or purple; nest of twigs, lichens, bark shreds; placed well out on branch of conifer, 2.5–16 m (8–51') high, in coniferous woods.

The White-winged Crossbill and its relative the Red Crossbill are found in the coniferous forests of North America and Eurasia. Though quite similar in general behavior, they are easily told apart. In both species, the adult males are reddish, and the females olive-green to olive-gray with yellowish rumps; however, the two bold wing bars of the White-winged Crossbill are distinctive in all plumages, and are readily seen in the field. Also, the males are different shades of red, the white-wing being a rose-red, the Red Crossbill an orangish brick-red. In the Northeast, the white-wing is the more common of the two species in most years, but in the West and especially in the Rocky Mountains Red Crossbills predominate.

The unique characteristic of crossbills that gives these birds their name, a crossed bill, is a specialization for feeding on the seeds of coniferous trees. The lower bill does not fit directly below the upper bill, but is crossed to one side or the other (there are both left- and right-billed birds). When feeding on a young spruce or pine cone, the crossbill tears the cone from the branch, holds it on a perch with one of its strong feet and inserts the tips of its bill under one of the scales of the cone. By sliding its lower bill sideways, it is able to lift up the scale and with its tongue—which is especially long for a finch of this size—pick out the seed. A bird often extracts only five or six seeds from a cone before it discards it and tears off another. When the cones are older and the scales are open naturally, crossbills simply cling to or hang onto them and pick out the seeds as other finches do.

Although they primarily eat the seeds of cone-bearing trees, they take other foods such as spruce buds, birch, alder, elm and maple seeds and (in summer) a few insects, most of which are taken from conifer branches. They even eat the seed heads of dandelion and ragweed. On more than one occasion, we have watched White-winged Crossbills on the ground picking seeds from fallen hemlock cones. But their crossed bills make it difficult for them to pick seeds off the ground. Drinking would also seem a problem with a crossed bill. But the crossbill has a solution—the bird turns its head to the side, parts its beak and laps up the water with its tongue which it is able to thrust out.

Crossbills are famous for their fondness for rock salt—a habit that often proves fatal in winter when they flock to salted roads and are struck by passing cars. We once found more than 20 crossbills that had been killed by cars in a single day along 50 km (30 mi) of road. (See p. 117 for an illustration of a male White-winged Crossbill.)

The vireos – Family Vireonidae

The relationship of vireos to other birds has long puzzled ornithologists. Conventionally, they have been considered the most primitive of the songbirds that are thought to have originated in the New World. Recent work on genetic similarities suggests that they belong instead to the songbird complex that includes the crows, nuthatches and chickadees. Whatever their origin, vireos are most easily confused with warblers. However they are less active; instead of flitting about looking for food, they search slowly and intently for insects.

Different species of vireos are more easily identified by their songs than by their appearance—for example, the eastern vireos are all basically green, which makes them hard to see in the dense leaves of deciduous trees. The Red-eyed Vireo—thought to be the most common bird in most wooded areas of eastern North America—is small and green. It is seldom seen, but often heard in spring and summer; some people think *too* often, for it sings all day, pausing only when it picks an insect off a leaf.

In the spring, if you follow the song of the Red-eyed Vireo, you might see it perched on a branch looking very strange indeed as it sways back and forth. When "swaying," the male puffs its breast feathers, smooths its crown, erects feathers just above each eye and begins to move back and forth; its head and neck move just a fraction of a second later than its body as it sways cobralike in a wide arc. In some vireos, such as Bells' Vireo (see Part II on *How birds woo*), the swaying is followed by copulation between a male and a female. Researchers have not seen Red-eyed Vireos copulate after the male sways.

People who have studied this behavior think that the act of swaying in birds originates from a conflict between two "drives" the birds have at this time of year—an aggressive drive and the sex drive. Putting it in terms of human understanding, we might say that the male "wants" to chase another male, but he also "wants" to copulate with a female.

All vireos are almost exclusively insectivorous, eating a variety of caterpillars, moths, bugs, beetles, ants, flies and so forth. On occasion, however, they will eat blackberries, or the fruit of the wax myrtle, holly, poison ivy, grape and other plants with fleshy pulp. All eastern species are highly migratory, and most winter in Mexico or South America.

The male Red-eyed Vireo displays before the female, swaying back and forth in front of her, with breast feathers puffed, and feathers just above each eye standing erect.

Red-eyed Vireo

Vireo olivaceus

Le Viréo aux yeux rouges

BREEDING
WINTER

Red-eyed Vireo 13–17 cm, 5.3–6.5″; 2–4 eggs, white, with tiny brown spots; cup-shaped nest of fine grasses, rootlets, bark strips; suspended from forked, horizontal branch, 2–8 m (5–25′) high in deciduous shrub or tree, in deciduous woods.

Vireo nests are easily recognized. Neatly woven from bark and grass, they hang like a cup between the arms of a forked branch.

Some call this bird "the preacher" because of its song—a long, continued series of two to five note phrases that ends with a rising inflection, like a question. They say it sounds as if the vireo has been giving a long sermon and then asks if it has been understood. A friend says it sounds to him as if the bird is saying: "Look at me. Over here. See me? Look at me...." These phrases, repeated with a brief pause between each group of several, reflect the song pattern of the Red-eyed Vireo.

After mating, the female Red-eyed Vireo starts to build a deeply cupped nest, but she often stops halfway through and starts a new one, using much of the material she had gathered for the first. The nests of vireos are distinctive. They are always neatly woven, and almost always hang between the arms of a forked branch.

These birds are found in trees with thick foliage where they pick insects from the surrounding leaves. Their main enemies are egg-eating birds, mammals and the parasitic Brown-headed Cowbird whose eggs they often incubate and hatch. Of 114 nests which were found in one area, 87 contained a cowbird egg. Young vireos do not usually survive to be fledged from nests where cowbirds are raised. The larger cowbird hatchlings get most of the food brought to the nest and the vireo hatchlings perish.

Though the vireo sings constantly in spring and summer, it migrates in silence, one or two mixed in with large flocks of warblers. You can distinguish the vireos because they fly more gracefully—in a less flitting way—than the warblers.

Social mimicry in vireos

Among the different vireos that occur in northeastern woodlands, two species, the Red-eyed Vireo and the Philadelphia Vireo, live in the same area, feed in the same habitat and sing similar songs. In fact, we shall see that the Philadelphia Vireo's song "mimics" that of the Red-eyed Vireo.

Like songbirds generally, male vireos sing to declare possession of a territory and generally an intruding male vireo is intimidated by hearing another male's song. By defending the area around his nest, the male ensures that there will be food available for his mate and offspring and less interference from other vireos.

A young biologist, who was studying the singing behavior of vireos in a northeastern forest, played tape recordings of different vireo songs to territorial male vireos. Interestingly he found that Philadelphia Vireos can distinguish between their song and that of the Red-eyed Vireo, but that the opposite does not hold true. When a Philadelphia Vireo comes into the territory of another, the latter sings and makes himself seen, backing up the threat with his presence. On the other hand, when a male Red-eyed Vireo enters a Philadelphia Vireo's territory, the Philadelphia Vireo sings, but stays out of sight. The Red-eyed Vireo, unable to see his rival, is fooled by this act and retreats, "thinking" that he has trespassed into a Red-eyed Vireo's territory. Were he to see the Philadelphia Vireo he would not be so misled. Red-eyed Vireos, being larger than Philadelphia Vireos, could easily chase them away. It therefore seems that the Philadelphia Vireo has developed a song that mimics the Red-eyed song as a way of preventing these two species that eat the same foods from occupying the same areas during nesting time when tremendous amounts of food are needed for the nestlings.

A simpler example of mimicry that might make it easier to understand the one just described is the case of mimicry between two common butterflies in North America, the Monarch and the Viceroy. Monarch caterpillars eat milkweed leaves that are bad tasting and poisonous to birds. Thus, when a bird tries to eat a Monarch, now poisonous from stored chemicals, it spits it out and often becomes ill. Experiments with caged jays have shown that they quickly learn to avoid Monarch butterflies. The Viceroy butterfly is not related to the Monarch and is not poisonous, but they look almost exactly alike. By mimicking the Monarch it gains some protection. When predatory birds see a Viceroy, they are deceived by its similar appearance and avoid it as they would a Monarch.

Similarly, the Philadelphia Vireo finds it advantageous to "sound" like a Red-eyed Vireo because this enables it to bluff Red-eyed Vireos from its territory.

Mystery birds

All that remains of Townsend's Bunting is a painting of it done by Audubon from a specimen given him in 1833. Did many of them exist? Was it aberrant? Did it really exist at all?

It would be intriguing to board a time machine, going back in time, to see North America as Audubon saw it, perhaps seeing some of the birds he saw that are now lost. Audubon and another early American ornithologist, Alexander Wilson, left us, through their writings and paintings, invaluable glimpses of the natural life of the early 19th Century— and a few mysteries as well. Among the mysteries are several species, described by these men, but never seen since. Perhaps the most famous is Audubon's "Carbonated Warbler," a distinctive little bird known only from Audubon's painting of two specimens that he collected in Kentucky in 1811. The "Small-headed Warbler" was known only by Audubon and Wilson, and apparently was uncommon, and the "Blue Mountain Warbler" was seen only by Wilson, in the Blue Mountains of Virginia. A single specimen of "Townsend's Bunting" was collected in Pennsylvania in 1833 by the naturalist John K. Townsend, and given to Audubon to paint; his figure is all that remains.

The specimens of all of these mystery birds have long been lost, and most biologists guess that they were aberrant—perhaps hybrid—individuals. It is also possible that some of them never existed. Though Audubon painted his figures from field sketches and fresh specimens, some of his paintings were destroyed; perhaps he redrew some of the rare birds (like the Carbonated Warbler) from memory, and simply misremembered. We do know, however, that Audubon was usually a careful observer, and most of the rare species he found have been known to later naturalists. For example, in the early 1800s the Chestnut-sided Warbler was rare—apparently as rare as the Carbonated or Small-headed Warbler. Had it become extinct instead of becoming common we could not know whether or not it ever really existed. The Carbonated Warbler and Townsend's Bunting are so distinctive it is hard to believe they were artifacts or hybrids. Perhaps they were species whose natural habitat was destroyed before they could be unquestionably described by science.

Endangered songbirds

Fortunately, few North American songbirds are in danger of becoming extinct. The best known of the endangered songbirds is Kirtland's Warbler, which breeds only in the Jack Pine second growth of Michigan and perhaps in Ontario. In spite of the fact that there is seemingly an abundance of suitable breeding habitat for this species, its numbers continue to decrease. The wintering habits of the Kirtland's Warbler are poorly known, and perhaps events during that season are causing its decline.

The rarest North American songbird is Bachman's Warbler, named by Audubon for his friend John Bachman of Charleston, South Carolina. Little is known of this secretive denizen of dense wooded swamps of the Southeast.

The wood warblers – Family Parulidae

If you've never seen a warbler, you've missed one of the world's most beautiful living creatures. Roger Tory Peterson, the noted ornithologist, calls warblers "the 'butterflies' of the bird world." This family of songbirds is represented in North America by many species. In the East alone, 39 kinds of these colorful, active, little birds can be found. All but 6 commonly breed as far north as Canada.

In summer when trees are in full foliage, these small, delicate birds are hidden by leaves. In late summer they skulk quietly and molt. In fall, most of them migrate by night and, in winter, they are in places few of us get to. Thus, spring is the time to find them. Most warblers return to their nesting places while the leaves are just emerging on the trees. They display their fresh colorful plumage as they flit from branch to branch in search of insects, and the males sing almost constantly.

You're particularly lucky if you live close to one of the resting places along their migratory route. A first major stop after they've crossed the Caribbean is the southern tip of Florida. You'll also see them in moderate numbers all the way up through the US as they pause every now and then. But the next spot to see huge numbers is on the north shore of the Great Lakes. After flying over one of these large lakes, they land, exhausted—especially on tips of land which jut out into the lake and point toward the south, such as Point Pelee and Long Point on Lake Erie. Even in cities like Toronto that border Lake Ontario's shore, the tired, hungry migrants pause to rest in wooded ravines and backyard trees.

Although many kinds of warblers fly northward together in their spring migration, they soon spread out, each to its own niche. Most are woodland birds; warblers occupy all parts of the woods from the ground to the treetops.

Few warblers actually warble (they were named after similar-looking Old World birds that do), but all have characteristic songs. Some are relatively easy to learn; others require more effort.

While warblers are distinctively colored in the spring, in their usually drabber fall plumage, many kinds are very difficult to identify. Peterson has written that if, after ten years of trying, you can say that you know each fall warbler from all the others, "you are doing very well."

But it's worth the try. If you're not already hooked on birdwatching, you will be after you've seen and heard the warblers.

Wood warblers tend to build cup-shaped nests and, except for a few species, in trees. The beautiful Prothonotary Warbler is one of few to nest in natural cavities, old woodpecker holes and occasionally birdhouses; they usually nest in holes near standing water and rarely go north of the US border. The nest of the Parula Warbler is also unusual: it looks like a scraggly beard. In the northern parts of its range, the Parula uses a lichen known as *Usnea;* it hangs its lichen nest from a tree branch and makes an entrance hole on the side or the top. In the South, it uses Spanish moss. Where no hanging lichen or Spanish moss grows, the Parula builds open nests of leaves or hanging clusters of twigs. (See Part II, A *variety of nests.*)

The Prothonotary Warbler nests in convenient cavities in trees (such as old woodpecker holes) and in birdhouses.

Black-and-white Warbler

Mniotilta varia

La Fauvette noire et blanche

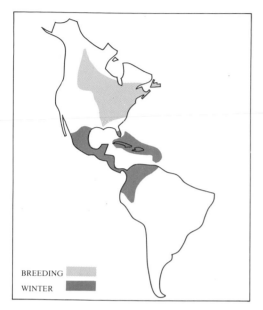

BREEDING
WINTER

Black-and-white Warbler 10–14 cm, 4.5–5.5″; 4–5 eggs, white or creamy white, with dots or blotches of shades of brown; bulky nest of bark strips, grasses, leaves, lined with finer materials; placed on ground, usually in a depression, in dead leaves at base of tree or rock, in deciduous or mixed woods.

This is one warbler that is not difficult to identify. In the fall, when many other warblers have molted into their drab winter plumage, the Black-and-white Warbler is as bright as it was in the spring. It is a common bird and easy to spot, as it tends to feed on lower branches and tree trunks. It uses its long claws to creep along tree trunks, but does not work around branches in a set pattern like the spiral movement of the Brown Creeper. And unlike creepers and woodpeckers, it does not use its tail for support.

Despite its name, the Black-and-white Warbler doesn't warble—it sings a high-pitched, thin *weesee weesee weesee weesee weesee weesee weesee* (at least seven times).

Black-and-white Warblers build their nests on the ground, usually at the base of a tree or stump, or beside a log or stone. The nest is well concealed with leaves.

In winter, Black-and-white Warblers are not restricted to certain altitudes or areas as are most warblers; they spread over a huge area, especially in Central America, and are found from sea level to high mountaintops. They are silent at this time, unless another Black-and-white Warbler comes around. Then they sing at each other until one is chased away. Though they sometimes attach themselves to small flocks of other warblers, for some reason still unknown to us, they won't associate with other Black-and-white Warblers. Perhaps their specialized way of feeding—by creeping along branches and trunks—means that they would compete too much for food with others of their kind.

The only other bird you could possibly confuse with this one is the Blackpoll Warbler, but there is an easy way to tell them apart. The top of the Blackpoll Warbler's head is solid black; the Black-and-white Warbler's is striped with black and white. The blackpoll also has a white cheek patch below its black cap and does not "creep" on tree trunks.

Yellow-rumped (Myrtle & Audubon's) Warbler

Dendroica coronata

La Fauvette à croupion jaune

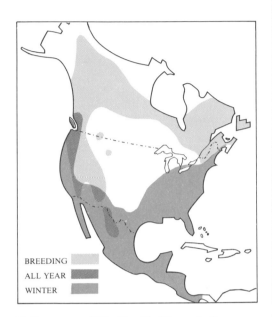

Yellow-rumped Warbler 13–15 cm, 5–6″; 4–5 eggs, white, creamy white, spotted with brown; cup-shaped nest of bark strips, grasses, weeds, bound with spiderwebs, lined with feathers, plant down; placed 1.5–15 m (4–50′) high in tree (usually conifer), in open coniferous woods.

BREEDING

ALL YEAR

WINTER

The western Yellow-rumped Warbler, called Audubon's Warbler in the past, is distinguished from its eastern counterpart by its yellow throat. Both eastern and western varities are very common birds.

Yellow-rumped Warblers are the most abundant wood warblers in the spruce forests of Canada and the northern and montane US. It's easy to distinguish the eastern from the western variety. The eastern birds have white throats; they used to be called "Myrtle Warblers" because of the large quantities of wax myrtle berries they eat along the Atlantic Coast in winter. The western birds have yellow throats; they used to be called "Audubon's Warblers." You'll find both kinds in northeastern British Columbia where they interbreed. Since they hybridize, most ornithologists combine them into a single species. The name Yellow-rumped Warbler is a good one for the two—they both have yellow rumps!

In the East in winter, "Myrtle" Warblers also eat a great many bayberries and, to augment their fruit diet, they search among seaweed along the seashore for flies that are stirred up on mild days. In the South you might see them drinking the sweet sap of sugar maples. (In the Great Plains we've seen myrtles, along with fox squirrels, eating hedge apples during these lean months.) In both spring and summer, watch for them at holes that have been bored into trees by birds called sapsuckers. There they drink sap (and eat the insects attracted to the sap). (See *Feeding on tree trunks* for more on sapsuckers.)

During spring courtship, males fluff their feathers, raise their wings, erect their crown feathers and hop from twig to twig after females, singing and fluttering all the while. After they have mated, Yellow-rumped Warblers build their deeply cupped nests, embedding feathers in the lining so that the tops bend inward over the cup. The feathers form a screen over the eggs. After the young have hatched, they are fed frequently by the parents—about once every 11 minutes.

The song of this bird is a slow, melodious trill. In fall and winter you'll never hear the full song, but its call note—a staccato *chip*—is quite distinctive. Identify the Yellow-rumped Warbler also by its jerky flight, the sharp flip of its tail when it lands and its yellow rump and crown.

126

Yellow Warbler

Dendroica petechia

La Fauvette jaune

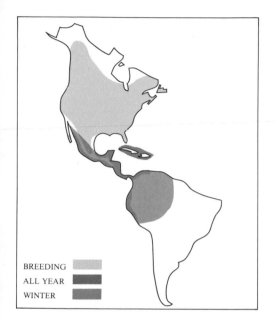

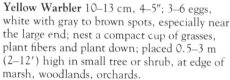

BREEDING
ALL YEAR
WINTER

Yellow Warbler 10–13 cm, 4–5″; 3–6 eggs, white with gray to brown spots, especially near the large end; nest a compact cup of grasses, plant fibers and plant down; placed 0.5–3 m (2–12′) high in small tree or shrub, at edge of marsh, woodlands, orchards.

Once you see this delicate, vociferous bird, you're not likely to forget it. It is a beautiful yellow, with thin reddish stripes on its breast. You're most likely to find it in orchards, gardens and open, shrubby, deciduous thickets along rivers, where it searches for insects.

The Yellow Warbler's song is a melodious, but thin, *tsee-tsee-tsee-tsee-ti-ti-wee,* which can be described as "wheat, wheat, sweet shredded wheat."

The Yellow Warbler is the most widespread of all New World Warblers. Like Song Sparrows, they show geographic variation, that is, Yellow Warblers from different regions are recognizably different. For example, along the coast in Mexico and the West Indies, Yellow Warblers are found in mangroves. These "mangrove warblers" are quite distinctive Yellow Warblers with rusty-red heads, the color of the stripes on the male's breast.

Yellow Warblers nest in low trees and shrubs, and like many other songbirds are often parasitized by the Brown-headed Cowbird. The female cowbird lays its eggs in the nest of the Yellow Warbler which has a rather novel reaction: upon finding this strange egg in its nest, it simply covers it over with a new floor and proceeds to lay its clutch in the "new" nest. If a cowbird lays yet another egg on the new floor, the warbler covers that one too. It will even cover some of its own eggs if the cowbird has parasitized the clutch.

Yellow Warbler nests have been found with as many as six floors, each of them covering a cowbird egg. As you can see, this warbler does not give up easily. In spite of these efforts, however, it is a frequent cowbird victim. For example, in Ohio 42% of the nests reported in one study were parasitized; in Michigan, 40.9%; and in Iowa, 29%. In one area in Michigan, interestingly, the incidence of parasitism was especially small because, biologists speculate, Yellow Warblers there were nesting close to Red-winged Blackbirds. These aggressive birds are known to chase away cowbirds, and they may have incidentally, with this behavior, helped the nesting Yellow Warblers.

How they compete

When different animals have the same basic requirements for survival, only one kind will end up occupying a certain habitat; the others will move, change their requirements or become extinct. In birds, it is sometimes competition for food that limits the number of kinds that can occur at the same place; sometimes it is competition for nest sites. For example, after the starling became widespread in North America, the number of Eastern Bluebirds decreased in areas where they competed with starlings for nest sites in tree cavities or birdhouses, and the more aggressive starling almost always successfully evicts a bluebird.

About 25 years ago, Robert MacArthur did a fascinating study on competition among wood warblers. This complex study has stimulated much of the exciting current work that is being done on competition and on natural animal communities. We will give only a few major points from the work; we suggest that the original paper be read for more detailed information.

Together yet separate

Five different kinds of closely related warblers, similar in size and shape, and all insect eaters, can be found in the same spruce and balsam fir forests of northeastern North America. How can five such similar birds live in the same habitat? Close study of these birds by MacArthur showed that they do not live in exactly the same habitat. Even though they may even inhabit the same tree, they live differently within that tree. Figure 1 shows precisely where in a spruce each kind of bird usually forages for food; Figure 2 shows where each nests; Figure 3 shows how each moves in search of insects.

In addition to the differences these figures show, there are others. For instance, peak periods for nesting vary slightly among the five warblers. Also, Cape May and "Myrtle" Warblers take long flights away from the trees more often than the others to hawk their prey (catch it in the air). The Black-throated Green tends to hover (wait in mid-air to spot prey on a branch); the Blackburnian is somewhere between the Black-throated Green and Bay-breasted in feeding behavior; the Bay-breasted is the most restricted in its habits: it is sluggish and uses its wings least often.

We do not wish to oversimplify, but we also do not want to confuse the problem by giving too much information. Let us summarize by indicating that the populations of these five different little birds were found to be regulated, not by just *one* factor, but by a combination, with any two species showing some overlap in all these activities: feeding in different positions, indulging in hawking and hovering to different extents, moving in different directions through the trees, varying from active to sluggish in their movements, having greatest need for food at different times of the season corresponding to different nesting periods.

The "Myrtle" Warbler is very versatile: it is found in many different habitats, but it is never abundant in any one place. Wherever it is found, it appears to maintain a low, constant population. On the other hand, Cape May and Bay-breasted Warblers have very specific needs. They depend on spruce budworm outbreaks, at which time they rapidly increase in number. When the budworm population is low, the numbers of these two warblers go down dramatically; sometimes they even vanish from some areas. These two species, then, depend upon periods of super-abundant food. They have erratic populations that are high when the food supply is rich and low when it is limited.

So here we have five kinds of birds that seem very similar in their living requirements, yet they can all survive at the same time in what appears to be the same habitat without depleting resources to such an extent that all die. This is possible because, basically, they do not have the same requirements after all.

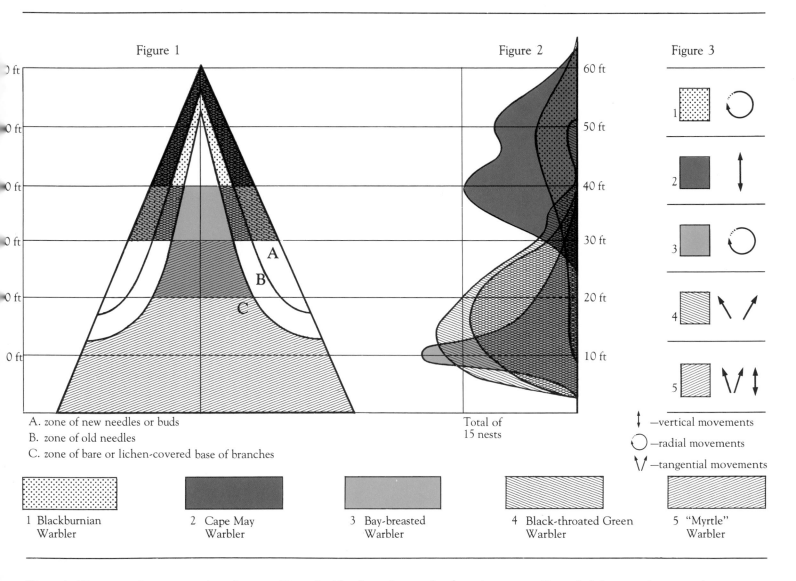

A. zone of new needles or buds
B. zone of old needles
C. zone of bare or lichen-covered base of branches

Total of 15 nests

↕ —vertical movements

◯ —radial movements

V —tangential movements

1 Blackburnian Warbler

2 Cape May Warbler

3 Bay-breasted Warbler

4 Black-throated Green Warbler

5 "Myrtle" Warbler

Figure 1. Diagrammatic representation of a spruce tree showing the main height and area where each of the five species of similar warblers searches for food.

Figure 2. Numbers of nests of each species found at various heights in a spruce tree.

Figure 3. Most prevalent type of movement used by each species as it searches for insects: horizontal movement around the tree, vertical movement or diagonal movement.

Chestnut-sided Warbler

Dendroica pensylvanica

La Fauvette à flancs marron

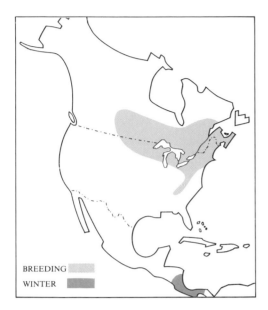

Chestnut-sided Warbler 11–13 cm, 4.5–5.3″; 3–5 eggs, white, spotted with browns or grays; cup-shaped nest of bark strips, grasses, plant fibers, lined with finer materials; placed 0.3–1.5 m (1–4′) in low shrub, sapling, in deciduous second growth.

If you hear the song "very very pleased to meet-ya," look for a colorful, little bird flitting about, its tail raised and its wings half spread. Between songs it sometimes hovers like a hummingbird to pick insects off leaves. This is the Chestnut-sided Warbler, one of the prettiest and commonest of the eastern wood warblers. Its song can be confusing, for sometimes the chestnut-side leaves the "meet-ya" off, and then it sounds much like a Yellow Warbler. Yellow and Chestnut-sided Warblers, however, are usually found in different habitats. If the song comes from a stream-side thicket, it's a yellow; if it comes from a shrubby hillside, it's a chestnut-side.

Chestnut-sided Warblers used to be rare in North America. Audubon saw them only twice in his life, once in Pennsylvania and once in what is now Missouri. Other early naturalists also found them to be uncommon. They nest in deciduous second growth; thus, the clearing of virgin woods in North America, though fatal for some species such as the Passenger Pigeon, benefited the chestnut-side. For example, the species was unknown in Massachusetts in the early 1800s, but was common there by 1860, breeding in the trees that were regrowing in abandoned fields.

The female builds the nest in a shrub or hedgerow. Nests are flimsy and loose walled, bound together by insect silk. When an intruder approaches, male and female react differently. The female drops to the ground and moves slowly away from the nest, as if injured. But the male flutters from branch to branch, vibrating his wings and spreading his tail in a way that will attract the intruder's attention. Both responses distract intruders, keeping them from finding the nest.

The Chestnut-sided Warbler molts in July so that in the fall the bird is very different in appearance: the chestnut color on its sides is greatly reduced, its upper parts are greenish yellow, the streaking is gone and the yellow and the black on the head are missing. In winter, the birds have another partial molt when all their feathers, except for those of the wings and tail, are replaced, and once again they acquire a bright yellow cap and chestnut sides.

Ovenbird

Seiurus aurocapillus

La Fauvette couronnée

BREEDING
WINTER

Ovenbird 14–17 cm, 5.5–6.5″; 3–6 eggs, white, with reddish-brown or lilac spots that form a wreath around the large end; bulky nest of grasses, leaves, bark strips, lined with finer materials; placed on ground in a slight depression among dead leaves, concealed by overhanging plants, in dense deciduous or mixed woods.

The Ovenbird always builds its nest in deciduous forests, using a depression in the ground. Leaf litter arching over the nest gives it the appearance of an old Dutch oven—thus the bird's name. The Ovenbird is also called "teacher bird" because it repeats "teacher-teacher-teacher..." 5 to 15 times, each note of the song being louder than the one before. Because the accent is on the second syllable, the song is better written "cherta-cherta-cherta...." The vibrating motion of the bird's tail and body when it walks has given it other names: "wood-wagtail" and "wagtail warbler."

Instead of foraging in trees and shrubs as most warblers do, the Ovenbird leads the life of a thrush. It walks along the forest floor scanning the fallen leaves for snails, insects and spiders.

The female leaves her well-hidden nest several times a day to feed since, unlike other warblers, male Ovenbirds rarely feed their mates. Before taking flight, she walks a great distance. When flushed, she may limp as far as 16 m (about 50 ft) from the nest to draw the intruder away before flying off.

By the sixth day after hatching, Ovenbird nestlings begin to preen themselves and peck at the bases of their feathers to help remove the sheaths from the developing new growth. Parents use food to coax their offspring out of the nest when fledging time arrives, and within three weeks the young birds can secure their own food.

In winter, the Ovenbird is quiet and solitary as it stalks among thickets at woodland edges and in canefields searching for food. When it returns north in the spring, the loud, ringing song—one of the least musical of warbler songs—makes it conspicuous and readily identifiable. But the Ovenbird can be difficult to see among the fallen leaves in the forest.

Common Yellowthroat

Geothlypis trichas

La Fauvette masquée

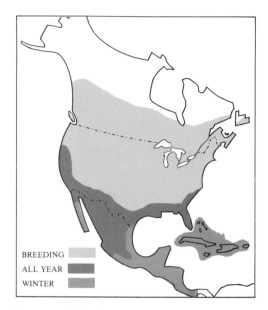

BREEDING
ALL YEAR
WINTER

Common Yellowthroat 11–14 cm, 4.5–5.7″; 3–5 eggs, white, dotted with gray and shades of brown that form a wreath around the large end; cup-shaped nest of dried grasses, lined with finer materials; placed on or near ground, in marshes, swamps, brushy thickets, dense grasslands.

With his black mask, the male yellowthroat looks a little like a bandit. His song is a rhythmical *witchity-witchity-witchity-witch* that sounds to some people like "I beseech you, I beseech you, I beseech you." It is one of the most distinctive of bird songs, and he may sing it persistently all day long, often starting well before sunrise. Sometimes he mimics the songs of marsh wrens and other birds that live in the same habitat. Because female and immature birds don't have a black mask and don't sing, they are more difficult to find and identify.

Yellowthroats are among the most widespread warblers, and are found in marshes, moist thickets and low-growing bushes in clearings. You may find their bulky, cup-shaped nests securely lodged in cattails, briars or even smaller plants such as skunk cabbage. Because they nest near or on the ground, yellowthroats fall victim to a variety of snakes and mammals. In marshes they face added danger from large fish, turtles and bullfrogs. They are also frequent victims of the parasitic Brown-headed Cowbird.

When an intruder comes near its nest, the yellowthroat assumes a wrenlike, tail-up posture and utters a husky *tscick* as if annoyed. Birdwatchers commonly "squeak-up" small birds by making a squeaking, kissing or "pishing" sound with their lips. Wrens, some sparrows and the yellowthroat are among those that react most strongly to this trick. They usually will hop up to look for the source of the sound, rewarding the observer with a good look.

Perhaps because they are both common and widespread, yellowthroats are among the birds most often killed by flying into TV towers or buildings. For example, out of 29,451 birds found from 1955 to 1966 beneath a TV tower near Tallahassee, Florida, 812 were Common Yellowthroats, that is, about 3% of the total; 176 out of 1090 tower-killed birds collected in 1954 near Topeka, Kansas, were yellowthroats, 16% of the total. (See *Migration kills.*)

Yellowthroats are typical warblers, constantly on the move as they glean insects from plants. One birdwatcher counted the number of aphids taken by a yellowthroat in a single minute—an amazing 69!

American Redstart

Setophaga ruticilla
La Fauvette flamboyante

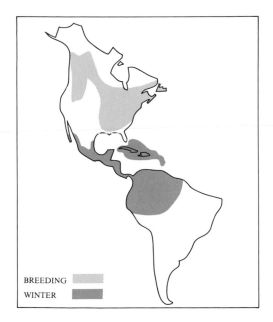

BREEDING
WINTER

American Redstart 12–14 cm, 4.7–5.7"; 3–5 eggs, white, spotted with browns and grays; cup-shaped nest of rootlets, plant fibers, bark strips, lined with finer materials; placed 1.5–9 m (4–30') high in hardwood sapling, bush, in woods.

"Redstart" is an Old English word meaning "red tail." The brightly colored American Redstart is not related to the British Redstart though both have brightly colored tails.

The commonly seen American Redstart is one of the most active of the little insect-eating wood warblers. As they hop from limb to limb, redstarts frequently spread their wings and tail, the adult males displaying their patches of black and orange. They "flycatch" more than other warblers, making lightning-fast dashes through the air to catch a flying insect. If you held one in your hand, you could see that its bill is especially adapted for this activity, being broader than those of most other warblers, with hairlike bristles on each side to help deflect insects into the open gape. After catching a moth, the redstart holds it in its beak, bangs it on a branch until its wings come off and then eats the body of the insect.

The redstart's song is varied, and similar to the Yellow Warbler's, so it takes practice to recognize. The song has a lispy, short, monotonous *weechy* sound. Males sing from spring until July.

The female redstart is a precise nest builder. After lining her nest with feathers and hair, she draws in any loose ends from around the cup of the nest and uses them to bind the lining to the frame of the cup.

If the female is incubating or brooding, she will not leave her nest if it is approached, whereas the male gives a distraction display. But if the young have just left the nest and are still nearby, both parents try to draw the intruder's attention by spreading their wings and tail, hopping around and singing. In this way, it is assured that *they* are watched, not their young who go into hiding as soon as a parent warns of an intruder.

Redstarts winter in Cuba and South America. Cubans call this bird *candelita* ("little candle") because it reminds them of a flickering flame as it darts from tree to tree.

The tanagers, cardinal-grosbeaks, New World sparrows – Family Emberizidae

A junco in flight is an easy bird to identify. Watch for a dark gray, House Sparrow-sized bird with a snowy white breast and white outer tail feathers. It can often be seen in small flocks with other seed-eating songbirds at woodland edges.

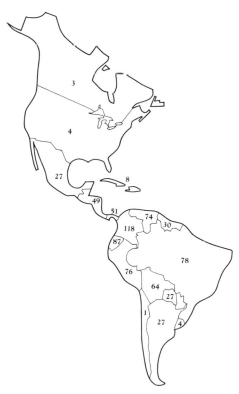

This map shows the number of species of tanagers in some North, Central and South American countries. It dramatically shows how rich is the variety of these birds in the New World tropics.

In Canada and the US, more species of birds belong to this family than to any other. It is also the most diverse family with its 61 species falling into three distinct groups (considered as separate families in some classifications): the tanagers, the cardinal-grosbeaks and the sparrows (more precisely, the New World sparrows).

It is easy to understand why tanagers are thought of as tropical birds. Only four kinds are commonly found north of Mexico, but a great many live in tropical and subtropical America. The map illustrates the great diversity in South and Central America compared with the few in North America. Fittingly, the name tanager comes from an Amazonian Indian name for these birds. Most tanagers are brightly colored—the tropical fish of the bird world—and of medium size. Some are extremely rare, known from only one or two museum specimens until they were rediscovered in the last 20 years. Several new species have also been found by recent expeditions into the deep forests of Colombia and Peru. It is interesting that only the four migratory tanagers that come to North America (and a very few others) have brightly colored males but duller females. Both males and females of most tropical and subtropical species are brightly colored. (This is also true of orioles.) Why migratory species have duller females is not known. Tanagers, in general, depend more on fruit and insects, and less on seeds, for food than do cardinal-grosbeaks and sparrows.

When it comes to beauty, our cardinal-grosbeaks surrender nothing to the tanagers, and like them the females of the North American species are not as gaudy as the males. In the East and Southwest, the Cardinal is the most familiar, but the Rose-breasted and Black-headed Grosbeaks and beautiful Indigo, Lazuli and Painted Buntings belong to this group as well. Though cardinal-grosbeaks eat a variety of foods—fruit, buds, insects—their large, cone-shaped bills are ideal for cracking and shelling hard-coated seeds. Like the New World sparrows they remove the seed coats before swallowing the seeds. They crack the coat with their powerful bill; then, using their tongue to hold the seed against a plate on the inside of their top bill, they rotate the seed, working off the coat with the edges of the bill. The pile of husks and shells below your feeder is evidence of this. We have illustrated this on p. 142 with a Fox Sparrow—a typical New World sparrow.

Most seed-eating birds in North America are New World sparrows, the least colorful of the North American Emberizidae. New World sparrows are so-called because they probably originated here, though some are found in the Old World. In England they are called "buntings," but most are called "sparrows" in North America. Most, but not all. Towhees, juncos, longspurs, and the Snow Bunting are all New World sparrows.

It may surprise some readers to learn that there are many different kinds of sparrows, for most of them look similar, with rather dull, streaked plumage (often with some yellow, ochre or rust in it). Most sparrows forage on the ground and eat many seeds—especially in winter. Towhees, White-throated, Fox and Song Sparrows scratch on the ground in a thicket; longspurs, Snow Buntings and Savannah Sparrows search in windswept, open fields; Chipping Sparrows sometimes feed up in trees like warblers, but will also search the ground for seeds. As you can see, there is a lot of diversity in these "little, brown birds."

Scarlet Tanager

Piranga olivacea
Le Tangara écarlate

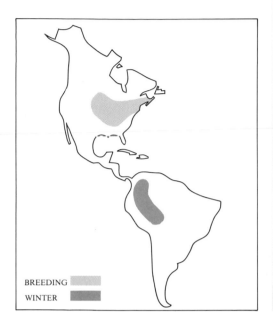

BREEDING
WINTER

Scarlet Tanager 17–19 cm, 6.5–7.6″; 3–5 eggs, pale blue or green, spotted with browns; thin cup-shaped nest of bark strips, weed stems, grasses, lined with finer materials; placed 2.5–23 m (8–75′) high near end of horizontal limb of deciduous tree, in deciduous woodlands.

Although the Scarlet Tanager has a loud song and brilliant plumage, it is seldom seen except during migration. It nests away from people in dense deciduous woods. Even when it is flying overhead, the Scarlet Tanager can go unnoticed; when seen from below without the sun's rays on its brilliant red plumage, it looks dark. Also its song resembles that of the robin and the Rose-breasted Grosbeak, but it is harsher. The *chip-kurr* call note, however, is distinctive.

During courtship, the male tanager displays his brilliant plumage, puffs out his feathers and drags his tail to attract a female. After this display, the two birds mate and the female begins to build a nest high in a tree. The simple, shallow nest is often so thin and loosely built that you can see the outline of the eggs through the bottom as you look up at it.

In spring migration, you might see tanagers at woodland edges or feeding in newly plowed fields along with blackbirds and other hungry migrants. Search for them as well among oak trees where they feed on the insects that eat the leaves. Tanagers move slowly and methodically as they pick up caterpillars and other insects from the foliage. These experts miss almost nothing—including the nocturnal moths that are almost impossible for us to see during the day when they are at rest on leaves and bark.

In late summer, you might see Scarlet Tanagers with red plumage mixed with patches of green feathers. These are molting males that will soon be entirely green and will look much like the females do year round. In March and April, while still in South America, the male tanagers molt again to return in spring as the brilliant scarlet birds with black wings that we know.

In the West, look for the Western Tanager—a close relative of the Scarlet. It, too, is a brilliant bird—bright yellow with a red head and black wings, back and tail. Both the male and the female have two bold, white wing bars; if it weren't for these, the female would be hard to tell from a female Scarlet Tanager. Western Tanagers are usually found in open coniferous forests. (See p. 143 for an illustration of the Western Tanager.)

(Northern) Cardinal

Richmondena cardinalis
Le Cardinal

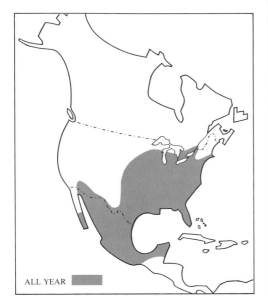

ALL YEAR

(Northern) Cardinal 19–24 cm, 7.5–9.3"; 3–6 eggs, grayish, bluish or greenish white, dotted with shades of brown, gray or purple; nest a loosely built cup of small twigs, strips of bark, weeds, grasses, lined with finer materials; placed 0.3–12 m or 1–40' (usually 2–3 m or 5–10') high in tree, vine, bush, in dense thickets, edge of fields, bushes in towns.

Cardinals were originally birds of the South. It was not until 1896 that the first Cardinal was seen as far north as the Canadian border. Since then, however, they have been steadily spreading northward, and now occur as far north as Ottawa.

A seed eater, the Cardinal has a short, pointed, cone-shaped bill, large jaw muscles, a strong skull and a powerful gizzard. Everyone loves to see this crested bird with its beautiful plumage and hear its pleasant, whistled song. While it sings most vigorously in the spring, you can hear it year round when the weather is nice. The Cardinal is so popular that Illinois, Indiana, Kentucky, North Carolina, Ohio, Virginia and West Virginia have all chosen it as their state bird.

When Cardinals begin courting, the female sings first; then the male repeats her song. She sings again, and if she changes her song slightly, the male will repeat it with the changes.

Nests are built in shrubs and small trees in towns and cities, along the banks of streams and in old fields. Male Cardinals look after their young as actively as the females. One observer saw a pair of Cardinals feed their young 178 times in a mere 6½ hours!

Cardinals are not migratory, and most stay in the same area year round. Some, however, wander as much as several hundred miles, on occasion even moving north in the fall. If food is plentiful, they will stay in an area and breed the next spring.

If you wish to attract Cardinals to your feeder in the winter, put out sunflower seeds, raw peanuts, apples and bread.

If you have thought that the male Cardinal seems brighter in spring, you're right. When the Cardinal molts fully in late summer, the male acquires red feathers with grayish tips. These tips gradually wear off, so that by spring the male returns to his brilliant red.

A note about feeders

Birds love many concoctions! Stick some peanut butter, cooked cereal, raisins or nuts in suet and you will be surprised at the number of birds attracted to your feeder. Even suet alone will attract nuthatches and chickadees. Many books and magazines suggest different grains to use in feeders, and give hints on how to keep away squirrels that will otherwise steal all the sunflower seeds so loved by Cardinals, chickadees and Evening Grosbeaks.

Black-capped Chickadees are tame enough that with patience you can get them to eat from your hand. One word of caution—birds become accustomed to getting food from certain feeders. If you are gone for even a few days, or if for some other reason you do not replenish the feeder that many birds have come to depend on, they will die if the weather is harsh. Before putting up a feeder, you should be aware that the cost of grain and sunflower seeds becomes substantial over a season and heavily used feeders require almost daily additions.

A chunk of suet placed in a wire basket will attract delightful birds to watch—woodpeckers, and songbirds such as chickadees and nuthatches.

If you wish to attract winter birds to your feeder, put out sunflower seeds, raw peanuts, apples and bread. (Lower left, female House Sparrow; upper left, Common Starling; top, Blue Jay; lower right, male Cardinal; below the Blue Jay is a male House Sparrow; to the left of the male House Sparrow is a female Cardinal.)

137

Rose-breasted Grosbeak

Pheucticus ludovicianus
Le Gros-bec à poitrine rose

BREEDING
WINTER

Rose-breasted Grosbeak 18–22 cm, 7–8.5″;
3–6 eggs, pale gray, blue to green, spotted with
brown and purple; wreathed or capped at the
large end; flimsy nest of twigs, grasses; placed in
fork of tree, 2–8 m (5–26′) high, in deciduous
woods, old orchards, suburban trees.

*The beautiful Black-headed Grosbeak
replaces the Rose-breasted Grosbeak in the
West. Where the two species overlap in the
western Plains, they occasionally hybridize.*

This bird is so beautiful, and its song so lovely, that it is captured and sold as a caged bird in Central America where it winters. Fortunately, songbirds are protected in North America and cannot be taken for commercial sale.

Small flocks of red-breasted males are the first to return in the spring; the duller females and one-year-old males follow. A male sings and displays with his head thrown back showing his colorful, rose-red breast feathers. Other males are intimidated by this display but the female is seemingly attracted by it and to the territory that he is defending.

The male and female often build their nest together. It is a flimsy structure so loosely woven that, like the Scarlet Tanager nest, you can see through its bottom. Unlike most songbirds, the male Rose-breasted Grosbeak sits on the eggs almost as much as the female. He even sings as he sits. After the eggs hatch, he also helps brood the young, keep the nest clean and teach the fledglings how to open seeds. Sometimes—after days of "teaching"—he pecks the fledglings on the head, seemingly to get them going "their own way."

The diet of Rose-breasted Grosbeaks consists of about 50% insects and 50% seeds and wild fruits. They also eat blossoms and buds, but whether they eat enough to damage trees or just enough to prune them is not clear.

Look for this bird in bushes, shrubs and among small trees. Listen for a song that is like the robin's but with shorter pauses between each element, and like the Scarlet Tanager's but less harsh. (The pauses between each element in the robin's song are about as long as the element itself.)

In the western Great Plains, the Rose-breasted Grosbeak is replaced by the closely related Black-headed Grosbeak. The males are quite different in coloration, but the females are similar. The two species interbreed where their ranges overlap in the western Plains.

Indigo Bunting

Passerina cyanea

Le Bruant indigo

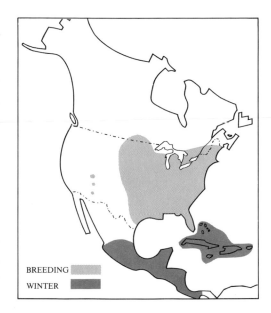

Indigo Bunting 13–15 cm, 5.25–5.75″; 3–4 eggs, white or pale bluish white, unmarked; compact cup-shaped nest of grasses, bark strips, weeds, dead leaves, lined with fine grass, feathers; placed 0.3–4 m (1–12′) high in dense bush, in deciduous thickets.

The song of the Indigo Bunting starts off loud, then becomes fainter. Though the songs are always clearly those of Indigo Buntings, each male sounds slightly different. They also have a call note, a sharp *chipping* sound, which may be easier to recognize than the song—it sounds like two pebbles being struck together.

The male Indigo Bunting is aggressive in territorial defense. After the males have learned the limits of each other's territory, the song—a warning—usually takes the place of a chase or a fight. But if a new male comes in—recognized as new because his song is different—the chasing starts again. The pale brown females stay low in thickets and are much less frequently seen. However, a female starts to give alarm calls and twitches her tail from side to side when an intruder approaches her nest. If her behavior is designed to distract, it works, for the bunting nest is among the hardest of all to find. Buntings will often abandon a nest with eggs in it if it has been disturbed, but they won't leave nestlings.

In fall and winter, male Indigo Buntings look almost like their mates. Males in their first breeding season have a mixture of the blue feathers characteristic of older males as well as the brown feathers of the females or wintering birds.

Watch for these birds in orchards and wooded roadsides where they feed on insects. In summer they eat mostly insects, especially beetles and caterpillars, but they frequent raspberry, blackberry and elderberry bushes when the fruit is ripe. In late summer they can be seen in cornfields where they find food among the silks of ripened corn.

The Indigo Bunting is replaced in the West by its close relative, the Lazuli Bunting. Like all members of this group (genus *Passerina*) the male is a beautiful bird—with a turquoise head, back and rump, an orange-red breast and a white belly and wing bar. The female looks much like the female Indigo Bunting. Indigo and Lazuli Buntings hybridize in a few places such as western Nebraska where their ranges overlap.

Savannah Sparrow

Passerculus sandwichensis

Le Pinson des prés

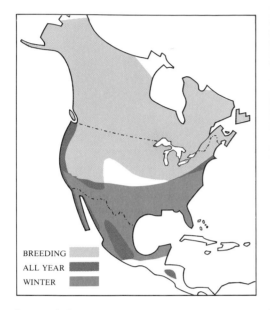

Savannah Sparrow 13–15 cm, 5–5.8″. **Ipswich Sparrow** 15–17 cm, 5.9–6.5″; 3–6 eggs, pale greenish blue, blotched with browns; cup-shaped nest of grasses, lined with finer grasses; placed in depression on ground near small bush, tuft of grass, low in bush (rarely), in short meadows, pastures, sedge marshes, arctic willow-birch, salt marshes (Mexico).

BREEDING
ALL YEAR
WINTER

The Savannah Sparrow is commonly found in hayfields and meadows, among dunes, around marshes and in scattered open willow thickets from the Arctic to the tropics. Though a bird of savannas, it was named, not for its habitat, but for the city of Savannah, Georgia.

In winter, Savannah Sparrows hop along the ground foraging for seeds; but in the nesting season, they eat mainly insects with a supplement of small crabs and snails where available. When Savannah Sparrows are disturbed, they crouch low with their heads down and run along the ground. If the female is flushed from her nest by an intruder, she will give a distraction display commonly known as a "rodent run" display. (See Part II, *How birds respond to intruders.*)

In spring, males give hostile displays to each other. They thrust their heads forward, open their bills wide and raise their wings with a quick jerk. It is not uncommon to see males chasing each other in fields where Savannah Sparrows are nesting.

Savannah Sparrows build their nests in hollows scratched out in the ground (or rarely, low in a bush). While the female incubates, the male sings from fence posts, thistle heads or whatever is highest in his territory. Once the young are hatched, the male helps with their care and feeding.

Males are polygamous in some parts of their range, but only after a male's first mate has begun incubating will he woo another. Then, while the second is incubating, he helps the first with her young who have hatched by this time. However, in the Far North where the nesting season is short, these sparrows are monogamous; they don't have time for two staggered broods and the female cannot raise the young alone!

The Savannah Sparrow's song is a high-pitched *buzz* similar to the buzz of an insect. Only males sing, but they rarely sing in migration. Males and females have a faint call note—*tseep*—given as they take off and repeated while flying.

The Ipswich Sparrow: Danger of extinction

Those who know the Savannah Sparrow may think that the bird illustrated on the page describing that species is too light in color. In fact, it is an Ipswich Sparrow, a member of an interesting, isolated population of the Savannah Sparrow that may be headed for extinction. Its breeding ground on Sable Island, a small island 150 km (about 100 mi) off the coast of Nova Scotia, is changing, and its wintering grounds may become reduced.

After spending the winter along a narrow coastal strip between Nova Scotia and Georgia, especially on some barrier islands off the coast of Virginia and North Carolina, Ipswich Sparrows start making their way north. When they reach approximately the latitude of Halifax, Nova Scotia, they reorient eastward and fly out across the North Atlantic to Sable Island where they breed.

Sable Island is a low, sandy, arc-shaped island about 32 km (20 mi) long. Livestock from shipwrecks and attempted settlements have drastically changed the island's surface over the last few hundred years. A population of wild horses (originally from domestic stock) continues to survive on this rather desolate sandbar. The delicate balance of the island has from time to time been disturbed. Well-meaning people have, in past winters, dropped bails of hay from planes for the horses who, thanks to the extra food, survived the harsh weather. More colts were then produced, and the population became too large for the island. The horses ate so much vegetation that nest sites for Ipswich Sparrows became fewer and fewer, and the dunes began shifting at an even greater rate than previously. The horses are now left on their own, but another intrusion on Sable Island has occurred. Vehicles involved in oil and gas exploration now threaten life on the island. How long can the Ipswich Sparrows hold out? Many think the sandbar on which the birds breed will disappear altogether within several hundred years by natural shifting of the island (it has become measurably smaller over the years). They may last that long only if other changes in either their breeding or their wintering grounds do not drastically reduce their numbers.

After wintering along the Atlantic Coast of the US, the Ipswich Sparrows return to Sable Island to nest.

Dark-eyed (Slate-colored) Junco

Junco hyemalis

Le Junco ardoisé

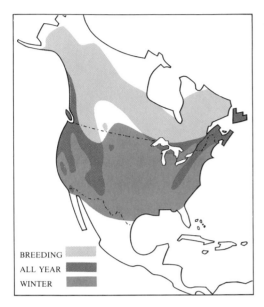

Dark-eyed (Slate-colored) Junco 15–17 cm, 5.75–6.5″; 3–6 eggs, pale bluish white, spotted with brown, purple or gray; cup-shaped nest of grasses, rootlets, bark shreds, lined with finer materials, hair; placed on ground to 2.5 m (8′) high, in coniferous, mixed woods.

The seed-eating finches and sparrows remove the seed coats from seeds before swallowing them. This illustration of the beak of a Fox Sparrow (close relative of the Song Sparrow, discussed in this book) shows how it removes the seed coat by holding the seed with its tongue against the rough plate on the inside of the top bill. A lateral movement of each jaw against the other rips off the seed coat. The side view shows the seed within and the seed coat falling, and the view from the inside of the bird's mouth shows its cup-shaped tongue holding the seed as the seed coat is being shucked off.

Juncos are sometimes called "snowbirds." The name is appropriate, for you'll often see flocks of them scratching through snow on the ground to find seeds.

Adult juncos are among the most distinctive of all sparrows—not dull brown and streaked like their relatives. The young, however, are streaked and sparrowlike, but only before they molt in the first fall of their lives.

Several kinds of juncos are found in North America. In the East, we have the "Slate-colored" Junco, illustrated here; in the West, the most distinctive is perhaps the "Oregon" Junco which looks like a Slate-colored but usually has a darker head and pinkish-brown sides and back. Another western junco, the "Gray-headed," is found in the Rocky Mountains south of Canada. It is light gray with a rusty-red back. At various places, these different juncos interbreed so that it is not possible to characterize every individual as being "Slate-colored," "Gray-headed," or what have you. Thus most ornithologists call them all "Dark-eyed Juncos"—to contrast them with the Yellow-eyed Juncos (which have a yellow iris) of southern Arizona and Mexico.

In the summer, juncos are birds of coniferous woods. They emit a simple, trill-like song; sometimes, when they are establishing territories in spring, they sing two or three trills on different pitches to produce a single song. When females appear in the area, males chase them with drooped wings and lifted tail, displaying their white outer tail feathers—a characteristic of all juncos.

During the rest of the year, juncos give a variety of call notes which differ depending on whether they are alarmed, scolding, fighting or feeding.

Like most songbirds, they feed their nestlings insects. They themselves eat insects at nesting time and in late winter when the early-hatching ones emerge.

In mid-October juncos start to move south in small, loose flocks—these gather into foraging flocks, each establishing itself in a different area; older birds often winter in the area they used the previous year.

Juncos are among the hardiest of all sparrows; in fall and winter, throw grain out in your yard or in a nearby park to attract these pretty little birds.

Why are some birds brightly colored and others dull?

The Western Tanager replaces its close relative the Scarlet Tanager (see its account) in the West where it is one of the most common and conspicuous birds in open coniferous woodlands. The female is less brightly colored than her mate and, except for her two wing bars, resembles the female Scarlet Tanager.

Most birds are well camouflaged in their natural environment. Streaked, brown sparrows crawl in and out of dead grasses, green vireos pick insects high in leafy trees and brown thrushes and wrens hunt for food in dark woodlands. Predators such as hawks have played an important role in the evolution of their colors. The conspicuous sparrows, vireos or wrens are the ones first taken by a keen-eyed hawk. But not all birds have camouflage. Think of the Scarlet Tanager, or Baltimore Oriole, or Yellow-headed Blackbird. Isn't it dangerous to be so bright?

Predators do catch some of these gaudy birds, but the advantages of being bright must be worth the added risk. The advantages are apparently "social." In most species only the adult males are brightly colored, which has led biologists to postulate that bright colors are beneficial because they make the bird distinctive. Since, in general, the female chooses a mate, the distinctive colors and patterns help her select a mate of the right species. The bright patterns also seem to serve an aggressive function, that is, a brightly colored individual has an advantage in combat, helping it hold a territory. The bright colors signal either a warning or a challenge. In species where both males and females defend territories, they are usually the same color and pattern. This is true of jays, chickadees and many tropical tanagers and orioles.

There are two advantages to "being dull." In addition to being hard for predators to see, a dull bird does not elicit aggression from others. If the male alone is fighting for a territory it may be necessary for him to be bright in order to be successful, but the female can remain dull and inconspicuous. Since, in songbirds, mainly the females sit on the nest, their dull colors do not lead predators to their nest.

In species with only brightly colored males, the young male birds often look like the dull females. Young Ruby-crowned Kinglets, like their mothers, lack a ruby crown. Young grosbeaks, buntings and orioles, too, look like their mothers. In many species with especially bright males —including grosbeaks, buntings, orioles and Purple Martins—the males do not get their bright feathers until their second summer. When they are one year old, they look like females, though rather more brightly colored. These young males are sexually mature and will mate if they can hold a territory and attract a female. Purple Martins are interesting in this regard. Since people have started putting out martin houses, the behavior of these birds has been closely studied. Most martin houses have several apartments, and the male martins are aggressive and chase off rival males *if* they recognize them as males. At houses where an old "purple" male is in residence, generally the only other males present will be young ones that closely resemble females. The older male doesn't recognize them as males, and therefore doesn't chase them away. And if they are allowed to stay, females usually mate with them.

It is clear that the answer to "Why are some birds brightly colored?" is not simple. The females do not need to see the bright feathers of a Purple Martin or a Baltimore Oriole to recognize a male of their species. We know this because they often mate with young males that "don't look like males." The older males, however, always have mates, and the younger ones only sometimes do. Perhaps this is because the bright color acts as a signal to other males that a bright bird is old and experienced, and these males, thus, have first choice of the best nest sites or territories. The females merely pick the best sites available to them, which happen to be those controlled by the brighter birds.

Other common sparrows

The Chipping Sparrow is a small, slim bird with a monotonous ''chipping'' rattle of a song—an almost insectlike sound.

The belly of the White-crowned Sparrow is grayer, and its back is not so rich a brown as that of the White-throated Sparrow. Though many white-throats have a bright white crown stripe, white-crowns never have a distinct white throat. Only the White-throated Sparrow has yellow between the eye and the bill.

Chipping Sparrow

The Chipping Sparrow is one of the most widespread and common of the North American sparrows. Its name describes its song—a dry, monotonous, "chipping" rattle—an almost insectlike sound on a single pitch.

Chipping Sparrows breed in open woods—either coniferous or deciduous—and in many parts of their range are commonly found in cities and parks.

Chipping Sparrows, and some closely related sparrows not illustrated in this book, are small, slim birds—more so than we usually expect a sparrow to be. Its body size, its distinctive markings on the head and its clear, unstreaked belly help identify this bird which, during migration, often gathers in small flocks.

Rufous-sided Towhee

One conspicuous and common "sparrow" that is brightly colored is the Rufous-sided Towhee. The males and females of this species are easily told apart by their plumage. The male has a black hood, back, wings and tail, with rusty-red on its sides and a clear, white belly; the female is a rich reddish brown where the male is black. In many parts of their range they have a bright red iris—hence, they are often called "Red-eyed" Towhee. Towhees are often seen—and heard—scratching among leaves on the ground, looking for insects and weed seeds. Though variable, the towhee's song is distinctive. Commonly there are three elements that sound like "drink your tea." The "tea" is a loud, buzzy trill. When calling, the towhee often just says "drink," which may have two distinct syllables—*chee-wink.* Hence, another common vernacular name for the towhee is "chewink." In fact the name towhee is supposed to describe their song—but we think chewink does so much better. (See Part II, *Hatching,* for an illustration of the Rufous-sided Towhee.)

White-crowned Sparrow

Though found throughout most of North America during one season or the other, the White-crowned Sparrow is especially common in the West. In the East, White-crowned Sparrows breed only at the edge of the tree line at high latitudes from Newfoundland across northeastern Canada; most apparently move southwest in the winter, as the species is uncommon along the eastern seaboard in migration and winter. In the West, White-crowned Sparrows breed in the mountains south to New Mexico and central California; in winter these birds move southward and to lower elevations. White-crowns along the California coast do not migrate, but those that breed along the coast of southern British Columbia and Washington move south in winter.

Though highly variable, the song of the White-crowned Sparrow is quite distinctive. It is a mixture of clear, plaintive whistled notes and burry, husky trills. These sparrows commonly sing during spring migration.

White-throated Sparrow

Zonotrichia albicollis

Le Pinson à gorge blanche

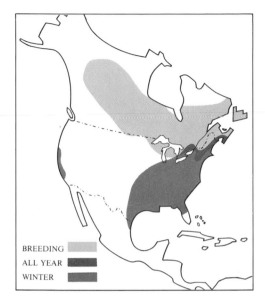

BREEDING
ALL YEAR
WINTER

White-throated Sparrow 16–18 cm, 6.3–7.2″;
3–5 eggs, grayish, bluish or greenish white,
blotched with shades of brown; cup-shaped nest
of grasses, leaves, bark strips, lined with finer
materials, hair; placed in hollow on ground, at
foot of tree, under fallen branch, in northern
deciduous or mixed woodlands, thickets.

New Englanders say the White-throated Sparrow sings "Old Sam Peabody, Peabody, Peabody," but Canadians claim it sounds more like "Oh Sweet Canada, Canada, Canada." Because of its distinctive whistled song, this bird is also known as the "Canadian song sparrow," "poor Sam Peabody," and "whistle bird." The song is a series of clear whistles, the first ("Old" or "Oh") lower or higher than the ones that follow. It is a common bird, easily recognized by the white patch on its throat and by its distinctive song.

When you see a flock of White-throated Sparrows, it doesn't take long to notice that some have white stripes on the top of their heads and others have tan stripes. In most birds, a color difference such as this often represents a difference in age or sex. In these birds the tan color is not just characteristic of young birds (although they do have tan stripes before their first molt), nor does it denote a sex difference. It appears that White-throated Sparrows have a unique system of forming pairs and choosing mates that is related to this color difference. About half the sparrows have white stripes; they are more aggressive than the tan-striped ones. When these birds mate, it is nearly always with birds of the other color. Perhaps if two tan-striped birds mated, they would not be able to defend their territory; or if two white-striped birds mated, they would waste too much time being aggressive—even to each other!—to raise their young. Nesting is more often successful when unlike birds mate.

If you see a White-throated Sparrow, watch for others; it will usually be one of a small flock. Notice how they forage. They scuffle the ground with outspread legs. After scratching the ground this way, they jump back throwing the dirt behind them. People have seen White-throated Sparrows scratching for seeds and insects for as long as an hour without stopping.

Bathing

White-throated Sparrows bathing.

Why do birds bathe? They doubtless do it to keep cool on hot summer days. They may do it to get rid of parasites such as lice, but they also seem to bathe for sheer "fun." As we watched a group of newly molted starlings and robins in their fresh fall feathers bathing on a *cool, wet* day recently, we had to wonder once again if they surely were not bathing just for enjoyment. They couldn't have been too hot, and it's unlikely that they had much of a louse or mite problem, having recently completed their molt.

If you find birds the least bit enjoyable to watch, we suggest putting out a birdbath. Birds will bathe in just about anything that holds water, including puddles and inverted garbage can lids. But ground bathing leaves birds easy prey for cats, so a bath on a pedestal is preferable. It gives the birds a much better chance to get away. Heated baths are now available; we put one next to our feeder in winter, and a number of different birds drink from it as well as bathe.

Songbirds also will bathe in dew or raindrops. Watch for them in wet foliage where you might see them hit wet leaves with their wings and bodies to knock drops of water onto their plumage.

Birds dust bathe and sun bathe as well. In summer, House Sparrows frequently dust bathe on gravel roads or on bare ground. They crouch in a depression in the dust, fluff their feathers and flip the dust over their bodies. Many other birds also dust bathe, especially those that live near the ground such as quail and Horned Larks. It might seem that the dust would soil a bird's feathers, but apparently this isn't the case. The dust absorbs oils in the feathers, then falls away as the bird resumes its normal activity. This probably makes the feathers fluffier and in that way increases their insulative value; it may also discourage feather mites.

Birds sun bathe to help keep warm. We see larger birds, such as cormorants, grebes and roadrunners, sun bathing more commonly than smaller species—perhaps because it is more dangerous for small birds to sit out in the open. Nevertheless, on a cool, sunny morning, it is not unusual to see a songbird sitting in the sunlight with its back to the sun and wings half spread. Laboratory experiments have shown that the heat absorbed by birds from sunlight can be substantial, and the hunched-down posture that sunning birds often assume increases the area exposed to the sun's radiation. Sometimes birds take advantage of solar energy by crouching on the hot surface of a paved road; swallows are especially bold about doing this, perhaps because they can outfly most predators.

House Sparrows dust bathing.

Song Sparrow

Melospiza melodia

Le Pinson chanteur

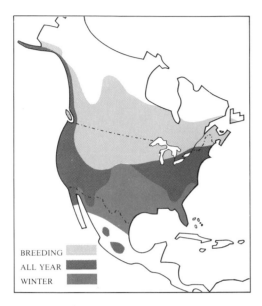

Song Sparrow 16–18 cm (19 cm on Aleutians), 6–7"; 3–6 eggs, pale bluish to grayish green, speckled with shades of brown; cup-shaped nest of grasses, weeds, bark strips, leaves, lined with finer materials; placed on ground to 1.5 m (4') high, in woodland edge, gardens, roadsides, salt marshes (West Coast).

BREEDING
ALL YEAR
WINTER

Listen for the Song Sparrow on a cold, clear morning in late winter. It begins early, singing as many as six to eight songs a minute, continuing all day though less frequently as the day wears on. To many people, the Song Sparrow signals the beginning of spring. It sings throughout the year, but does so much more often and more vigorously as spring approaches.

When a male sets up his territory in spring, he flies from bush to bush with head and tail held high, wings vibrating rapidly and neck outstretched. As soon as he lands, usually on an exposed perch, he bursts into song. The same male and female often mate year after year and may produce as many as three broods in a season.

At one time of the year or other, the Song Sparrow is found almost everywhere in North America—near our houses (in bushes or thickets, but not in barnyards), along riverbanks, along the brushy edge of woods, fence rows and ponds and in wet meadows. You can recognize it by the bold blackish or brownish spot on its breast, its streaked underparts, its rather long, rounded tail, and by its actions. Look for a sparrow that flies only short distances from perch to perch, with tail flopping to one side as it flits about in search of food.

Song Sparrows sing variable, musical songs of two general types. They seem to learn their particular phrasing by listening to other Song Sparrows in the vicinity. Thus, a Song Sparrow in Montreal would sound much like one in Quebec City, but different from one in a more distant place such as St. Louis or Cincinnati. All songs, however, start off with one to three clear whistles and would be recognized as the rich song of the Song Sparrow—a bird welcomed not only for its sound, but also for its beneficial role in eating millions of weed seeds and insects.

All of one kind, but so different

Song Sparrow from the south-western desert (Arizona).

Song Sparrow from southern Ontario.

Song Sparrow from the dark, wet coastal forests of Oregon.

Not only may birds of the same kind from different localities sound different; they may not even look precisely the same. You might, for instance, identify a bird in the southwestern US as a Song Sparrow and a bird in eastern Canada also as a Song Sparrow, but if Song Sparrows from different regions were all lined up in a row, you would notice dissimilarities in size and color.

Illustrated here are four Song Sparrows from four parts of North America. The birds are painted to scale.

It is clear that the Song Sparrow from the Aleutian Islands, Alaska, is the largest; the one from Arizona, the smallest and lightest in color; the bird from Oregon, the darkest. The Song Sparrow from Ontario is more or less typical of Song Sparrows found east of the Rocky Mountains and throughout the Northeast—though some are a bit more rust colored than the one we have shown here.

These four birds illustrate what biologists call *geographic variation,* that is, variation among individuals of a species from geographically different parts of their range.

It is thought that geographic variations in size and color occur because the birds have adapted to different environments. For example, Song Sparrows from the colder parts of the range are larger than those from the warmer regions. A large bird is better adapted to a cold climate because it cools down less rapidly than a small one. We see this in humans, too: healthy adults get chilled on a cold day more slowly than do small children. Heat is lost from the surface of an animal. Since large animals have less surface area *for their mass* than do small ones, they cool down more slowly.

The large Song Sparrows that live on the Aleutian Islands are residents—they live there year round. These islands, being surrounded by water, do not get as cold as the mainland of Alaska, but it is still quite cold there in winter, and chilly in summer. The Song Sparrows in southern Canada (represented here by the bird from Ontario) live in a milder climate; they winter mainly in the South and breed where it is warm in the summer. The small Arizona birds are residents where it is rarely cold in winter but can be very hot in summer. In their case, losing heat efficiently is critical for survival!

Biologists believe these size differences are adaptations to different climates and find this trend to be common among birds and mammals; the colder it is, the larger the animals of a particular species are.

The color variation shown here is also a result of adaptation. Song Sparrows are dark where it is moist, and pale where it is dry. This is probably due to the need for camouflage. Song Sparrows spend a lot of time on the ground when feeding. Moist soils contain dark humus and promote the luxuriant growth of plants, which shade the ground. Dark-colored Song Sparrows are difficult for hawks and other predators to see against moist, shady ground. Lighter sparrows are less easily seen against light, sandy soils. Thus, the Oregon sparrows are as well adapted for their moist environment as the Arizona sparrows are for theirs.

Song Sparrow from the Aleutian Islands of Alaska.

The blackbirds – Family Icteridae

Some of our most familiar birds are members of the blackbird family though not all are black. If you know only the black species, such as grackles, cowbirds and Red-winged Blackbirds, you might find it strange that their family name, Icteridae, comes from the Latin *icter* meaning "yellowness."

Yet *icter* is certainly appropriate for the beautiful orioles, meadowlarks and Yellow-headed Blackbirds of the West. The blackbirds are a varied lot, as you will see, and include "look-alikes" such as the Eastern and Western Meadowlarks, distinguished at a distance only by their different songs, and the notorious cowbird which doesn't make a nest of its own, but forces others to be foster parents for its young.

Blackbirds are generally medium-sized birds and powerful fliers. They have strong legs that allow them to spend a large amount of time walking on the ground—they seldom hop. Only the orioles are not commonly seen on the ground. Most blackbirds have long pointed wings and long rounded tails. Their beaks are quite variable: the cowbird and Bobolink have finchlike, cone-shaped bills; orioles and meadowlarks have long, pointed insect-picking bills; the Red-winged Blackbird's is in between.

On the whole, blackbirds are a gregarious lot. Some species nest in colonies—rather unusual for songbirds. Often large numbers of the "black" blackbirds gather in flocks, and usually several species will be represented. Most commonly, grackles, red-wings and cowbirds—joined by the "black" starling, not a member of the blackbird family—will predominate in these flocks, which become so large as to represent a hazard in some cases. A few years ago in southern Missouri in December, we drove for 20 minutes parallel to a flock of blackbirds—mostly grackles—and still had not seen the beginning or the end of the flock when we turned off and went in another direction.

Every winter, large flocks of blackbirds make the news because people become outraged by the noise and mess or fear that they constitute a health hazard. Drastic measures have been taken at various times to reduce blackbird numbers. As early as 1695, one village in Massachusetts passed a law forbidding a man to marry unless he presented to the town clerk six blackbird heads! Today, modern technology has, at times, been used to reduce blackbird flocks. In February 1975, a "detergent" was sprayed on a flock of about 2 million blackbirds in eastern Kentucky. The detergent destroyed the birds' natural waterproofing, so that when authorities sprayed the flock with water, many of the birds froze to death.

Blackbirds are so closely related to tanagers and Cardinal-like finches that there is some question as to which group some of them actually belong. For example, the Bobolink has finchlike characteristics such as a short, stout beak and a short tail, and yet it has many other features in common with blackbirds.

Though well represented in North America, many blackbirds are confined to the New World tropics. Some tropical orioles are especially interesting— they build long hanging nests in colonies so that one tree might be loaded with these magnificent woven gems. North American orioles all build similar woven baglike nests, but they are solitary nesters.

This lovely western oriole, the Bullock's Oriole, hybridizes with the Baltimore Oriole where their ranges overlap in the Great Plains, and replaces the Baltimore in the West. Some ornithologists consider these orioles to be a single species, and call it the "Northern Oriole."

Bobolink

Dolichonyx oryzivorus

Le Goglu

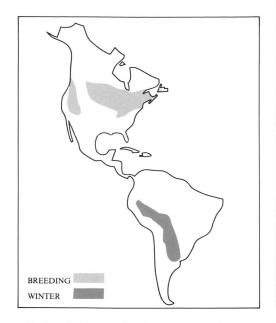

BREEDING

WINTER

Bobolink 17–20 cm, 6.5–8″; 4–7 eggs, pale gray or pale brown, spotted with shades of brown; flimsy nest of grasses, lined with finer grass; placed in shallow depression on ground, in tall hayfields, moist meadows.

The rich song of the male Bobolink is spectacular: it is a loud, clear series of short notes that begins on a low pitch and rises as it continues. Bobolinks fly over meadows with rapid, shallow wing strokes, singing as they fly. When they land in fields and meadows, they continue to gurgle their songs and display their plumage.

In contrast with the gaudy males, the females look like big sparrows and are well camouflaged. They stay low in the grasses while nesting. Bobolinks make it practically impossible for an intruder to find their nest. They hop or run along the ground for a great distance before flying away, and when they land, it is far from the nest. Then, hidden in the grasses, they run back to the nest.

After the breeding season is over, the male Bobolink molts so that he resembles his less showy female partner. Bobolinks, like all birds, tend to be quieter while molting, but they give a distinctive *clink* note as they migrate south in the fall.

Bobolinks stop to eat and roost in the rice fields of the southern US on their way to and from the marshy areas of Argentina and Brazil where they winter. Huge numbers of these "rice birds," as they are often called, were shot by farmers in the past because of the destruction they caused to crops. And because they were considered a restaurant delicacy, plump from the rice on which they fed, many more were shot for the table.

They are now protected by law, but the number of Bobolinks in the East has been vastly reduced since the 1800s when they could be seen hovering over every tall grass meadow and hayfield. Now they are more common farther west in the prairies where hayfields and meadows are plentiful.

Eastern Meadowlark

Sturnella magna
La Sturnelle des prés

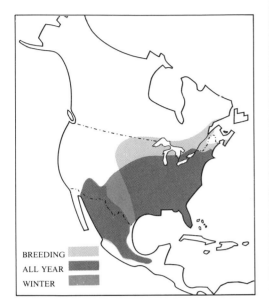

BREEDING
ALL YEAR
WINTER

Eastern Meadowlark 22–28 cm, 8.5–11″; 3–7 eggs, white, greatly spotted with lavender and shades of brown; nest of weeds and grasses, usually dome-shaped; placed on ground, in open fields, short pastures, prairies.

Farmers in southern Canada and the northern US welcome the Eastern Meadowlark, probably the best known of all meadow and grassland birds. Meadowlarks eat large quantities of destructive insects and noxious weed seeds, especially in breeding season. It has been estimated that, in a 10-day period after hatching, nestlings are fed 5000 to 7000 grasshoppers by their parents.

The female meadowlark builds her nest on the ground in a hoofprint or some other depression. She remodels the spot with her sharp, pointed bill and covers it with surrounding grasses. Eventually she builds a dome-shaped roof over the nest; she enters and leaves through a side opening. About eight days after the nestlings hatch, they become so active that they completely destroy the nest. With no roof over their heads they are exposed to the sun's rays and have to pant vigorously to keep their body temperature from soaring. Within a few days, they leave the nest, returning only to be fed.

Meadowlark males have territories of about three hectares (seven acres) in the breeding season. Sometimes a male mates with more than one female and spends most of his time perched at a spot between the nests of the two (sometimes three) females.

Meadowlarks sing their pleasant clear whistled song that sounds like "spring-o-the-yeeeear" year round except while incubating and molting.

In parts of the Midwest of the US, in central Canada and in the West, you are likely to see a bird that looks and acts almost exactly like the Eastern Meadowlark, but that sounds quite different. What you are seeing is a Western Meadowlark, a different species. In some areas of the Midwest, these two can really confuse you—they occur in the same fields and meadows. Eastern Meadowlarks, however, usually nest in the more moist areas, and Western Meadowlarks in the drier parts of the fields.

Baltimore (Northern) Oriole

Icterus galbula
L'Oriole de Baltimore

BREEDING
WINTER

Baltimore (Northern) Oriole 18–21 cm, 7–8.2″; 4–6 eggs, pale grayish white, streaked or blotched with browns and blacks; nest a neatly woven sac; suspended from small branch, 2–21 m (6–70′) high in deciduous tree (commonly maple, cottonwood), in open deciduous woods.

This pretty bird was named for the British colonist Lord Baltimore, whose family colors were orange and black. Baltimore Orioles are said to be like spring flowers: they arrive suddenly and dramatically, then disappear too soon. Watch for them in late spring when northern woodland flowers such as trilliums are in bloom and apple blossoms are opening in the orchards. Perhaps we should say "watch and listen"—besides being one of the prettiest of our songbirds, the Baltimore Oriole is also a persistent and spectacular singer, especially before mating. Most do not leave until fall, but after their flurry of nest building and singing, they become so inconspicuous that you rarely see them.

If you see a long, hanging nest suspended high in a tree, you will know it was made by a Baltimore Oriole. (See Part II, *Nest building,* for more about this intricately woven nest.) After nesting season, the young birds and females form feeding flocks; adult males remain alone until migration.

Orioles eat huge quantities of caterpillars, even the hairy and spiny ones that many birds avoid. They also eat other insects, spiders and some wild fruits. Unfortunately, they like cultivated peas and small fruits and can damage crops in areas where flocks are large. More delicate eaters than the robin, they do not gulp whole cherries and grapes, but pierce the skin with their beak and drink the juice. Ripe mulberries, they swallow whole.

Baltimore Orioles migrate to areas of low elevation in central and northern South America to spend the winter. Some arrive as early as July on their wintering grounds where they can be found foraging in small flocks—in shrubs and cactuses in dry areas, and treetops in humid rain forests.

Baltimore Orioles are replaced in the West by the slightly larger and less colorful Bullock's Orioles. In the Great Plains from central Texas to southern Alberta, the Baltimore and Bullock's Orioles often hybridize.

Red-winged Blackbird

Agelaius phœniceus
Le Carouge à épaulettes

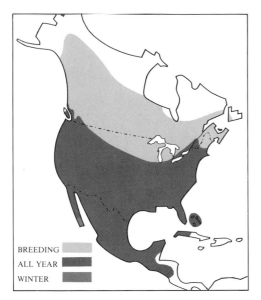

Red-winged Blackbird 19–25 cm, 7.5–10″; 3–5 eggs, pale bluish green, spotted or streaked with shades of brown and purple; nest a loosely woven, bulky cup of cattails, grasses, weeds, lined with finer materials; attached to cattails, other emergent vegetation 8 cm–4 m (3″–14′) high over water, or small tree over ground, in marshes, swamps, wet meadows.

This beautiful bird of marshes, wet fields and roadside ditches is one of the most common North American songbirds. Many males return to the northern US and Canada to establish their territories in early spring, often when the water in marshes is still covered with ice. Females join them later, but because they keep low in the vegetation and are less bright and vocal than the males, they are not so readily seen.

Early in spring the males do not sing vigorously, and only the yellow margins of their colorful wing patches show. Later, they display their brilliant red shoulder patches as they sing their *konk-la-reeee* song.

Red-wings often nest in colonies, especially in marshes, and a male may have several mates. He doesn't help feed the young, but he does help his mates defend them. When an intruder approaches the marsh, each male red-wing circles the nests of his mates and scolds the unwelcome visitor. If the intruder is another male red-wing, he is vigorously chased; if it is a hawk, it is harassed, and often physically attacked, by several males.

You will hardly see a red-wing in early August. They stay low in the marshes and remain quiet while molting. But by September they're out in their new feathers. The males keep their red shoulder patches through the winter.

In summer, red-wings eat large numbers of insects and thus are beneficial to local farmers. But in migration large flocks—often mixed with other blackbirds—can damage crops.

BREEDING
ALL YEAR
WINTER

154

Some western blackbirds

Like its cousin, the Red-winged Blackbird, the male Yellow-headed Blackbird often has several mates at the same time. The yellow-head is more strictly a bird of marshes than the red-wing, and its nests are almost always placed in tall vegetation (cattails or tules) over standing water. The female is brownish, with a yellow throat.

In the northern prairies and west another blackbird is common in marshes—the Yellow-headed Blackbird. The yellow-head is more strictly a marsh bird than the red-wing, and is somewhat larger. Where both red-wings and yellow-heads nest in the same marsh, the yellow-heads form denser colonies in cattails in the middle, the red-wings staying at the periphery. Yellow-head males are easily identified by their bright yellow heads and large white wing patches, especially noticeable in flight. The female yellow-head is a bit smaller than the male, brownish with dull yellow on the cheeks and throat.

The western Brewer's Blackbirds look like small grackles with shorter tails, and they are found in many of the same habitats as grackles—parks, gardens, irrigated fields and pastures. Though the males are iridescent blue on their head and shoulders, they are not so bright as grackles; females are brown. Male Brewer's Blackbirds are frequently polygamous, like many other blackbirds. Since Europeans settled this continent, Brewer's Blackbirds have become closely associated with cattle, and in recent years have been extending their range eastward. Today they are found as far east as Wisconsin and western Ontario.

Common Grackle

Quiscalus quiscula
Le Mainate bronzé

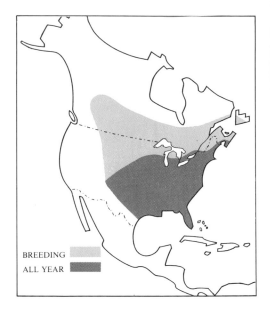

Common Grackle 28–34 cm, 11–13.5″; 3–6 eggs, pale greenish white, blotched with dark browns or purples; bulky cup-shaped nest of sticks, grasses, leaves, bark strips, mud, lined with finer materials, feathers; placed 2–18 m (6–60′) high in tree, in parklands, towns, swampy thickets.

This beautiful shiny blackbird, whose metallic colors change with the angle of the sun, is common in backyards and city parks. Noisy and aggressive, the grackle is sometimes called "crow blackbird" because it acts and looks a bit like a crow. But the crow is much larger and stockier and not closely related.

The male's hoarse, grating song has been described as sounding like the squeak of a rusty hinge. His song and aggressive "head-up" display keep other males away.

When a female comes into his territory, the male struts before her with feathers fluffed and tail dragging stiffly on the ground behind him. Shortly after mating, the female begins building her nest in shade trees or orchards. During mating and nest building all grackles in the area disappear at night, flying off together to some favorite roosting spot. It is unwise to go near a grackle nest once it is built and the female is incubating. Not only will you be met with scolds and dives, but grackles sometimes strike directly at an intruder who is too close to their nest.

The grackle is one of the goats of the bird world: it will eat almost anything. It frequents areas where there is garbage. Like the Blue Jay, it robs the nests of other birds, eating eggs and killing the young. Grackles have been seen wading body-deep in water and even plunging in from overhanging tree roots to catch insects and snails, and to dig crayfish from under stones. Holding a crayfish in its bill, the grackle hammers the hard shell against rocks to open it. Grackles will even seize goldfish from small pools and frogs from ponds. They often eat seeds, and take in sand or gravel to help grind the seeds. A special pointed projection attached centrally on the inside of their upper beak is a handy tool for acorn cracking.

Grackles are among the first birds to return north in the spring. Like red-wings, the males arrive first, and by early March a few will arrive in southern Canada.

Brown-headed Cowbird

Molothrus ater
Le Vacher à tête brune

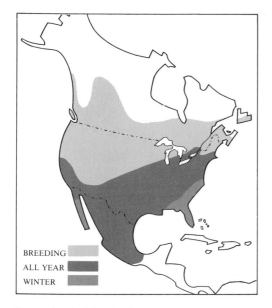

BREEDING
ALL YEAR
WINTER

Brown-headed Cowbird 18–21 cm, 7–8.25″; eggs white or grayish white, dotted with shades of brown; eggs are placed in nests of other species; females probably lay several "clutches" per season, with perhaps 6 eggs in a clutch.

Now we come to the culprit—the bird that makes life difficult for so many other songbirds! The cowbird's Greek name, *Molothrus*, means "vagabond" or "parasite," and it is apt, for this blackbird is the only parasitic songbird in most of North America (the Bronzed Cowbird of the extreme Southwest is also parasitic). It neither lives inside another animal nor attaches itself to the body of another animal (as a lamprey might). Rather, the cowbird is a "social parasite" because the female cowbird builds no nest; instead, she lays her eggs in the nests of other birds. The reaction of "host" birds to a strange egg in their nest is varied and fascinating. (See *What to do with a foreign egg in the nest!*)

The cowbird is the smallest North American blackbird. Like the Bobolink, this bird has a short beak that is more like a sparrow's than a blackbird's. Males are iridescent black with brown heads, while females are totally grayish brown.

The cowbird is common in pastures, fields, along woodland edges and in city parks. Like many birds in this kind of habitat, the cowbird became widespread with the clearing of virgin forests.

In spring males emit squeaking, shrill whistles and perform elaborate displays to keep other males away and to attract females. These "bill-pointing" and "ruff-out" displays are described in other sections. Cowbirds are promiscuous birds, establishing no pair bonds. In late spring you'll see single females each followed by several males vying for her attention.

Cowbirds eat mainly seeds, but they also search the grass for insects that are stirred by grazing cattle, a habit which gives them their name. In the past they were known as "buffalo birds" because they followed the great herds of bison. They now often forage along roadsides for insects that have been stunned by passing cars. Watch for a bird that seldom hops but walks or runs, with tail held high and wings drooping.

What to do with a foreign egg in the nest!

A young cowbird opens its mouth to be fed by a female Blackburnian Warbler half its size.

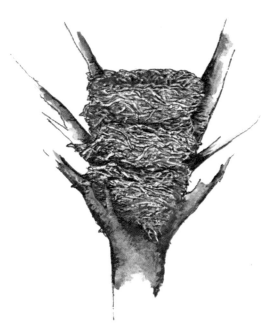

Sometimes a female Yellow Warbler will build a new nest over one in which a Brown-headed Cowbird has laid an egg. In this picture, the female warbler has built three nests because of persistent cowbird parasitism.

We have mentioned several times in this book an extraordinary habit of the female cowbird. She builds no nest, nor does she incubate her eggs or brood her young. She simply deposits her eggs in several nests of other birds in the vicinity. Often before laying her own egg, she will throw one of the "host's" eggs out of the nest. The responses of the birds whose nests she has "parasitized" are not all the same.

Blackburnian Warblers, Common Yellowthroats, Ovenbirds, most vireos, Cardinals, Indigo Buntings and many other birds incubate the cowbird egg, brood the nestling and raise it as their own—often at the expense of their young. The cowbird incubation period is very short, so the young cowbird often hatches before the other eggs in the nest and, thus, begins getting food earlier. The cowbird also grows faster (cowbirds average 13 times their hatching weight in only 9–13 days). Its wider gape is seen more easily by the adult birds than the gapes of their own smaller young. This means that the cowbird nestling gets most of the food, while the birds' own nestlings may die of starvation. We have frequently seen the rather sad and ridiculous sight of a young cowbird following a tiny warbler less than half its size, gaping to be fed—a sure sign that the warbler had raised the young "vagabond."

Some birds do not accept the strange egg in their nest. Robins and catbirds are almost never successfully parasitized because they invariably throw the cowbird egg out of their nest as soon as they see it there (they also chase away any cowbird they see in the area). Other birds throw the egg out sometimes, but not other times. Many birds abandon nests containing a cowbird egg if it appears *before* they have laid their own eggs, or if they have not yet started to incubate. Remarkably, some birds, especially the Yellow Warbler, often bury the cowbird egg by building a floor on top of it, and then laying a new clutch on this new floor. Thus, the cowbird egg does not hatch.

Occasionally, the cowbird lays an egg in the nest of a bird whose body would seem to be too tiny to keep so large an egg warm and properly incubated, but very small birds such as kinglets and gnatcatchers do raise young cowbirds. More rarely, the cowbird will lay an egg in the nest of a Killdeer or sandpiper whose young are precocial, needing no care by the parents after they hatch. Since cowbird nestlings require feeding and brooding, they do not survive if they hatch in such a nest. Fairly frequently, cowbirds lay in swallows' nests, but even though swallows incubate and feed nestlings while they are in the nest, young cowbirds probably rarely survive to adulthood. Swallows do not feed their young after they leave the nest, as most songbirds do. Young swallows, like their parents, soon learn to catch insects "on the wing."

Female cowbirds have been seen feeding young cowbirds—possibly their own offspring—in the nest of hosts, but they do this rarely, and do not help to feed the hosts' young. In fact, she pecks at them if they try to take food from her.

Certain other birds are also parasites. The European relatives of the American cuckoos have perfected parasitism to the point where their newly hatched young throw the hosts' nestlings or eggs out of the nest! And some lay eggs that look almost exactly like the eggs of the species they parasitize, making it difficult for their unwilling host to reject them. Unlike the Brown-headed Cowbird, these birds are very choosey about which nests they lay their eggs in. Some kinds of cowbirds are not parasitic at all and one South American species sometimes builds its own nests and other times lays its eggs in the nests of others.

A female Brown-headed Cowbird throws a vireo egg out of a vireo's nest.

How birds show their age

Some young songbirds are easily distinguished from their parents. Surely everyone has seen a spotted-bellied fledgling robin chasing its "red-breasted" parents for a worm. Young bluebirds, close relatives of the robin, also have spotted breast and bellies. These spots are lost in their fall molt; by winter the young look like the adults. Young waxwings have streaked breasts till their first fall, and many don't get the wax on their wings until their second year.

The young of many other species, however, look just like the adults. Unless you are fortunate enough to be involved in a bird-banding program, you'll not be able to age vireos, kinglets and most thrushes in the fall. But if you have a bird in the hand, there are some features to look for. The Red-eyed Vireo does not get its red iris until its first winter, so a "brown-eyed" Red-eyed Vireo is a young bird. Adult Mockingbirds and Brown Thrashers have yellow eyes, but are "gray-eyed" until their first winter. You can only be certain of eye color if you are very close to a bird. Often the feathers of young birds are a different texture or shape than those of older birds, but most age differences in feather shape are difficult to learn.

All songbirds can be aged in the fall by the technique known to bird banders as *skulling*. The skull of a young songbird is single layered (or at least it appears to be without magnification) and is nearly transparent. Because you can see through to the tissues below (the brain), the skull appears to be pinkish. In older birds (ones that are at least five to seven months old) the skull becomes two layered and appears to be whitish (because of the air space between the layers) and flecked with whitish dots; the layers are connected to each other by tiny bony columns, the ends of which look like dots. If you wet and part the feathers on top of the bird's head, you will be able to see these differences through the skin—with a little practice.

Except for the pink patch on his breast and under his wings, the male Rose-breasted Grosbeak in his first winter molts to the same color as the female. In subsequent winters, he has black wings and tail, and a larger rose patch on his breast.

The first-year breeding plumage of the male Rose-breasted Grosbeak looks much like the plumage of the female, too, except for his pink breast patch and pink under his wings (the female is yellow under her wings). First-year males may also have some of the adult male black feathers when they return in spring to breed for the first time. Compare this young male with the spectacularly colored adult male shown in the account of that bird.

How long do birds live?

In captivity, birds may live very long lives. Songbirds in captivity commonly live 10 to 15 years, and some large birds live from 20 to over 50 years (cockatoos have lived over 100 years). But in the wild, the average life expectancy for songbirds that live through their first year is only 1 to 2 years more. Wading birds and gulls live an average of 2 to 3 years after their first year, while large birds like the Yellow-eyed Penguin live 9 to 10 years more after the first year and the Royal Albatross may live an average of 30 to 40 years more. For all birds, the mortality rate is especially high in the first year of life—during the time the young bird is learning to cope with the rigors of existence.

To determine how long wild birds live, they must be individually marked. This is done by banding—using a small metal ring or band with a number on it that fits loosely around one leg. Of the millions of birds banded over the years, only a small percentage have been found again. For example, in one study of Purple Finches, more than 20,000 were banded, and slightly fewer than 1800 were recovered (six of these birds lived for 8 years, only one was found alive after 10 years).

Banding studies have shown the longest life known for a songbird in the wild is 16 years—for a Barn Swallow, a Common Starling and a Common Grackle. Other records for great longevity are 14 years for an American Crow, 13 years for a Cardinal and 11 years for a Black-capped Chickadee.

How do birds die?

The most common cause of songbird deaths is probably a combination of starvation and inclement weather. A late freeze in spring can destroy a berry crop on which a species depends, or it may cover seeds of plants or insects embedded in the bark of trees. A storm, excess rainfall or an exceptionally cold winter may be more than the birds can withstand.

Mortality rate of full-grown birds is probably highest in the winter when food is the scarcest or hardest to find, and competition for what is available is highest (because of the presence of all the young birds that were hatched the previous summer). Foggy nights during migration contribute almost yearly to the death of huge numbers of songbirds. On starless nights birds are attracted to the lights of towers and fly into them. (See *Migration kills* for more on this topic.) And marvelous though birds' navigational abilities are (see *Migration*), many do become disoriented and fly out over an ocean only to drop ultimately from exhaustion.

Other accidents of many kinds, predators, parasite infestation, disease caused by various microorganisms, poisons and the absence of certain requirements in their diet (vitamins, etc.) also cause the death of songbirds. Great loss of life owing to newly introduced diseases is exemplified by the accidental introduction of a species of mosquito that carried a bird-infecting malarial parasite and other disease-causing microorganisms to the Hawaiian Islands early in the 1800s. Many species became extinct and others survived only at higher altitudes where the introduced mosquitoes could not live. Even today, these birds live only above certain elevations on the islands; when they wander to the lower elevations, they become diseased and die.

Among songbirds, about 80% die in the first year of their lives. Of those that survive, about 55% die each of the following years of their lives. One

Song Sparrow study showed that for every 100 eggs laid, 26 were lost before hatching and 22 were killed as nestlings. Of the 52 birds that fledged, 42 died in the first year. This left only 10 birds to breed as adults in the next spring, and 4 or 5 of those died before their second breeding season!

Without these deaths, of course, the numbers of birds in each backyard would be staggering. For example, if all offspring of one pair of Song Sparrows (they produce eight eggs in a season, usually two broods of about four young each) survived and reproduced through 10 years of breeding with no death of parents or offspring, this one pair of sparrows would have grown to 19,531,250!

How food supply determines population levels

In reality, however, the number of songbirds nesting in each garden probably remains about the same from year to year; if you are fortunate enough to have Song Sparrows in your neighborhood, the number of pairs present each year is fairly constant so long as the habitat in the area is not modified. It is the amount of habitat available—not the birth or death rates—that primarily limits a species' numbers. Thus, when the House Sparrow and Common Starling were introduced into North America, their numbers increased almost as rapidly as the hypothetical increase calculated for Song Sparrows—at least until they had filled up the habitat for House Sparrows and Common Starlings (the maps in Part III in the sections about these birds graphically show their spread across North America). Most of their populations are now fairly stable because they have filled most of the habitat available to them.

The mortality figures given—that about 80% of songbirds die in their first year, and 55% during following years—are based on studies of bird populations that have been stable from year to year. Those figures vary according to how many birds there are in the area and how much habitat there is for them. For example, in one study done in The Netherlands, eggs were removed from nests so that the number of young fledged from the nests of a species of chickadee was artifically reduced by 40% during four years; the mortality rate of the remaining chickadees during these four "experimental" years was then compared with that of five "normal" years (years during which the nestlings were allowed to fledge normally). *Remarkably,* the average number of pairs of birds present on the study area (an isolated island in the North Sea) stayed about the same even though 40% fewer young were produced from the experimental birds. The population remained the same because though more young fledged in normal years, more also died the following winter, primarily from starvation. (In a normal year 89% of the young died during their first year of life and 74% of the adult birds. But following experimental removals, only 80% of the young and only 46% of the adults died.) Therefore, it seems that for these birds the winter food supply decides the numbers. Probably there is enough food in winter for only a small percentage of the population to survive and the greater number of birds fledged in the normal years was too many for the winter habitat.

Song dialects and communication

In North America, we don't speak English with quite the same pronunciation as our British friends. Nor is the speed with which we speak—nor are all the words—the same. We're acquainted with the very different accents such as the distinct Scottish accent or the southern US drawl, even subtle regional differences, but it's difficult to imagine songbirds having dialects too. Yet it appears that they do. There are both individual differences and regional differences in the songs of birds of a given species.

Sonagrams—pictures depicting bird songs—are valuable in helping us describe differences among bird songs. Sonagrams of Indigo Buntings, Cardinals, Song Sparrows, White-crowned Sparrows and others show us that the males in a certain area all sing a few similar songs, but these may be quite different from the songs of the same species from other regions. The birds are sensitive to these differences, too. When Cardinals were exposed to recordings of other Cardinals from their region they responded very aggressively. But when they were exposed to songs from populations 11 to 3000 km away, they responded most strongly to the closest and least strongly to those from farther away.

In the San Francisco Bay area of California, different populations of White-crowned Sparrows all have different song dialects. When young birds were taken early in the nesting season and raised in isolation, their songs differed from the dialect of their area. But if they remained in the area until fully fledged and then kept in soundproof chambers, they developed their normal dialect. Once it was "set," the dialect wouldn't change if they were isolated or if other dialects were played to them. Thus, these birds learn their dialect while still in the nest.

Indigo Buntings, on the other hand, seem to learn their dialect during their first spring. Young males return from their wintering ground singing a full, normal Indigo Bunting song, but then change their song to be like that of another nearby male, generally one that has successfully established a territory and attracted a mate.

Several studies have shown that birds recognize individuals. Dr. Bruce Falls, a Canadian biologist, and his students noted that once territorial boundaries were established among White-throated Sparrows, the response of a territorial bird to its neighbor declined as the season progressed. Its response to strangers, however, remained strong. And if the song of a neighbor was played from the wrong side of a male's territory, he responded to it as vigorously as to a stranger's song. Therefore, the position of the neighbor was also known by the territorial bird! In light of some other experiments, Dr. Falls concluded that this continued vigorous response to a "strange" bird is appropriate since, when males are removed from their territories, they are more often replaced by strangers than by neighbors for the latter will usually have already set up territories of their own.

For birds, songs are an important means of communication—just as our language is important to us. Lincoln Chew, a student at Dalhousie University in Nova Scotia, recently completed a study of the "language" of Savannah Sparrows by studying the sonagrams of many of these birds from eastern Canada. The song of Savannah Sparrows always starts with a series of very high (8–10 kHz) zeeps. To those people who can hear them (they are too high and faint for many) they usually sound like two or three notes or elements, zeep zeep or zeep zeep zeep. On the sonagram illustrated here, we can see that there actually are five zeeps (although that varies a bit from bird to bird). These zeeps are then followed by a highly variable set of two or three notes;

the arrangement of these notes is unique to each bird Chew studied. Then, commonly, comes the *buzz* (at about 7 kHz)—the part of the song we most easily hear. Often (as in this song) there is a sharp, terminal *chip* note, but not all birds include this in their song. The *buzz* and the *chip* are the parts of the song that show the most dialectical variation in eastern Canada. By studying these notes, one can tell what part of the country the bird is from.

Mr. Chew has tried to interpret what a male Savannah Sparrow is telling other Savannah Sparrows when a male hops on top of a weed, throws back his head and "speaks a sentence," that is, sings his song: (1) "I am a Savannah Sparrow." Those *zeeps* at the beginning are unique to Savannah Sparrows and are sung by all. They are valuable for "species recognition." (2) "I am Mr. X." The middle notes are unique to the singer and identify him as an individual. They are valuable for "individual recognition." (3) "I am from Nova Scotia." The *buzz* or trill varies from place to place. It is useful for "regional identification." Each male sparrow repeats it over and over, all day long (especially in the morning and evening) as it flies from one dried weed to the next—just to be certain, so it seems, that no other Savannah Sparrow forgets it. The trill at the end also varies throughout the season and might indicate the male's reproductive readiness. It is doubtful that we yet have a full "translation" of this song, but a good start has been made.

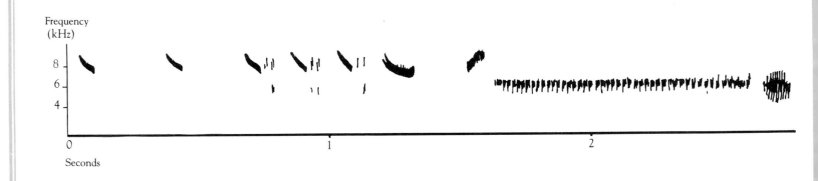

A sound spectrogram (sonagram) of the song of a male Savannah Sparrow is shown here. The frequency, in kilohertz (kHz), is indicated on the vertical axis, and the passing of time, in seconds, on the horizontal axis. There are four parts to this sparrow's song: first, five ZEEP elements, at about 8 kHz), then two "transitional" elements, followed by a BUZZ at 6-7 kHz that lasts for about 1 second, and lastly a terminal CHIP. Different birds sing different songs. For example, some individuals have two buzzs, separated by the transitional notes, in their songs. The songs generally last from 2½ to 3 seconds.

Audubon and conservation

The name "Audubon" is today closely associated with conservation in North America—and appropriately so. Audubon frequently collected specimens of birds and eggs in order to draw and study them. This may give the impression that he was not concerned with the preservation of wildlife, but this was not the case. Nowhere was Audubon's concern about the future of the wild animals of North America stated more emphatically than in the journals that he kept while collecting and drawing birds in the Gulf of St. Lawrence ("Labrador") in 1833. From near Natashquan, Quebec, Audubon wrote (June 22): "We ascertained to-day that a party of four men from Halifax took last spring nearly forty thousand eggs [of nesting seabirds], which they sold at Halifax and other towns at twenty-five cents per dozen, making over $800; this was done in about two months. Last year upwards of twenty sail were engaged in 'egging'; so some idea may be formed of the birds that are destroyed in this rascally way. The eggers destroy all the eggs that are sat upon, to force the birds to lay again, and by robbing them regularly, they lay till nature is exhausted, and few young are raised. In less than half a century these wonderful nurseries will be entirely destroyed, unless some kind government will interfere to stop the shameful destruction."

Audubon's wish has been granted, at least in part. Today it is strictly illegal in North America to collect either wild birds or their eggs, or even to sell for food wild birds that have been legally hunted. But the widespread destruction of habitat continues, often opposed by conservation groups that bear Audubon's name.

When the habitat is gone, the wildlife, for lack of a place to live, must emigrate or become extinct. Again from "Labrador" Audubon wrote (June 23), "Where can I go now, and visit nature undisturbed?" That was 1833. Where could he go today?

Glossary

altricial   Young that are not able to leave their nests soon after hatching; they are incapable of either feeding themselves or maintaining normal body temperatures without intensive parental care. Contrasts with precocial. Young songbirds are altricial.

amnion   A thin, membranous, fluid-filled sac that surrounds the embryo of a reptile, bird or mammal. The amnion helps to prevent the embryo from losing water (dehydrating).

amphibians   Literally "animals that lead a double life." Amphibians are a taxonomic group of animals that characteristically breed in water but spend some of their life on land; frogs and salamanders are the most conspicuous modern representatives. Through many interesting specializations, some modern amphibians need no longer return to water to breed. It is thought that reptiles evolved from amphibians, perhaps 325 million years ago, and that birds, in turn, evolved from reptiles.

anthropocentric   Centered on humans. In biology, an anthropocentric explanation is one that interprets a feature or action of any animal as though that animal were a person.

Archaeopteryx   The first known bird, known only from fossil remains. *Archaeopteryx* existed in the Upper Jurassic (or late in the Jurassic) Period, and has many reptilian features. See also JURASSIC PERIOD.

barbs   The individual lateral branches on either side of the rachis or shaft of a feather.

barbules   The tiny "hook-shaped" structures that project laterally on either side of a barb of a feather. The barbules on adjacent barbs hook together to fuse or connect the barbs into the vanes of the feather. Barbules can barely be seen with the naked eye.

bird   An animal with feathers; in many ways, birds are much like some reptiles, such as crocodiles and dinosaurs. See also DINOSAURS.

brood   The young hatched from a set or clutch of eggs; a set of young.

brood patch   See INCUBATE.

calcium   An element essential to give strength to bones and the shells of eggs.

clavicles   Shoulder bones ("collarbones"); in birds, the clavicles in most species are fused to form the "wishbone."

cloaca   The area common to the digestive and urogenital tracts of a bird, where body digestive waste products and urinary waste products accumulate. These, then, are passed simultaneously through the bird's cloaca. Eggs and sperm from the reproductive system also exit via this opening.

clutch   A set of eggs; the number of eggs that a female or pair will incubate at a single time. See also BROOD.

cold-blooded   An animal that regulates its body temperature primarily by behavior and whose body temperature might fluctuate greatly during a single day; when active, cold-blooded animals may have body temperatures as high as warm-blooded ones. See also WARM-BLOODED.

colony	Two or more pairs of birds breeding gregariously; the birds of a species seek a nest site that is near the nests of similar birds.
contour	The outline or shape. In birds, the feathers that cover the body and give it "its shape" are called *contour feathers* (includes wing feathers, tail feathers, but not down or rictal bristles).
convergence	Coming together. In biology, convergence means that a characteristic has independently arisen (evolved) in two different lineages.
copulation	A part of the mating process; specifically, sexual intercourse.
courtship	The interactions between a male and female that precede the formation of a pair bond.
Cretaceous Period	A geological period, occurring from 135 to 65 million years ago.
desiccation	Dehydration, drying out.
dinosaurs	A group of prehistoric reptiles existing from about 220 to 65 million years ago, many—but not all—attaining large size. Dinosaurs, crocodiles, pterodactyls and birds are thought to be closely related; some features of birds are so similar to those of these ancient reptiles that it has been said that birds should be known simply as "dinosaurs with feathers."
display	Ritualized signal used for communication, primarily with other individuals of the same species; songbird displays can involve actions, postures or vocalizations, or a combination of these.
down	A type of feather with no rachis, or central shaft. Down is especially important for insulation, and some birds use the soft down feathers to line their nests.
egg tooth	A specialized sharp, pointed structure at the tip of the bill of an embryonic bird that is used to puncture the egg.
embryo	An unborn or unhatched animal.
eye ring	A ring of feathers around the eye that contrasts in color with other feathers on the side of the face.
family	A taxonomic category more inclusive than a genus; a family is a group of fairly similar birds (e.g., blackbirds, wood warblers, vireos) that can still be subdivided into smaller distinct groups of species or genera (e.g., blackbirds [family] divided into orioles, meadowlarks, Red-winged Blackbirds, grackles, etc. [genera]). Some families, however, contain only a few distinctive species (e.g., waxwings, dippers), and hence contain only one genus.
fecal sac	A mass of feces and semisolid urine (uric acid), enveloped in a mucous coat. Fecal sacs are produced by the nestlings of many species; the parents remove these from the nest, commonly dropping them some distance from the nest.
fledgling	A young bird that has fledged, that is, one that has acquired its first set of "true" feathers and is able (in most songbirds) to fly. A fledgling can leave the nest and the nesting area; it may or may not be accompanied by its parents.
flock	A group, usually an organized group, as contrasted with a mere aggregation of animals at a food source, watering hole, etc.

forage To seek and obtain food.

fossil Remains of a plant or animal, long dead. Most fossils are bones or teeth in which much of the original tissue has been replaced by minerals from the soil; but some are impressions of soft parts (like leaves, skin, feathers), gizzard stones, coprolites (feces) or other parts.

gape The line along which the upper and lower bills meet; baby birds open their gape when begging for food. This open-mouthed—open-gaped—display is called *gaping*.

genus One or more species having characteristics shared with no other group of organisms at this same level of separation (see also FAMILY).

geographic variation Differences among geographically separated populations of a single species. In birds, there is commonly geographic variation in size, coloration, song and clutch size.

gizzard The stomach of birds. This is a specialized portion of the digestive tract that has thick muscular walls. In birds and many reptiles, food is "chewed" in the gizzard; these animals swallow gravel or stones that are used to grind the food. The gizzard is especially well developed in seed-eating birds. In many birds, the gizzard is preceded in the digestive tract by a crop, a thin-walled chamber that holds food before it moves into the gizzard to be milled.

guano The combined digestive (feces) and urinary (primarily uric acid) wastes of a bird.

habitat The special place where a particular species of bird or other animal normally lives (depends largely on the size and kinds of plants in an area).

hatching muscle A muscle that helps the baby bird break the shell of the egg and hatch. This muscle gradually disappears after the bird hatches.

homing Returning to home, a nest site or roosting site.

hybridize Breeding between individuals of two different species. Many different kinds of birds are known to hybridize, especially several kinds of ducks. If hybridization occurs commonly (such as it does between Baltimore and Bullock's Orioles and between Myrtle and Audubon's Warblers), many ornithologists consider the two types of bird to be a single species.

incubate To transfer heat from a parent's body to an egg. In songbirds, only females have specialized incubation or "brood" patches—defeathered and highly vascularized areas that are specialized to pass heat efficiently from the adult bird's body to the eggs; males of these species may sit on the eggs to conceal or shade them, or to slow down their rate of cooling, but they, strictly speaking, cannot incubate the eggs. Males of many other kinds of birds (e.g., sandpipers, some flycatchers) do help incubate; in a few species (ostriches, phalaropes, etc.) only the males are capable of incubation. In songbirds, the brood patch develops just before the female starts to incubate, usually while the last or next-to-last egg in the clutch is being produced.

inherit Inherited features or characteristics are those carried in the genes of an individual. Genes are segments of chromosomes; hence, each chromosome carries many genes, each of which influences an individual in a specific way. Most animals carry two of each chromosome, one from their maternal parent and the other from their paternal parent. Many physical features are inherited; in humans, eye color, hair color and blood type are examples. Often, however, many different genes influence a physical feature, such as stature in people. Some features are also influenced by the environment; for example, nutrition affects human stature. Certain behavioral characteristics are inherited, though many are learned (that is, independent of inheritance) or modified by learning. For example, scientists now think that simple human facial expressions such as smiling or frowning are inherited (inherent), although in some cultures people learn to modify these expressions and, say, frown when they are happy. Human language, and much bird song, are learned.

instinct A behavioral reaction that does not need to be taught, and hence is programmed in the inherited characteristics of every individual. See also INHERIT.

interbreeding Breeding between individuals of two different types of the same species (such as between individuals from different populations of Song Sparrows).

irruptions Irregular migratory movements, often involving large numbers of a single species of bird, but perhaps not the entire population of that species in a given area.

Jurassic Period A geological period in the Mesozoic Era, occurring from 190 to 135 million years ago.

keel See STERNUM.

mammal An animal that possesses hair; females have specialized glands (teats) that secrete milk used to suckle the young. Examples are whales, bats, mice, cattle, humans.

mate Used sometimes as a synonym of copulate but, more broadly, refers to the interactions between a male and female associated with producing and raising young. In some species, the male and female are together only to copulate; in others, there is elaborate cooperation between the mates in many aspects of reproduction (territorial defense, care of young, building the nest, etc.). In some species, an individual may have two or more mates (polygamous); most songbirds are monogamous. Some species mate for life; most only for a single season.

migration The seasonal movement of birds from one region to another. Commonly, migration of North Temperate species consists of a northward movement in spring to a breeding site, and a southward movement in late summer or autumn to a wintering site.

mimicry Mimicry exists when two different kinds of organisms have evolved a close resemblance to each other. Commonly, one species ("the mimic") has developed a resemblance to the other ("the model"), but sometimes the mimicry is mutual.

molting The loss and replacement of feathers; changing often from one type of plumage to another. Molts can either be complete (involving all of the feathers on the bird's body—though not at the same time—or partial, involving only the feathers of a specific region (e.g., head) or type (e.g., body feathers, but not wing or tail feathers).

monogamous	A pair bond consisting of only one male and one female (cf. polygamous).
nestling	A baby confined to the nest or the immediate vicinity of the nest.
order	A taxonomic category more inclusive than a family, i.e., containing several families. The Order Passeriformes contains all of the families of perching birds, including the songbirds; the Order Anseriformes contains all of the families of ducks, geese and swans.
ornithology	The scientific study of birds.
ovary	A gland of females that produces not only eggs (ova) but also several hormones that influence behavior, growth and the development of specialized structures (such as the brood patch) and colors used in courtship.
pair bond	The bond formed between members of a pair. This bond might last only for copulation, for an entire season or for life, depending on the species.
parasite	An organism that lives at the expense of another organism, usually of another species. Brood parasitism is of special interest in birds. In brood parasitism, a female lays her eggs in the nest of another bird, usually a bird of another species. Among North American songbirds, cowbirds are the only species that are commonly brood parasites (see the account of the Brown-headed Cowbird).
Passeriformes	One of the major orders of birds (comprises more than one-half of the kinds of living birds); all members of this group are similar, having four toes that all emerge at the same level, with three pointing forward, and one backward for excellent grasping. The spermatozoa are a distinctive shape (the adjectives "passeriform" and "passerine" refer to this group). Most of these birds are songbirds (Suborder Passeres).
photoperiod	The number of hours of sunlight per day.
pigment	A substance that imparts color to feathers, skin or the shells of eggs.
pip	To break through the shell of an egg. See also EGG TOOTH.
Pleistocene Epoch	A part of the Quaternary Period, occurring from about 2 million years ago to a few thousand years ago. See also QUATERNARY PERIOD.
plumage	The complete set of feathers. Birds have a series of different plumages, starting with a *natal plumage,* consisting of down feathers which are molted, and followed by a *juvenal plumage,* the first contour feathers. Various "adult" plumages follow (such as "winter" and "breeding" [nuptial] plumages, which are sometimes called "basic" and "alternate" plumages).
polygamous	One male mates with two or more females (polygynous); or one female mates with two or more males (polyandrous). Polygamy includes both polygyny and polyandry. In songbirds polygyny is commoner than polyandry.
precocial	Young that are able to leave their nests soon after hatching; these can forage and maintain normal body temperature with little or no help from their parents. Young ducks, sandpipers and grouse are precocial.
precopulatory display	The special behavior shown by a male or female immediately before copulation.

predator	An animal that eats another kind of animal. Most birds are predators of insects; some are predators of other kinds of birds.
pygostyle	The distal-most (farthest from the body) tail bones of birds are fused to form a single element, the pygostyle.
Quaternary Period	A geological period, occurring about 2 million years ago to the present day; divided into two epochs, the Pleistocene and Recent.
regurgitate	Literally, to "pour back." Many birds feed their mates and young by regurgitation, that is, they pour back food from their crop into the open gape of their mate or young.
resident	Strictly speaking, a resident bird is one that stays in a single area year round. More loosely, resident means a species is "present at all seasons" (even though individual birds of the species may move so that different ones are present during different seasons).
rictal bristles	Stiff, vaneless feathers located to the sides of the beaks of many birds. These bristles probably help funnel insects into the mouth; they resemble the whiskers of mammals.
roost	A place where a bird sleeps or, more commonly, a place where a flock of birds (often of several different species) gather to sleep.
scales	See SCUTES.
scutes	The scales of reptiles and birds. Strictly speaking, scutes develop differently than the scales of fish. Thus, it is not thought that the scutes of reptiles evolved from the scales of fish.
selection	In biology, selection refers to choosing or selecting one type of individual relative to another type. At the most fundamental level, for example, a predator may select an individual that is not well camouflaged—merely because it is easy to see. Selection can also take place within a species; for example, a female bird might not select a male of her species if he were to sing an atypical song. If the differences among types of individuals are inherited, then selection against a certain type (such as a conspicuous as opposed to a camouflaged type or one that sings the "wrong" song rather than the normal song) will result in its disappearance.
skeleton	The framework of bones (or cartilage) of an animal, providing support and protection.
skulling	A method of determining the age of a songbird by looking at the skull (see *How birds show their age*).
sonagram	An image of a bird's song or call. Sonagrams are usually drawn by a special machine that converts taped songs to visual images. On the horizontal axis or scale of a sonagram the time sequence (usually in seconds) is illustrated; on the vertical axis the frequency (usually in hertz—cycles per second) is indicated. Thus a sonagram illustrates the timing and the frequency of a song or call. These are also called "sound spectrographs," "spectrograms" or "audiospectrograms."
songbird	A member of the taxonomic group, Passeres, the major suborder of the Order Passeriformes. Members of this group have seven to nine pairs of "syringeal

muscles" that enable them to sing elaborate songs. See also SYRINX. Most small, familiar birds of gardens and parks are songbirds.

species   A group of individuals that are similar to each other—so similar that they tend to select only each other (of appropriate sex) as mates.

sperm   A male gamete; a motile cell containing one complete set of chromosomes from the male; this will combine with a female gamete or egg in a process called *fertilization* to form a single cell (zygote) containing two complete sets of chromosomes, one from the male and one from the female (see also INHERIT). The zygote develops into an embryo, then into a chick or baby.

spicules   Small slender spikes.

sternum   The breastbone; in birds that fly (including all passeriform birds) the sternum has a distinct keel, similar in shape to the keel on the bottom of a ship. The keel serves as an area of attachment for the large muscles that are used for flight—the "breast muscles" (the bone under the breast of a chicken).

subspecies   A well-marked population of a species that is confined to a region that is only a portion of the area occupied by the species as a whole. Most individuals of one subspecies are distinct from those of another subspecies.

syrinx   A specialized part of the trachea or "windpipe" of a bird that serves as its voice box.

taxonomy   The scientific study of classification.

terrestrial   Referring to the land. A terrestrial animal is one that lives on land (rather than in the water); a terrestrial feeder or nester is an animal that either feeds or nests on the ground.

territory   A defended area. Ornithologists differentiate between two types of territory: (1) where only a nest site and the area immediately adjacent to the nest site are defended, (2) where both a nest site and an area used for feeding are defended. A bird that is involved in the defense of a territory or spends much of its time on the territory is *territorial.*

testis   A gland of males that produces not only sperm but also several hormones that influence behavior, growth and the development of specialized structures and colors used in courtship. See also SPERM.

vane   The more or less fused or connected barbs on either side of the rachis or shaft of a feather.

vertebrate   An animal with a backbone (includes fish, amphibians, reptiles, birds, mammals).

warm-blooded   An animal that regulates its body temperature by behavioral as well as physiological means, and consequently maintains a fairly high constant body temperature throughout the day, regardless of environmental temperature. Mammals and birds are warm-blooded animals, though many—especially small species—do not regulate their body temperature so precisely as humans do.

Bibliography

Allen, A. A. 1961. *The Book of Bird Life.* D. Van Nostrand Co., Princeton, N.J.

Audubon, Maria R., ed. 1960. *Audubon and His Journals.* Dover Publications, Inc., N.Y. Originally published by Charles Scribner's Sons in 1897.

Austin, Oliver L., Jr. 1961. *Birds of the World.* Golden Press, Inc., N.Y.

Barlow, J. C. 1962. Natural history of the Bell Vireo. *University of Kansas Publications of the Museum of Natural History,* vol. 12, pp. 241–296.

Barlow, J. C. and Rice, J. C. 1977. Aspects of the comparative behavior of red-eyed and Philadelphia vireos. *Canadian Journal of Zoology,* vol. 55, no. 3, pp. 528–542.

Bent, A. C. 1942–1958. Life histories of North American songbirds. *U.S. National Museum Bulletin,* vols. 179, 195, 203, 211, 237.

Brown, J. L. 1975. *The Evolution of Behavior.* W. W. Norton & Co., N.Y.

Cade, T. 1967. Ecological and behavioral aspects of predation by the Northern Shrike. *The Living Bird,* vol. 6, pp. 43–86.

Dwight, J., Jr. 1900. The sequence of plumage and moults of the passerine birds of New York. *Annals of the New York Academy of Sciences,* vol. 13, no. 2, pp. 73–360.

Emlen, S. T. 1970. Celestial rotation: Its importance in the development of migratory orientation. *Science,* vol. 170, pp. 1198–1201.

Emlen, S. T. 1971. Celestial rotation and stellar orientation in migratory warblers. *Science,* vol. 173, pp. 460–461.

Farner, D. S. and King, J. R., eds. 1971. *Avian Biology,* vol. 1. Academic Press, N.Y.

Ficken, M. S. and Ficken, R. W. 1962. The comparative ethology of the wood warblers: A review. *The Living Bird,* vol. 1, pp. 102–122.

Godfrey, W. E. 1966. *The Birds of Canada.* Bulletin 203. National Museum of Canada, Ottawa.

Hamilton, W. J. and Orians, G. H. 1965. Evolution of brood parasitism in altricial birds. *The Condor,* vol. 67, no. 4, pp. 361–382.

Lincoln, F. C. 1950. *Migration of Birds.* Doubleday & Co., Garden City, N.Y.

MacArthur, R. H. 1958. Population ecology of some warblers of northeastern coniferous forests. *Ecology,* vol. 39, pp. 599–619.

McAtee, W. L. 1938. "Anting" by birds. *Auk,* vol. 55, no. 1, pp. 98–105.

Miller, F. W. 1952. Blue Jay, *Cyanocitta cristata,* "Anting" with burning cigarettes. *Auk,* vol. 69, no. 1, pp. 87–88.

Nero, R. W. 1964. Comparative behavior of the Yellow-headed Blackbird, Red-winged Blackbird, and other icterids. *Wilson Bulletin,* vol. 75, pp. 376–413.

Newton, I. 1973. *Finches.* Taplinger Publ. Co., N.Y.

Nichols, D. G. 1960. Notes on the icterids. *Atlantic Naturalist,* vol. 15, no. 3, pp. 169–174.

Odum, E. P., Connell, C. E., and Stoddard, H. L. 1961. Flight energy and estimated flight ranges of some migratory birds. *Auk,* vol. 78, pp. 515–527.

Orians, G. H. and Christman, G. M. 1968. A comparative study of the behavior of Red-winged, Tricolored, and Yellow-headed Blackbirds. *University of California Publications in Zoology,* vol. 84, pp. 1–81.

Perdeck, A. C. 1958. Two types of orientation in migrating starlings, *Sturnus vulgaris* L., and chaffinches, *Fringilla coelebs* L., as revealed by displacement experiments. *Ardea,* vol. 46, pp. 1–37.

Peterson, R. T. 1980. *A Field Guide to the Birds.* 4th ed. Houghton Mifflin Co., Boston.

Pettingill, O. S., Jr. 1970. *Ornithology in Laboratory and Field.* Burgess Publ. Co., Minneapolis.

Portmann, A. 1950. Le développement postembryonnaire. In *Traité de Zoologie,* par Grassé, P. Tome 15, *Oiseaux.* Masson et Cie, Paris.

Rice, J. O. and Thompson, W. L. 1968. Song development in the Indigo Bunting. *Animal Behaviour,* vol. 16, pp. 462–469.

Robbins, C. S., Bruun, B., and Zim, H. 1966. *A Guide to Field Identification: Birds of North America.* Golden Press, N.Y.

Romer, A. S. 1971. *Vertebrate Paleontology.* University of Chicago Press, Chicago.

Saunders, A. A. 1951. *A Guide to Bird Songs.* Doubleday, N.Y.

Stobo, W. and McLaren, I. 1975. The Ipswich Sparrow. *The Proceedings of the Nova Scotia Institute of Science,* vol. 27, pp. 9–105.

Storer, R. W. 1971. Classification of birds. In *Avian Biology,* edited by Donald S. Farner and James R. King. Academic Press, N.Y.

Summers-Smith, D. 1963. *The House Sparrow.* Collins, London.

Terres, J. K. 1968. *Songbirds in Your Garden.* Thomas Y. Crowell Co., N.Y.

Thomson, A. L., ed. 1964. *A New Dictionary of Birds.* McGraw-Hill Book Co., N.Y.

Welty, J. C. 1975. *The Life of Birds.* W. B. Saunders Co., Philadelphia.

Wing. L. 1943. Spread of the starling and English sparrow. *Auk,* vol. 60, pp. 74–87.

Ziswiler, V. 1965. Zur Kenntnis des Samenoffnens und der Struktur des horneren Gaumens bei Kornerfressenden Oscines. *Journal für Ornithologie,* vol. 106, pp. 1–48.

In drawing the maps, we used extensively our own field experience, especially for northern Canada and the Great Plains. Many regional lists were also consulted; the following is a list of the ones most extensively used.

General

A(merican) O(rnithologists') U(nion). 1957. *Checklist of North American Birds.* 5th. ed. Lord Baltimore Press, Inc., Baltimore, Md.

Canada

Godfrey, W.E. 1966. *The Birds of Canada.* Bulletin 203. National Museum of Canada, Ottawa.

Todd, W.E.C. 1963. *Birds of the Labrador Peninsula and Adjacent Areas.* University of Toronto Press, Toronto.

Austin, O.L., Jr. 1932. *The Birds of Newfoundland and Labrador.* No. 7, Memoirs of the Nuttall Ornithological Club, Cambridge, Mass.

James, R.D., McLaren, P.L., and Barlow, J.C. 1976. *Annotated Checklist of the Birds of Ontario.* Life Sciences Miscellaneous Publications, Royal Ontario Museum, Toronto.

United States

Gabrielson, I.N. and Lincoln, F.C. 1959. *The Birds of Alaska.* Wildlife Management Institute, Washington, D.C.

Gabrielson, I.N. and Jewett, S.G. 1970. *Birds of the Pacific Northwest.* Dover Publs., N.Y.

Kessel, B. and Gibson, D.D. 1978. *Status and Distribution of Alaska Birds.* Studies in Avian Biology, No. 1. Cooper Ornithological Society, Los Angeles, Ca.

Mexico

Blake, E.R. 1953. *Birds of Mexico.* University of Chicago Press, Chicago.

Peterson, R.T. and Chalif, E.L. 1973. *A Field Guide to Mexican Birds.* Houghton Mifflin Co., Boston.

Caribbean

Bond, J. 1971. *Birds of the West Indies.* Collins, London.

Central America

Ridgely, R.S. 1976. *A Guide to the Birds of Panama.* Princeton University Press, Princeton, N.J.

Land, H.C. 1970. *Birds of Guatemala.* Livingston Publ. Co., Wynnewood, Pa.

South America

Meyer de Schauensee, R. 1970. *A Guide to the Birds of South America.* Livingston Publ. Co., Wynnewood, Pa.

Index

Where there is more than one page number in an entry, the main discussion is indicated in bold-face type. Illustrations are indicated in italic type.

Agelaius phoeniceus. See *Blackbird, Red-winged*
Aggression, significance of plumage color for, 143
Aging birds, 160
Air sacs, 10
Albatross, Royal, longevity of, 161
Altricial young of birds, 50–51
Amnion, 9
Anthus spinoletta. See *Pipit, Water*
Anting, 105
Archaeopteryx lithographica, 12, 13, 14, 14
Audubon, John James, 86, 93, 123, 165

Barb(s) of feather, 17
Barbule(s) of feather, 17
Bathing, 146–47, 146–47
Beak(s), 16, 16, 19, 19; of finches, 114, 114; of sparrows, 134, 142
"Bee bird." See *Kingbird, Eastern*
"Bee martin." See *Kingbird, Eastern*
Bill(s). See *Beak*
Blackbird(s) (Family Icteridae), 150; Brewer's, 26, 155; displays of, 26, 28–29; European, 88, 88; feeding of, 19; flocks of, 150; fossils of, 13; migration of, 55
    Red-winged, 150, 154, 154; aggression of, 27; beak of, 19; copulation of, 31; displays of, 26, 33; habitat preference of, 69, 155; nesting of, 127; significance of colors of, 27; territory of, 25, 25
    Yellow-headed, 155; coloration of, 143, 150; habitat preference of, 155
Bluebird(s): aging of, 160; anting by, 105; boxes for, 93; competition with House Sparrows, 112; competition with starlings, 109, 128
    Eastern, 94, 94; eggs and nest of, 40; feeding of young by, 49
    egg of, 95; Mountain, 94, 94; Western, 94
Bobolink, 151, 151; bill shape of, 150, 157; coloration of, 27; habitat preference of, 69; migration of, 54, 54, 55 table, 56
Bombycilla cedrorum. See *Waxwing, Cedar*
Bone, 9, 10, 12, 13
Bristle(s) of feathers, 17, 17
Brood (incubation) patch, 41
Brood size of birds, 32, 40–41
Bullfinch: function of calls of, 113; relationships of, 114
Bunting(s): coloration of, 143
    Indigo, 27 caption, 139, 139; orientation of, 60, 61; relationships of, 134; songs of, 163; as victim of cowbirds, 158
    Lazuli, 27 caption; relationships of, 134, 139
    Painted, 27; relationships of, 134
    Snow: feeding of, 134; relationships of, 134; in winter, 66
    "Townsend's," 123
"Butcher bird." See *Shrike*

Calls, 26, 113
Camouflage, 46, 75, 143, 149
Canary: relationships of, 114; "wild," see *Goldfinch*
"Cankerbird." See *Waxwing, Cedar*
Cardinal (= Northern Cardinal), 136, 136; attracting to feeders, 137, 137; egg of, 95; feeding of, 114; feeding instinct of, 48; function of song of, 20, 20; longevity of, 67, 161; relationships of, 110, 134; song of, 163; as victim of cowbirds, 158; young of, 50
Cardinal-grosbeaks (Family Emberizidae, in part), 134; relationships of, 110, 150
Cardueline finches (Family Fringillidae), 114
Carduelis flammea. See *Redpoll, Common*

Carduelis tristis. See *Goldfinch, American*
Cassowary, 12
Catbird, Gray, 87, 87; anting of, 105; response of, to cowbird, 42, 158
Cats, as enemies of birds, 93
Certhia familiaris. See *Creeper, Brown*
Chaffinch, relationships of, 114
"Cherry bird." See *Waxwing, Cedar*
Chickadee(s) (Family Paridae), 100; attracting to feeders, 137
    Black-capped, 100, 101, 101, 137; irruptions of, 65; longevity of, 161; song of, 70; territory, of, 23, 24
    Boreal, 56, 100, 100; Carolina, 100; Chestnut-backed, 100; coloration of, 143; feeding of, 98; migration of, 56; mortality of, 162; Mountain, 100; relationships of, 120; in winter, 8, 66–67, 68 caption
Chicken (= Domestic Chicken): brood size of, 40; eggs of, 95; young of, 50
Cloaca, 10, 31
Clutch size of birds, 32, 40–41
Cockatoo, longevity of, 161
Color (coloration of birds): as camouflage, 46, 143; display colors, 27, 143; of eggs, 95, 95; pigments, 27, 95
Competition: for food, 122, 128–29, 161; for nest sites, 84, 93, 94, 109
Convergence, 16, 77, 110
Copulation, 27–31
Corvus brachyrhynchos. See *Crow, American*
Courtship of birds, 28–31
Courtship feeding, 30
Cowbird(s), 26, 150; Bronzed, 157
    Brown-headed, 157, 157; courtship display of, 29; egg of, 95; energetic cost of molt of, 53; as nest parasites, 34, 158–59, 158–59; parasitism of Common Yellowthroat, 132; parasitism of vireos, 121; parasitism of Yellow Warbler, 127
Creeper(s) (Family Certhiidae), 8, 98, 98
    Brown, 98, 99, 99; beak of, 19; feeding of, 125; feet of, 18, 18; molt of, 52; in winter, 67, 101
    "Tree." See *Creeper, Brown*
Cretaceous Period, 12
Crossbill(s): feeding of young by, 48; function of calls of, 113; irruptions of, 64; nesting of, 45; opportunistic feeding of, 115; Red ("Common"), 118, 118, 119; White-winged ("Two-barred"), 116, 118, 119; beak of, 19
Crow(s) (Family Corvidae), 11, 102; American (Common), 106, 107, 106–7; anting by, 105; calls of, 113; compared to chickadee, 100; compared to grackle, 156; courtship of, 28; feeding of, 19; longevity of, 161; mobbed by kingbirds, 46, 46; navigation of, 58; relationships of, 120; skeleton of, 14
Cuckoo(s), 13; as nest parasites, 159
Cyanocitta cristata. See *Jay, Blue*

Dendroica coronata. See *Warbler, Yellow-rumped*
Dendroica pensylvanica. See *Warbler, Chestnut-sided*
Dendroica petechia. See *Warbler, Yellow*
Dipper, American, 85, 85
Display(s): begging for food, 48; "bill-pointing," 26, 26; "broken wing," 47, 47; courtship, 28, 28, 29, 29; distraction, 46–47, 47; "head-up," 26, 26; "rodent run," 47; "ruff-out," 29, 29; territorial, 25–30; "wings out," 25, 25
Dolichonyx oryzivorus. See *Bobolink*
Dove, 13
Down (feathers), 14, 17, 17, 52
Duck: foot of, 18; migration of, 55; molt of, 52; penis of, 31; young of, 45, 50
Dumetella carolinensis. See *Catbird, Gray*

Eagle, 18, 18, 24; Golden, 24
Egg: color of, 95, 95; hatching of, 42, 42; incubation of 41–42; laying of,

40–41; number of, 32, 40; recognition of, by parents, 43; shell thinning, 41; shells of, 41; tooth, 43
Emu, 12
Eremophila alpestris. See *Lark, Horned*
Extinct birds, 123
Extinction, in danger of, 123, 141, 165

Falcon, 16; Merlin, beak of, 16
    Peregrine: egg shell thinning of, 41; flight speed of, 11
Fat, deposited for migration, 54–55
Feather(s): of *Archaeopteryx,* 12, 13, 14; bristle, 17, 17; as a characteristic of birds, 9; colors of, 27, 143; contour, 17, 17; to determine age by, 160; down, 14, 17, 17, 52; evolution of, 14, 17; for flight, 10, 14; for insulation, 10, 14, 17; molt of, 52–53; pigments of, 27; primaries, 52; secondaries, 52; structure of, 17; tail, 10, 14; tertials, 52; tracts, 52; wing, 14, 17
Fecal sac(s), 44, 44
Feeders, for songbirds, 137, 137
Feeding, 19; courtship, 21, 30, 30; on seeds, 114, 114, 134, 142; in winter, 161; of young, 48–49, 49
Feet. See *Foot*
Fertilization, 31
Finch(es): beaks of, 19; cardueline, 114; cut-throat, 110; feeding of, 114, 134 caption; feeding of young by, 48; Gouldian, 110; Purple, longevity of, 161; relationships of, 110; weaver, 110
Flight, 11, 15; feathers, 14; speeds, 11
Flocks, 24, 76, 108, 109, 113, 150, 154
Flycatcher(s) (Family Tyrannidae), 17, 72; compared to kinglets, 96
    Great Crested: nest of, 39; nesting of, 72
    Least, territory size of, 24
    migration of, 55; Scissor-tailed, 72, 72
Foot: diversity of, 18, 18; of larks and longspurs, 16; of shrikes, 80; of songbirds, 11
Fossil birds, 12, 13

Gannet, 18, 18
Geese, migration of, 55
Geographic variation: of Song Sparrows, 149, 149; of songs, 148, 163–64; of Yellow Warblers, 127
Geothlypis trichas. See *Yellowthroat, Common*
Gizzard, 10
Gnatcatcher(s) (Family Muscicapidae, in part), 96; Blue-gray, 44, 96; relationships of, 88, 96
Goldfinch, American (Common), 116, 116; beak of, 19; compared to redpolls, 117; courtship feeding of, 30; feeding of young by, 48; flight of, 69 caption, 116; relationships of, 113; in winter, 68
Grackle, Common, 156, 156; defense of nest by, 46; flocks of, 150; "head-up" display of, 26, 26; identification of, 71, 71; locomotion of, 18; longevity of, 161
Grebe: feet of, 18, 18; molt of, 52; penis of, 31; sun bathing of, 147
Grosbeak(s), 100, 114, 134, 143; Black-headed, 134, 138, 138
    Evening, 115, 115; attracting to feeders, 137; feeding of, 114; in winter, 67
    Pine, 114
    Rose-breasted, 138, 138; anting by, 105; coloration of, 160; incubation by, 42; relationships of, 110, 134; song of, 135
Guano, 10
Gull: Herring, orientation of, 59; longevity of, 161; migration of, 55; orientation and navigation of, 58

Hatching: muscle, 42; synchrony, 42
Hawfinch, feeding of, 114
Hawk(s): bills of, 16; migration of, 55; penis of, 31; as predators, 46, 143

Red-tailed: call of, mimicked by Blue Jay, 104; territory size of, 24 responses by starlings to, 109; territory size of, 24; young of, 50
Heart, 10
Hesperiphona vespertina. See *Grosbeak, Evening*
Hesperornis, 12
Hirundo rustica. See *Swallow, Barn*
Hummingbird, 13, 130; Bee, weight of, 11; size of, compared to kinglets, 96
Hybrid, 90; buntings, 139; grosbeaks, 138; "mystery birds," 123; orioles, 155; redpolls, 117; warblers, 126
Hylocichla mustelina. See *Thrush, Wood*

Ichthyornis, 12
Icterus galbula. See *Oriole, Baltimore*
Identification of birds, 69–71
Incubation (brood) patch, 41
Incubation period, 42
Iridoprocne bicolor. See *Swallow, Tree*
Irruptions, 64–65

Jay(s) (Family Corvidae), 100, 102, 143
    Blue, 104, 104; attracting to feeders, 137; beak of, 19; irruptions of, 65; migration of, 56; nest defense by, 46; as predators of nests, 92, 156
    Gray (Canada), 44, 103, 103; migration of, 56; nesting of, 45; in winter, 66
    Mexican, 23; Pinyon, irruptions of, 65; Scrub, 23; Steller's, 102, 102
"Jenny Wren." See *Wren, Winter*
Junco, 68, 134, 134; Dark-eyed (Gray-headed, Oregon, Slate-colored), 142, 142; Yellow-eyed, relationships of, 142
Junco hyemalis. See *Junco, Dark-eyed*
Jurassic Period, 12

Keel of sternum, 12, 14
Killdeer: disruptive coloration of, 75; as hosts of cowbirds, 159; young of, 50
Kingbird(s), 73
    Eastern, 15, 73, 73; feet of, 18; mobbing predators, 46
    Western, 73
Kingfisher, 13
Kinglet(s) (Family Muscicapidae, in part), 88, 96
    Golden-crowned, 96, 97, 97; egg of, 95
    Ruby-crowned, 97, 97; coloration of, 143

Landmarks, significance for orientation, 59
Lanius ludovicianus. See *Shrike, Loggerhead*
Lark(s) (Family Alaudidae), 74
    Horned, 75, 75; distraction display of, 46; dust bathing of, 147; feeding nestlings, 48, 48; feet of, 16, 18, 18, 74; habitat preferences of, 69; territorial display of, 29, 29, 93; in winter, 66
Locomotion of birds, 18
Longevity of birds, 161–62
Longspur(s), 134; Chestnut-collared, 74; feet of, 16, 74, 74; Lapland, in winter, 66
Loon(s): flight speed of, 11; migration of, 55; molt of, 52
Loxia curvirostra. See *Crossbill, Red*
Loxia leucoptera. See *Crossbill, White-winged*
Lungs, 10

Magnetism, used for navigation, 60
Magpie, Black-billed, 102, 102
Martin, Purple, 76; coloration of, 143; competition for nests, 112; egg of, 95; identification of, 76, 77; migration of, 55; nesting of, 36, 36
Mating systems, 32–33
Meadowlark(s)
    Eastern, 74, 150, 152, 152; eggs and young of, 51, 51; habitat preferences of, 69; locomotion of, 18

Western, 150, **152**
Melospiza melodia. See *Sparrow, Song*
Merlin, head and beak of, *16*
Migration: dangers of, 55, 57, 62, 132, 161; evolution of, 58; routes of, 54–56, 124; speed of, 55–56; triggering of, 56. See also *Navigation; Orientation*
Mniotilta varia. See *Warbler, Black-and-white*
Moa, 12
Mockingbird (= Northern Mockingbird), 86, **86**; aging of, 160; resemblance of, to shrikes, 80, *80*; responses of, to predators, 46
Molothrus ater. See *Cowbird, Brown-headed*
Molt, 52–53
Monogamy, 25, **32–33**
Mortality: during migration, 54, 55, 56, 57, **62**, 132, 161; in winter, 161–62
Muscle, 10, 11, *12*, 14, 18, 42, 80; hatching, 42
Myna(s) (Family Sturnidae), 108; Crested, 108

Navigation, 58; by local landmarks, 59; by magnetic cues, 60; by smell, 62; by stars, 61; by sun, 60
Nest(s): construction of, **34–37**; parasites of, 110, 157, **158–59**; robbery from, 92, 156; sanitation of, **44**; variety of, **38–39**; young in, 45
Nestlings: feeding of, 48; solicitation of food by, 48
New World buntings (= New World sparrows), Family Emberizidae, 134
New World Warblers. See *Warblers*
Nightingale, 88; song of, 86, 92
Nutcracker, Clark's, irruptions of, 64
Nuthatch(es) (Family Sittidae), **100**, 120; feeding of, 98; migration of, 56; nest sanitation by, 44
Red-breasted, 100; beak of, *19*
White-breasted, 100, *101*, **101**; irruptions of, 65; in winter, 8, 66

Orientation, 58; by local landmarks, 59; by magnetic cues, 60; by smell, 62; by stars, 61; by the sun, 60
Oriole(s), 134, 150
Baltimore, *153*, **153**; aggression of, 27; dispersal of, 25; egg of, 95; nest of, 36, **36–37**; significance of coloration of, 143
Bullock's, *150*, 153; nest of, 36, **36–37**; migration of, 55; Northern, see *Oriole, Baltimore; Bullock's;* Orchard, anting, 105
Ostrich, 14; feathers of, 17; penis of, 31; weight of, 11
Ovenbird, *131*, **131**; "broken wing" display of, 47, *47*; convergence of, with thrushes, 16; habitat preference of, 69; as victims of cowbirds, 158
Owl(s): convergence of, with hawks, 16; irruptions of, 65; mobbed by jays, 104; penis of, 31; Snowy, irruptions of, 65; young of, 50
Oxpecker, 108

Parus atricapillus. See *Chickadee, Black-capped*
Passer domesticus. See *Sparrow, House*
Passerculus sandwichensis. See *Sparrow, Savannah*
Passeres. See *Songbird*
Passeriformes. See *Songbird*
Passerina cyanea. See *Bunting, Indigo*
Pelican, egg shell thinning of, 41
Penguin, 14; Yellow-eyed, longevity of, 161
Penis, 31
Perching bird, 13, 18
Peregrine Falcon: egg shell thinning of, 41; flight speed of, 11
Perisoreus canadensis. See *Jay, Gray*
Petrels, orientation of, 62
Pewee, Eastern Wood: mimicked by starling, 109; nest of, 39; song of, 70, 72

Pheucticus ludovicianus. See *Grosbeak, Rose-breasted*
Pigeon(s), 13; flight speed of, 11; orientation of, 59, 60, 62
Pigments: of eggs, 95; of feathers, 27
Pipit(s) (Family Motacillidae), *16*, 74, **93**; Sprague's, aerial display of, 93; Water (Rock), *93*, 93
Piranga olivacea. See *Tanager, Scarlet*
Pleistocene Epoch, 12, 13
Plover, 18
Golden: egg of, *51*, 51; young and adult of, *51*, 51
Semipalmated, disruptive coloration of, 75
Plumage, **52–53**, 160; breeding, 52, 160; coloration, 143; "nuptial," 52, 53, 160; winter, 52, 53, 160. See also *Feather*
Polygamy, 25, **32–33**
Posture, 25–29
Precocial young of birds, 50–51
Predators: responses to, 25–26, **46–47**; select for coloration, 143
Preen, 17

Quail: dust bathing of, 147; young of, 50
Quiscalus quiscula. See *Grackle, Common*

Rachis, 17
Rail, feet of, 18
Raven, Common (= Northern Raven), 96, **107**; calls of, 113; egg of, 95; migration of, 56; size of, 11
Recognition: by plumage, 143; by song, 90–91, 163–64
Redpoll, Common, *117*, **117**; feeding of young by, 48; Hoary, 117; relationships of, 113; in winter, 68
Redstart, American, *22*, *133*, **133**; distraction display of, 47, *47*; nest and eggs of, 40; territorial display of, *24*
Regulus calendula. See *Kinglet, Ruby-crowned*
Regulus satrapa. See *Kinglet, Golden-crowned*
Reptile, 9, 12, 13, 17
Richmondena cardinalis. See *Cardinal*
Rictal bristle, *17*, 17
Robin
American, 88, 89, **89**, 96; aging of, 160; anting by, 105; beak of, *19*; dispersal of, 25; egg of, 95, 95; feet of, *18*, 18; inebriation of, 83; migration of, 55; reaction of, to cowbirds, 158; recognition of eggs by, 42; song of, 70, 135
European ("Redbreast"), 88, **88**; orientation by, 60; territorial display of, 27

Sandpiper(s): feet of, 18; as hosts for cowbirds, 159; young of, 50
Sanitation of nests, 44
Sapsuckers, feeding of, 97, 98, 126
Scales, 9, 14, 17
Scutes, 9, 17
Seiurus aurocapillus. See *Ovenbird*
Setophaga ruticilla. See *Redstart, American*
Shore Lark. See *Lark, Horned*
Shorebirds: feet of, 18; young of, 45, 50
Shrike(s) (Family Laniidae), *16*, *20*, 20, 80, **80**, 107
Loggerhead, *20*, *81*, **81**; beak of, *19*, 19
Northern, *23*, **81**; beak of *16*
Red-backed, 80
Sialia sialis. See *Bluebird, Eastern*
Siskin, Pine: function of calls of, 113; relation of, with redpolls, 117; in winter, 68 caption
Sitta carolinensis. See *Nuthatch, White-breasted*
Skeleton, 10, *14*; determine age by, 160
"Skulling," to determine age, 160
Skylark, 74; flight of, *74*
"Snowbirds." See *Junco*
Sonagram, 163–64, *164*
Song(s), 11, 20–21; dialects of, 148, **163–64**; functions of, 23, 25, 26,

90–91, **113**, 122, 139, 163–64; identification by, 70, 163–64; variation of, 21, 163–64
Songbird(s): aging of, 160; anting by, 105; bathing by, 146–47; behavioral traits of, 20–21; bills of, 19; body temperatures of, 45; brood patches of, 41; characteristics of, 11; color of, 27, 143; competition among, 128–29; convergence of, 16; copulation of, 31; courtship of, 28–31; deaths of, 161–62; distraction displays of, 47; egg laying by, 40–41; eggs of, 95; feathers of, 17; feeders for, 137; feet of, 18; fossils of, 12–13; geographic variation of, 149, 163–64; identification of, 69–71; incubation of eggs by, 41–42; irruptions of, 64–65; mating systems of, 32–33; migration of, 54–58; nest of, 34–37; nest sanitation by, 44; number of, 11; orientation and navigation of, 58–62; plumage and molt of, 52–53; response of, to intruders, 46–47; songs and calls of, 26, 113; territoriality of, 23–26; in winter, 66–67; young of, 48–51
See individual entries for more complete information on each topic.
Sparrow(s) (Family Emberizidae, in part), 16, 18, 55, 62, **134**
Chipping, *144*, **144**; feeding of, 134
Field, call of, 113; Fox, 134, 142
House (English) (Family Ploceidae), 110, *111*, **111–12**; attracting to feeders, 137; dust bathing of, 146, 147; mortality of, 162; nesting of, in bluebird boxes, 93, 94; nesting of, in wren boxes, 84; nest of, *112*; relationships of, 114; in winter, 67
"Ipswich," *140*, 141; Java (Family Ploceidae), 110
Savannah, *140*, **140**, 141; brood size of, 40; distraction display of, 46; feeding of, 134; habitat preferences of, 69; locomotion of, 18; song of, 163–64; territory size of, 25
Song, *148*, **148**; brood patch development of, 41; egg of, 95; feeding of, 134; geographic variation of, 127, *149*, **149**; habitat preferences of, 69; migration of, 56; mortality of, 162; nest site fidelity of, 25; song of, 163
Tree, 68; hatching synchrony of, 42
White-crowned, 9, *144*, **144**; bathing of, *146*; song of, 163
White-throated, *145*, **145**; compared with White-crowned Sparrow, 144 caption; feeding of, 134; habitat preferences of, 69; migration of, 55 table; orientation of, 61; polymorphism of, 24; song of, 163
Sperm, 31
Starling(s) (Family Sturnidae), **108**
Common (European), 108, *109*, **109**; anting by, 105; attracting to feeders, 137; flight of, *116*; flocks of, 108; foods of, 19; identification of, 71, 71; locomotion of, 18; longevity of, 161, 162; navigation of, 59, 59, 60; nest sanitation of, 44; nesting in bluebird boxes, 93, 94, 128; nestling, 48; in winter, 67
Stars, cues for navigation from, 61
Sternum, 12, 14
Stomach, 10
Stork, 31
Sturnella magna. See *Meadowlark, Eastern*
Sturnus vulgaris. See *Starling, Common*
Sun, used for navigation, 60–61
Swallow(s) (Family Hirundinidae), 57, **76–77**
Bank, 76, 76; nesting colony of, 34; nestlings of, 45, 48; territory of, 23, 24
Barn, 76, 76, 77, *79*, **79**; longevity of, 161; migration of, 55; nest of, 34; beaks of, 19
Cliff, 76, 76; beak of, *19*; homing of, 59; migration of, 55, 55; nesting of,

34, **34–35**
myth about migration of, 63; nest sanitation by, 44; Rough-winged, 76, 76; sun bathing of, 147
Tree, 25, 76, 78, **78**; competition with starlings for nest sites, 109; diet of, 76; identification of, 76; migration of, 57; nest of, *34*, **34**; nesting of, in bluebird boxes, 93; nesting of, in wren boxes, 84
Violet-green, 78
Swift, 13, 16; Chimney, convergent with swallows, *77*, 77
Syrinx, 11; of shrikes, 81

Tachycineta thalassina. See *Swallow, Violet-green*
Tanager(s) (Family Emberizidae, in part), **134**; coloration of, 143; habitat preferences of, 69; migration of, 55; migration kills of, 62; relationships of, 110, 150
Scarlet, *135*, **135**; color of, 143; migration of, 54, 55 table, 56; molt of, 53
Summer, migration of, 55 table
Western, *135*, *143*
Temperature, body: of songbirds, 49; regulation of, 41–42, 49–50
Tern, Arctic, migration of, 54
Territory, 23–26
Testes, 10, 31
"Thistle bird." See *Goldfinch*
Thrasher(s) (Family Mimidae), **86**
Brown, *86*, **86**; aging of, 160; anting by, 105; resemblance of, to Wood Thrush, 92
California, 86; Curve-billed, 86; Sage, 86
Thrush(es) (Family Muscicapidae, in part), **88**; convergence of, with Ovenbird, 16; feeding of, 19
Gray-cheeked, 90–91, *91*; migration of, 55
habitat preference of, 69; Hermit, 88, 90; locomotion of, 18; migration kills of, 62; Swainson's, 90, *91*; Veery, 90
Wood, 16, 88, 90, 92, **92**; egg of, 95; eggs and nest of, 40; hatching of, 42; song of, 70; young of, 51
Tinamou, 31
Titmice (Family Paridae), 100; Tufted, 100, *100*
Toe, 18
Tongue, use in feeding, 114, 134
Tooth (teeth), 10, 12, 13
Toucan, 31
Towhee, 134; Rufous-sided, 43, 144
Troglodytes troglodytes. See *Wren, Winter*
Turdus migratorius. See *Robin, American*
Tyrannus tyrannus. See *Kingbird, Eastern*
Tyrant flycatchers. See *Flycatchers*

Uric acid, 10
Urine, 10

Vane of feather, 17
Variation, geographic: of Song Sparrows, *149*, **149**; of songs, 148, **163–64**; of Yellow Warblers, 127
Vireo(s) (Family Vireonidae), 19, **120**; Bell's, swaying of, *28*, 28, 120; compared with kinglets, 96; habitat preferences of, 69; migration of, 55; migration kills of, 62; nests of, *121*; Philadelphia, territoriality and songs of, 122
Red-eyed, *121*, **121**; aging of, 160; bill of, *19*; courtship display of, 28; feeding nestlings by, 48; migration kills of, 62; song of, 69 caption, 70; swaying of, *120*, 120; territoriality and song of, 122
as victims of cowbirds, 158
Vireo olivaceus. See *Vireo, Red-eyed*

Warbler(s) (Family Parulidae), 16, **124**; Arctic, 48; "Audubon's," see *Warbler, Yellow-rumped;* Bachman's, 123; Bay-breasted, habitat selection of, 128–29;

175

beaks of, 19
Black-and-white, 98, *125*, **125**; migration of, 55
Black-throated Blue, *22*; Black-throated Green, *22*; habitat selection of, 128–29
Blackburnian: habitat selection of, 128–29; as victim of cowbird, *158*, 158
Blackpoll, *54*; fat of, 54; speed and route of migration of, 55–56, *56*
"Blue Mountain," 123; Canada, *45*; Cape May, habitat selection of, 128–29; "Carbonated," 123
Chestnut-sided, *130*, **130**; aggressive display of, *25*, 25; change in abundance of, 123
distraction displays of, 47; habitat preferences of, 69; killed in migration, 62; Kirtland's, 123; Magnolia, *19*, *22*; migration of, 55; "Myrtle," see War-

bler, Yellow-rumped; Old World, 96; Parula, nest of, *38*, 124; Pine ("Pine Creeping"), 98; Prothonotary, nest of, *124*, 124; "Small-headed," 123; songs of, 70
Yellow: egg of, *95*; habitat preference of, 69; song of, 133; as victim of cowbird, *158*, 158
Yellow-rumped ("Audubon's," "Myrtle"), *126*, **126**; habitat selection of, 128–29; migration kills of, 62
"Water Ouzel." See *Dipper, American*
Waxbill, 110
Waxwing(s) (Family Bombycillidae), **82**; behavior of, 20; "berry passing" by, 82; Bohemian, 82
Cedar, 82, *83*, **83**; incubation of eggs by, 42; petal passing by, 21; territories of, 23
irruptions of, 65; opportunistic feeding by, 115; territories of, 24

Weaver, Social, nesting of, 110, 112
Weaver finch(es) (weaverbirds) (Family Ploceidae), 110
Weights of birds, 11
Wheatear, migration of, 56
"Whistle bird." See *Sparrow, White-throated*
Widow weaver, as nest parasite, 110
Widowbird, as nest parasite, 110
Wood Pewee, Eastern: mimicked by starling, 109; nest of, *39*; song of, 70, 72
Wood warbler(s). See *Warbler*
Woodpecker(s), 13; Acorn, 98; competition with starlings, 109; Downy, in winter, 8, 68 caption; feeding of, 98, 125; feet of, *18*, 18; Hairy, in winter, 8 caption; penis of, 31; Red-headed, 98; young of, 50
Wren(s) (Family Troglodytidae), **84**; Cactus, nesting of, 84

Carolina, 84; brooding of young by, 45
House: body temperature of, 49; care of young by, 48; competition with starlings by, 109; dispersal of, 25; incubation by, 41–42; nesting of, *37*, 37, 84; nesting of, in bluebird boxes, 93
Long-billed Marsh: nest of, *39*; nesting of, 84
nest sanitation of, 44; nests of, 34; resemblance of, to Mockingbirds, 86
Winter, 84, *85*, **85**; mating systems of, 33; nest of, *38*; singing of, 69 caption
Wrentit, 84

Yellowthroat, Common, *132*, **132**; coloration of, 27; habitat preferences of, 69; as victims of cowbird, 158
Zonotrichia albicollis. See *Sparrow, White-throated*

About the Maps

It is difficult to summarize a bird's range on a map. Most species are found in a characteristic habitat, say pine forests. If, on a map, we shade in areas where there are pine forests, and hence the birds, we also incidentally include many spaces between the pine forests. In using these maps, then, it is advisable to get a general impression of the distribution of the bird from looking at the map, and then to consult the text for a general indication of the specific habitat in which you would expect to find that species within its geographic range.

We have attempted to indicate regions where the species regularly occurs, not necessarily to include every record of occurrence known. For example, Baltimore Orioles have been known to winter north to Ontario, but in general they winter in Mexico, southward. The maps we have made show the "usual" or "characteristic" ranges of the species discussed.

We have used three different maps in the book, one of North America, one of North and South America, and one of the Northern Hemisphere. The ranges of species that occur only in North America are indicated on the first type of maps; those whose range, in summer or winter, includes South America are shown on the second. A few of the species discussed in this book occur in both the Old and New Worlds, and we have illustrated the world-wide distributions of some of these. (For others, in order to emphasize details of their New World distributions, we have shown only their North American ranges, and discussed their overall distributions in the text.)